MISSOURI

American Historical Press
Sun Valley, California

MISSOURI

CROSSROADS OF THE NATION

Charles Phillips & Betty Burnett

© 2003 American Historical Press
All Rights Reserved
Published 2003
Printed in the United States of America

Library of Congress Catalogue Card Number: 2003096190
ISBN: 1-892724-36-7

Bibliography: p. 257
Includes Index

CONTENTS

Kansas City glows
with the festive
lights of Christmas
in this Kevin Sink
photo. Courtesy,
Midwestock

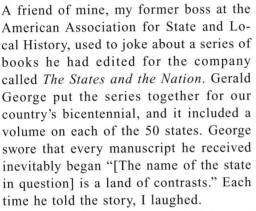

Preface

A friend of mine, my former boss at the American Association for State and Local History, used to joke about a series of books he had edited for the company called *The States and the Nation*. Gerald George put the series together for our country's bicentennial, and it included a volume on each of the 50 states. George swore that every manuscript he received inevitably began "[The name of the state in question] is a land of contrasts." Each time he told the story, I laughed.

When writing an illustrated history of one of those 50 states, I found myself in the embarrassing situation of having to say, *"No, really,* Missouri is a land of contrasts." Other states, of course, do have various geographical regions, but in few are they so marked that a simple compass direction won't suffice to identify them. And, true, other states have more or less official nicknames for geographically and politically distinct regions, but few have names for virtually all of them. Still, I do not invoke the hoary old shibboleth of state history lightly; I do so only because there is no adequate understanding of Missouri without it.

From its tumultuous entry into the Union till the present, Missouri has struggled with the political consequences of those sharp contrasts, making its story, in the words of Paul Nagel (who wrote the Missouri volume for *The States and the Nation* series), "as often disillusioning as it is inspiring." Located at mid-continent and bounded by one of America's greatest rivers, Missouri's variety of social and economic ties prevented it from casting a clear sectional image, and its relationship to the Union was often confused and contradictory. Most of the history of the state revolved around the axis formed by the Missouri River in mid-state between the two major urban settlements at each extreme—Kansas City, looking resolutely westward, and St. Louis looking longingly to the East. Unlike its Midwestern neighbors, Missouri's economy was from the beginning both commercial-industrial and agricultural.

Such variety and contrast fed the rivalries common to most states, exaggerating them, until they became the key to Missouri's journey from *Crossroads of the Nation*, when all trails to America's destiny had their origins in the state, through a period of lawlessness and decline, to the archetypal conservative state, where caution was the prime political virtue. What follows is the story of that journey, one that has its triumphs, but also its embarrassments and no little despair. For Missouri's history is nothing if not colorful, and colorful stories are never painless—that's part of their fascination.

This Herman J. Meyer lithograph shows Kansas City in 1850. Kansas City, like St. Joseph, had become a major center for the cattle trade. During the gold rush in 1849 and the subsequent mining excavations in the West, a head of cattle purchased in Missouri for $10 often brought $100 or $150 in Colorado or California, and huge drives started on the long trek from the banks of the Missouri to the shores of the Pacific—in excess of 100,000 head a year by the mid-1850s. Courtesy, Missouri Historical Society

The beauty of the Lake of the Ozarks glowing in the sunset has awed visitors from the early explorers to modern-day tourists. Photo by Harry Rogers

The Land of Lewis and Clark

The Native Americans considered it a fertile hunting ground, and called it home. The French crown thought it an expensive colony with disappointingly little in the way of mercantile treasure to exploit, and gave it away at first opportunity to the Spanish. Spain wanted it mainly as a buffer, first against Britain and then against the United States. The English king treated it as a mere pawn in the empire's international games. Thomas Jefferson bought it to avoid a war with European powers. He also hoped to satisfy his great intellectual curiosity about its flora, fauna, geography, and native cultures. Most Americans, unlike their president, saw in it the promise of cheap land, low taxes, and a better life. But nature had the final word on what would become the state of Missouri, having broken it down into three very different terrains—prairies, alluvial plains, and Ozark highlands—and located all of them at the meeting place of three great rivers, the Missouri, the Ohio, and the Mississippi.

While Missouri's topography would tend to divide its people, economy, and political interests along sectional lines, creating disputatious citizens famous for their wariness, the state's geographical position ensured its central role in the drama of the country's "manifest destiny," making Missouri, in the words of historian Paul C. Nagel, "the key to America's western kingdom." But only after the new American republic had finally wrested the land from the Indians, more or less laid to rest the problems of its European tradi-

The abundance of game drew early inhabitants to Missouri—from the Sac and Fox Indians to the fur trappers who would later live along the rivers, reaping the benefits of the unspoiled wilderness. This photo was taken in the Squaw Creek National Wildlife Refuge and captures snow and blue geese in flight. Photo by Harry Rogers

tions, and reshaped the area politically through territorial wrangling could Missouri assume its natural place as mother of the American West.

In prehistoric times the ancestors of such tribes as the Yuchi, Creek, Chickasaw, Natchez, Quapaw, and Osage built the low mounds in which they buried their dead all over Missouri. Other tribes, even more ancient, made their homes in the caves and rock shelters of Taney, Stone, Barry, McDonald, and Newton counties. But by the time the first Europeans arrived, these primitive bluff dwellers had long disappeared, as had the mound-building Woodland and Mississippi cultures. Throughout the colonial period, two main linguistic groups occupied the Missouri wilderness. The Northeastern part of the state belonged to the Algonquin tribes—the Sac, the Fox, and the Illinois. Their hereditary foes, the Sioux—tribes like the Iowa, Kansa, Missouri, Oto, Quapaw, and Osage—held the rest.

The French drove the Sac and the Fox into Missouri. Originally, the home of the Sauk and the Mesquakie, as the Sac and the Fox called themselves, had been to the north—the former in the upper Michigan peninsula and the latter along the south-

ern shores of Lake Superior. Early in the seventeenth century, the Mesquakie, eased off their lands by the Chippewas, moved southward gradually until they occupied the area around Lake Winnebago and along the Fox River, from which they received their French name. Midway through the same century the Iroquois and the French chased the Sauk south to Green Bay. It was there that the Sac and the Fox forged their close alliance. When the French tried to punish the Fox for attacking French fur traders, the tribe sought refuge with the Sac. And when the Sac—at that point on good terms with the French—refused to give up their new allies, the Europeans vented their wrath on both tribes, forcing them to migrate south yet again.

They arrived in the Mississippi Valley implacably bellicose, and they remained that way till the bitter end. They attacked and displaced the Illinois, whose land they coveted, then undertook wars of extermination against the Missouri and the Peoria. After smallpox finished what the Sac and the Fox began, the Missouri disappeared as a nation; a few joined the Osage, others the Kansa tribe. The Peoria, their ranks greatly depleted, established villages near St. Louis and Ste. Genevieve, seeking the protection of the whites from their relentless enemies. But long before that, in fact by the beginning of the eighteenth century, the Sac and the Fox held in undisputed possession all the territory north of the Missouri River and east of the Grand River to the Mississippi. And here, this time, they meant to stay.

To the whites—the French, the Spanish, and the Americans in turn—the Sac and the Fox appeared intensely savage, rude, untrustworthy, and disposed to wander. But each group in turn respected the fighting prowess of both tribes, and the efficient political administration of the Sac. From Algonquin stock, mixing the cultures of eastern Woodland Indians with practices adopted from the Plains tribes, the Sac and the Fox were proud, vain, and intemperate. The imposing appearance of the young Sac or Fox brave—physically well developed and attired in breechclout and beaded moccasins, his scalp lock treated with vermilion and yellow, his face streaked with red, blue, and yellow, a string of wampum or bear claws around his neck with ear bobs to match—announced clearly that combat was at the center of his existence.

Though tribal authority rested nominally with a civil chief, backed by a council of adult males, much depended on personality. Any brave who could attract sufficient followers for a war party became a war chief and wielded influence with the tribe and on the council so long as his exploits succeeded or his dreams and visions remained vivid and inspiring. A highly organized social structure fueled the tribes' propensity to war. Each family among the Sac and the Fox belonged to one of a dozen or so great gens, or hereditary groups, with names like Bear, Buffalo, Sturgeon, or Thunder, which had religious significance and dictated the transmission of property. In addition, the males of each tribe belonged to one of two non-religious orders chosen at birth by their parents, who daubed the face of every male child with either white or black paint. From that point on, the Indian youth teamed with those of his order in tribal games and competed in feats of daring and stratagem during war.

The Sac and the Fox, constantly at war with their Indian neighbors and with the French, severely hindered French colonial trade on the upper Mississippi throughout the early eighteenth century. Louis XIV sent expeditions against them in 1717, 1728, and 1734, the last commanded by Nicholas Joseph De Noyalles. After a dispirited campaign, De Noyalles arranged an indecisive peace the following year.

The Sac and the Fox began their winter hunt each year after a fall harvest and continued through March or April, when the tribe returned to their villages to plant crops. Their agriculture was rather more extensive than that of the Sioux tribes. Cultivating land near the Mississippi, they raised as much as 8,000 bushels of corn annually, as well as beans, pumpkins, and melons. During the summer, young braves went on a hunt while the women stayed behind to weave rush mats and bark corn bags. The older men dug and smelted ore at the lead mines belonging to the tribe, mines that produced 5,000 pounds of lead a season. Whatever surplus they produced in corn, lead, and furs they sold to the white traders. Not surprisingly, given their prior history, the Sac and the Fox much preferred to do business with the English when they could. It was a habit that did little to endear them to the French (or the Spanish and Americans who came after), reinforcing their image as the archetypal "bad" Indians.

The Osage were much more to the French taste. Of all the Indian tribes living within Missouri after the arrival of Europeans, it was the Osage who excited the interest and admiration of the whites. When the first French explorers reached the region late in the seventeenth century, the tribe lived near the mouth of the Osage River, but by 1718 the Great or Big Osage, who called themselves Pa-he'tsi, or "campers on the mountain," had moved

This view of the Lake of the Ozarks captures the cedars that line Horseshoe Bend on Osage Beach. Early inhabitants found abundant water and ample fuel for fires in the Missouri area. Photo by Harry Rogers

The Founding of St. Louis was captured on canvas in this August Becker oil painting in 1861. Courtesy, Missouri Historical Society

a girdle, dressed-deerskin leggings concealing their legs but for the thighs, unadorned moccasins of dressed deer, elk, or buffalo skin, and blankets thrown over their torsos. They then returned to the cone-shaped huts and oblong lodges of their irregular villages to harvest the modest crops of corn, beans, and pumpkins they left unhoed and unfenced all summer. Late in September the fall hunts began, ending around Christmas. They stayed in camp until February or March, whenever spring came, and then hunted bear and beaver. Those families fortunate in the

Above and right: Karl Bodmer traveled Missouri in the early 1830s, painting and sketching what he saw. These two views capture the Missouri that belonged to the Indians and the fur trappers. Above is an idyllic, quiet scene no doubt experienced by the earliest explorers; at right is a scene of the Bellevue Indian Agency, when the Indians were no longer in power in the territory. Courtesy, Iowa Historical Society

upstream and established villages at the river's headwaters. The rest of the tribe, the Little Osage, moved (along with their defeated cousins, the Missouri) westward up the Missouri River into present-day Saline County, and called themselves U-tsehta, "campers in the low lands."

When the famous naturalist and painter John James Audubon encountered the Osage in the 1840s, he thought them "well formed, athletic and robust men of noble aspect," and, indeed, they were impressively tall, averaging six feet or more, and prodigious runners. Subsisting chiefly through hunting, the Osage often traveled 60 miles a day; their war parties trekked even greater distances. ,Osage braves hunted from May until August, decked in breechclouts of blue or red held tight by

hunt provided for the destitute, sending provisions to the homes of the poor, the widowed, and the fatherless.

Osage politics in general operated with the same spirit of consideration, without a regular code of laws. The tribe was governed instead by a tacit understanding of the right to command. Though they vested nominal authority in a small number of usually hereditary chiefs, those chiefs never made important decisions without consulting the warriors' council.

Early on, the Osage established a reputation among the whites for general sobriety that made them conspicuous among the various Indian tribes. Constantly forced to defend their hunting grounds against encroachments by whites and enemy Indians alike, they developed as well a reputation for being warlike and hostile, but not, like the Sac and the Fox, treacherous. They grew especially close to the prominent St. Louis family, the Chouteaus, who maintained exclusive trading privileges with the tribe throughout the eighteenth century.

Though envied by the other tribes for the special treatment accorded them by the whites, the Osage had their pride. As the old Chief Big Soldier once told a white friend: "You are surrounded by slaves. Everything about you is in chains, and you are in chains yourselves. I fear if I should change my pursuit for yours, I too should become a slave." The sad truth was that Big Soldier and his fellow braves were already all but economic slaves to the Europeans, for the Indian trade was carried on by credit. Regardless with which group of whites a tribe deigned to traffic, over the course of a century and a half the Indians would become completely dependent upon the traders. And however much an Osage chief like Big Soldier or a Sac and Fox leader like Black Hawk might hotly deny the term, they were essentially hirelings for the fur companies—pawns in the struggle for empire between the great European mercantile powers.

The entire early history of the state, like that of its Indians, can only be understood as part of the struggle for empire, especially between England and France. By the mid-1600s both were in a position to challenge Spain's New World monopoly. The English had established compact little settlements along the Atlantic coast, while the more adventurous French had spread westward down the St. Lawrence and into the expanses of the interior. From the time Champlain founded Quebec in 1608, coureurs de bois—as casual with their lives as any old English sea dog and as good at woodcraft as the natives— chased furs ever deeper into the wilderness. In their wake came soul-seeking French Catholic missionaries, undaunted by the dangers of the forests and dubbed "Black Robes" by the Indians. These hardy explorers established settlements and built forts all along the far reaches of

the Great Lakes. To such remote outposts came the Indians, with animal hides for sale and strange tales about a great "father" of rivers they called the "Mesippi."

The French government, however, did not much appreciate the exploits of its wandering subjects. Louis XIV had taken over New France from a French trading company in 1663, and ruling by royal decree through a governor and an intendant, he consistently discouraged the coureurs. Led by his great minister Charles Colbert de Croissey, Louis wanted New France populated by hardworking and docile farmers. Sending women to entice the wild fur traders into a more settled life, he placed a bounty on large families, forbade all but a privileged few from engaging in the fur trade, and urged the Church to excommunicate men who left their farms without permission.

Canada's governor, the Comte de Frontenac, however, chose not to enforce the king's decrees. Immediately upon his arrival in 1672, he perceived the strategic significance of what the coureurs were doing. East of the Appalachians, English settlers had nearly subdued the Indians, and the English could supply more cheaply than the French the textiles and hardware the Indians demanded in exchange for fur. Despite that handicap, the French remained competitive chiefly because they were better at winning the Indians' friendship. Instead of evicting the Indian from his land, the Frenchman more often lived in his wigwam, married his daughter, and taught him to like Catholicism and hate the English. And, Frontenac realized, only those Indians led by the French would stand ready to halt English expansion at the mountains.

Before the count arrived in Canada, the French intendant Jean Talon had commissioned a fur trader, Louis Jolliet, to explore the unknown river described by the Indians. Talon hoped this father of waters might prove to be the fabled passageway to the Pacific. Without hesitation the new governor approved the plan, despite the fact that the French king had only recently rejected another scheme by two

Black Hawk and his Sac and Fox followers soon found that their lives had been irreversibly changed by the influx of European fur traders into the area, embroiled in the white man's struggle for empire. From Cirker, *Dictionary of American Portraits,* Dover, 1967

Rene Robert Cavelier, Sieur de La Salle, followed the Mississippi River to its mouth, laying claim to the river, its branches, and the surrounding land, as he searched in vain for the elusive Northwest Passage. Courtesy, Arkansas History Commission

coureurs to create a trading company that would service the northern fur supply by sea using just such a passageway. French-Canadians Pierre Radisson and Medart Chouart Grosseilliers turned to the English and established the Hudson's Bay Company in 1670. In June 1673, Jolliet and a Jesuit priest, Jacques Marquette, lowered their two birchbark canoes into the muddy waters of the Mississippi. Sometime that summer, with the help of their five other passengers, they became the first white men to set foot on Missouri soil.

The two of them reported many strange sights along the way—fish so large they threatened to rip apart the canoes, huge herds of grazing buffalo, wildly vivid Indian paintings of savage monsters that glared down at them from the river bluffs a bit upstream from the mouth of the Missouri—but they never did find the Northwest Passage. They turned back when they reached Arkansas for fear they might stumble into Spanish territory and create problems for themselves and their reluctant king. Nor did they find any gold or silver, and not for want of trying. Marquette chose to remain in the wilderness and convert the natives while Jolliet dashed off to Quebec to report on their journey. Within two years, worn out by the rugged climate, the Jesuit died. Jolliet, deprived of the recognition he believed he deserved, wandered from one minor government post to another for the rest of his life.

Not deterred by their failure, Rene-Robert Cavelier, Sieur de La Salle, came back scarcely a decade later looking for the passage that, despite the faith and desire of the explorers, simply did not exist. Assured by the Indians en route that the Missouri ran all the way to the Pacific, La Salle came to believe that the Missouri was the main river, the upper Mississippi merely its tributary. He followed the Mississippi to its mouth and laid claim to the river, its branches, and all the land thereabouts. He called it "Louisiana," after a king who couldn't have cared less.

La Salle's plans for empire collapsed when he was murdered by one of his own

men on a second trip to the wilderness, but he had managed to pave the way for Frontenac's French Canadians to carry out the count's clever strategy. All King Louis had to show for his efforts was a meager scattering of agricultural settlements in Nova Scotia, along the St. Lawrence, and now in Louisiana and Illinois country. In contrast, the divines and the trappers traveled up and down the Mississippi, filled with missionary zeal, searching for precious metal, and looking for the mythical Northwest Passage that would open direct trade with the Orient. They explored much of the Missouri, mapped and named many of its streams, and made peace with the Indians. They ruled the wilderness, though it was at best a vague sort of rule, resting not on force of arms but on native good will, and they had little need for permanent settlements.

The French called a section of upper Louisiana, running roughly from the Alleghenies to the Rockies, Illinois Country, after the Indian confederation displaced by the Sac and the Fox along the Mississippi. Since prehistoric times, the Indians had mined small amounts of lead in present-day Illinois and Missouri, and now they showed small specimens of the ore to the Europeans. In 1700 French mineralogist Joseph LeSueur investigated the Illinois mines. Based on his report one Le Moyne d'Iberville petitioned the French king for a concession, but the petition fell on the deaf ears of an all-but-bankrupt French court.

Antoine de la Mothe Cadillac, founder of Detroit, had better luck when he was appointed governor of Louisiana a decade later. A rigid, pompous, overbearing man, Cadillac frequently engaged in pointless disputes with his subordinates. Though a poor administrator, he fared better as a promoter, and when he returned to Paris in 1710 he managed to persuade Antoine Crozat, a French banker and wealthy merchant with connections at court, to underwrite the cost of French activity in Cadillac's new province.

In return the French government granted Crozat a 15-year trade monopoly for all of Louisiana, and the banker instructed Cadillac, now *his* agent, to open up silver mines in the Illinois Country. But silver proved as elusive as the Northwest Passage. Late in 1714 Captain Claude Dutisne arrived at Cadillac's garrison in Mobile with ore samples containing silver supposedly obtained from mines near Kaskaskia. When Cadillac arrived on the spot, he found the silver had come from Mexico. The Indians had given it to Dutisne as a joke. A still-determined Cadillac dug for silver at Mine la Motte, named in his honor, and found only lead. He evidently tried to hide his failure from his patron, reporting that he had discovered abundant silver at the mines and sending back several samples he said he had mined in the area. Ultimately, of course, the mining ventures collapsed, as did Crozat's hope for trade with the Spanish due to opposition from the viceroy of New Spain. By 1717 Crozat had lost his shirt and asked to be released from his obligations under the charter.

Convinced that the task of developing Louisiana was too great for one individual, the king allowed himself to be persuaded by Scottish financier John Law that a stock company could handle the job. Law, who had amassed a fortune at the gaming tables and naturally enough gained acceptance in the highest circles of the French court, became the driving force behind the formation of the Company of the West in 1717. A promoter on a much grander scale

than Cadillac, Law promised to send to Louisiana in the next 10 years 6,000 whites and 3,000 blacks in return for a trade monopoly, ownership of all Louisiana's mines, use of all its forts, depots, and garrisons, the right to import French goods duty-free and export American goods under reduced duties, control of Louisiana's commercial and Indian policies, and the right to name all officials in the province. Eager Frenchmen clamored to invest, and within two years Law expanded his operations by creating the Company of the Indies, consolidating the Company of the West with several other trading enterprises. Under his flamboyant direction, big capital flocked to the speculative venture.

Back in Louisiana the new governor, Jean-Baptiste Le Moyne, sieur de Bienville, reported that rich silver mines had been found, and the company's stock soared. By this time the company had sent Etienne De Bourgmont to handle Indian affairs. He put a stop to the unscrupulous practices of some traders, who actually encouraged warfare between various tribes to enhance the Indian slave trade. He traveled up the Missouri as far as the Platte River, keeping an accurate log of his journey, and becoming an idol of the Indians along the way. He took a group of the natives back with him to France, creating a sensation in Parisian society. He also checked the encroachment of the Spanish on the king's province. When an Iberian military expedition of about 60 entered French territory around Nebraska in 1720, they were massacred by some of De Bourgmont's new friends. That same year Captain Dutisne explored southwest Missouri and visited the Osage, strengthening the tribe's ties to the French. Also in 1720, Philip Renault, agent of the Company of the Indies, arrived in Illinois with about 50 miners and the future state's first black slaves. He worked his men hard. Prospecting and mining in the southeastern portion of the state expanded. But Renault, like Cadillac, found no precious metal in Missouri. Within months John Law's great "Mississippi bubble" burst, wrecking the French economy and aborting the devel-

Francisco Cruzat had been lieutenant governor of Upper Louisiana for a year when this portrait was painted in 1776. The popular Spaniard became the only man to serve two separate terms in that office, from 1775-1778 and from 1780-1787. Courtesy, Missouri Historical Society

opment of the Louisiana colony.

The company withdrew Renault's credit, but he hung on, harassed by debts and a desultory war between the Fox and the French, until 1744, when he returned, defeated, to France. De Bourgmont, still in the company's employ, built Fort D'Orleans in 1723, only to abandon it six years later when the company decided it had failed to pay its way. Though stockholders, eager to recoup their losses in the wake of the 1720 collapse, continued to operate the company, most Frenchmen had grown more prudent and few would invest additional money. Increasing trouble with the Sac and the Fox in Illinois finally prompted the company to petition the king in 1731 to take Louisiana back, which he did.

Though the king, the court, and French investors had good reason to be unhappy with the company, its activities had helped the traders, missionaries, miners, and saltmakers in the region by increasing their trade with the Indians and more firmly establishing France's claim to the area. Not long after the Company of the Indies withdrew from Louisiana, a few Creole families from Kaskaskia crossed the river and established the first permanent settlement west of the Mississippi at Ste. Genevieve. It was a damp and muddy place, which the white residents in Illinois called *Misere*— French for "misery."

The French king had problems in Europe much vaster than those his hapless subjects faced in Louisiana. Beginning around 1689 with the War of the League of Augsburg, called King William's War by the British colonials, England and France opened a century-long contest for colonial possessions throughout the world. And just as Frontenac had foreseen, when war did break out with England, the coureurs were ready to lead their Indian friends in raids on the outlying English settlements in New England and New York. And they did so throughout the intermittent conflicts that followed, such as the War for the Spanish Succession (Queen Anne's War), and the War of Austrian Succession.

During these conflicts, the French sent their Indians to raid thinly populated British villages, and the English protected themselves by an uneasy alliance with the Iroquois, who controlled the Mohawk Valley. The Osage and the Missouri rescued the French from the Fox at Detroit in 1712, creating a lasting enmity between the Fox and the other tribes. By the treaties that followed the wars, sovereignty shifted back and forth over various American lands with the signing of each new soon-to-be-violated peace.

In Europe the decisive war came to be called the Great War for the Empire, but the American colonists dubbed it the French and Indian War. Britain ultimately humiliated the French, who surrendered Canada on September 8, 1760. The Sac and the Fox, of course, fought with the British, and the Osage were with the French at British General Braddock's defeat at Fort Duquesne.

In 1762 the New Orleans firm of Maxent, Laclede and Company received from the French government a monopoly on the fur trade along the Mississippi and in the area between the Missouri and St. Peters rivers as part of an official attempt to speed postwar economic recovery in Louisiana. Pierre Laclede, directing the company's activities and assisted by a precocious 14-year-old stepson named Auguste Chouteau, established St. Louis as his headquarters in 1764. By the Treaty of Paris in 1763, French losses in the war had become official—Canada and her possessions east of the Mississippi went to England.

Suddenly, Missouri's strategic position at the crossroads of this new international boundary gave the region a new prominence, which Laclede brilliantly foresaw. He actively recruited settlers from among the disheartened and dispirited French across the river in Illinois, and by winter St. Louis was already a well-established village of some 40 or 50 families. Then in November or December of 1764, the word came: by secret treaty of November 3, 1762, two years before, France had ceded all of its colony west of the Mississippi and the city of New Orleans to Spain. The King of France had abandoned them, and the New World, entirely.

Spain was in no hurry to occupy its new lands in North America. In fact, it took seven years for Spanish officials to arrive in the territory and pick up the reins of government. In the meantime St. Ange de Bellerive, the French commander of Fort Chartres, served in their stead as both the civil and military authority. In 1765 he surrendered the French capital of Upper Louisiana to the British and moved his garrison to St. Louis. There he awaited the tardy transfer of the colony west of the Mississippi to its new Iberian masters in 1770.

Even after the transfer to Spain, the colony continued for the most part to observe the laws and customs of Paris. Spain invited French settlers east of the river to relocate on good terms, and they did so, preferring to live under the flag of their erstwhile allies rather than that of their bitter enemies. For Spain looked at Louisiana mainly as a buffer against English ambitions, and sent few colonists of its own. Probably not more than 20 Spanish families settled in the area during the 40 years of Spanish rule, and hence Upper Louisiana remained thoroughly French until its transfer to the United States in 1804.

Spanish became the official language, of course, but the inhabitants still spoke French. Many Frenchmen were appointed to office, though the appointments now carried Spanish titles. Spain changed only the laws providing for the acquisition of lands and regulating dower and intestate inheritances, and kept the structure of its government in Upper Louisiana simple. A governor general in New Orleans appointed a lieutenant governor, who resided in St. Louis and superintended all affairs of state for the entire territory stretching from the Arkansas River to the Canadian border. His authority, while extensive, was not absolute. Residents could appeal decisions over his head to New Orleans. To deal with purely local affairs, Spain broke the settlements along the Mississippi into districts, five of them falling within present-day Missouri: St. Charles,

St. Louis, Ste. Genevieve, Cape Girardeau, and New Madrid. The lieutenant governor appointed commandants for each district.

About 1,000 whites lived in the area when the Spanish arrived in 1770, almost all of them Frenchmen from Illinois, Indiana, Lower Louisiana, and Canada. Though the population would increase tenfold under the Spanish, the territory remained a remote, sparsely populated frontier. It was a society dominated by fur traders rather than colonists—the inhabitants of Missouri suffered little land hunger. They clustered along the banks of the Mississippi in settlements that were not much more than trading posts. Their very existence depended upon friendly relations with the Indians. From the first, the Spanish followed the French lead and promoted unity with the natives. Unlike the British colonials to the east, they adopted the practice of recognizing all Indian land claims. They did not fortify their villages against the Indians, and few if any of Louisiana's Creoles fell victim to the tomahawk. Not until the British and Americans threatened invasion did Spain take military precautions, fortify St. Louis, and build forts and blockhouses throughout

The Carre Gabriel residence, shown here in 1770, is typical of well-to-do homes built by early French pioneers. The steep-roofed, multi-roomed mansion, with its gardens, outbuildings, barn, and orchard, was surrounded by a cedar-picket fence. The property bordered four narrow, rutted, dirt lanes—Main, Levee, Vine, and Washington. Courtesy, Pierre Chouteau Collection, Missouri Historical Society

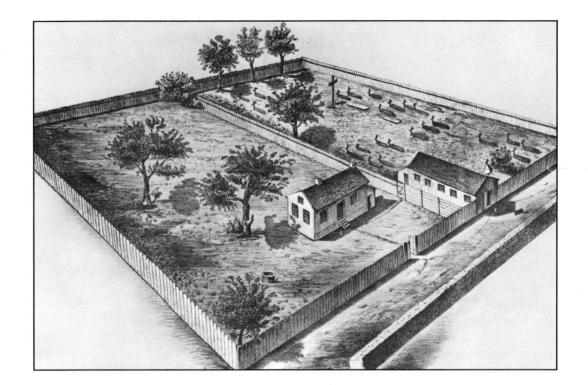

Missouri's first Catholic church, with its adjacent priest house, was built in 1770. From the time of the earliest settlements, when Jesuit missionaries traveled the upper Mississippi Valley, Roman Catholicism was an important force in the life of the community. Courtesy, Missouri Historical Society

the territory.

They lived leisurely, these easy-going and uncomplicated French pioneers in their sleepy French villages. They surrounded their homes, which doubled as places of business, with gardens, orchards, barns, stables, and outbuildings. They fenced them round with cedar-picket stockades or high stone walls. The houses varied in size and elegance from one-room dwellings with dirt floors to the multi-room mansions of the wealthy merchants. They had steep hipped roofs, and all but the simplest had porches.

Along the narrow, dusty lanes that ran between the houses (and turned to mud with every rain), they allowed their cattle, horses, sheep, and other livestock to wander. Most of the villagers worked sporadically in the common fields on the village outskirts. Each villager had his own strip to cultivate. Richer residents secured larger tracts and sometimes used slaves to work them, but generally they did not draw class lines too strictly. Wealthy men dominated local affairs, but they mingled freely with the poorer members of the village—at cards, at billiards, or around a muddy race track. They loved to gamble and often wagered quite sizable sums. Gracious and hospitable, they opened

their doors to strangers and travelers. Sometimes a band of Indians might appear in the village, seeking to confer with the local officials. Occasionally the return of a party of traders might create some excitement. But otherwise the calm was mostly punctuated by frequent and elegant balls and by the normal Saturday night dances.

The Spanish, like the French, established Catholicism as the official state religion, granted financial assistance to the Church, and continued the purge of the Jesuits that the French government, fearful of the order's growing wealth and power, had begun. Expelled from the territory, their property confiscated, the Black Robes gave way to the Capuchins as the dominant religious order. The Spanish even began to import young Irish priests, educated in Spanish seminaries and hesitant to return to a homeland ruled by English Protestants, to serve in Upper Louisiana and ease the chronic shortage of clergy.

As French Catholics, then, Missouri's inhabitants saw no reason for harsh distinctions between religious and social life. For them Sunday was not only a day for worship, but also an excuse for celebration. The church holidays featured music and dancing, and everyone—old, young, rich, poor, free and slave—joined in the festivities. So much so that Spanish officials and the priests often complained about the lax moral standards of their fun-loving subjects.

Only the fur traders strayed far from the village, trekking expertly into the interior along a few poorly marked trails. Except for the trails and the village lanes, roads hardly existed, and when folks traveled at all, they used the river. They plied up and down the Mississippi in pirogues, hollowed-out logs shaped like canoes. To move larger loads, they turned to a flat-bottomed boat called a bateau. Enclosed at the rear and covered with a roof, the bateau floated easily downstream, but it took hardy rowers to make the arduous journey back upstream against the current. A trip to St. Louis from New Orleans could easily take three months.

A few French merchants residing in the principal villages controlled the river traffic and dominated economic activity in Upper Louisiana, trading, buying, and selling any commodity they believed would turn a profit. Though profits could be huge, frontier ventures also called for great risks, and Louisiana's resourceful traders often dabbled in more than one of the major local enterprises—fur trading, farming, lead mining, and saltmaking. St. Louis merchants in particular controlled the fur trade, though residents in other villages often exchanged goods with local Indians for fur and peltries. In fact, because of a chronic shortage of money, the Spanish authorities approved the use of peltries as legal tender, and barter in fur became the common form of exchange, enhancing even more the position of St. Louis merchants like the Chouteaus.

But once again the indolent life of the French on the frontier was about to be seriously disrupted, this time by the American Revolution.

At first they were all for it, this revolt of their fellow North Americans. Even before Spain declared war against Britain in 1779, the St. Louis authorities unofficially helped George Rogers Clark in his conquest of the lands above the Ohio River, and they kept open the Mississippi-Ohio supply route to the American army by defeating a combined British and Indian attack on their city in 1780. But soon the French residents and the Spanish rulers found their enthusiasm waning in the face of the harsh and disorganized government established by the American Yankees in the territory they took from the British. Even before the war ended, great numbers of Creole families moved west across the Mississippi. When the United States passed an ordinance in 1787 prohibiting slavery in the Northwest Territory, American slaveholders began to follow them.

Suddenly it seemed as if Spain had been left holding the bag in the New World. Though England had relinquished its possessions east of the Mississippi to the

George Rogers Clark was unofficially assisted by authorities in St. Louis in his conquest of lands above the Ohio River during the American Revolution. Older brother of renowned explorer William Clark, George Rogers Clark helped to keep open the Mississippi-Ohio supply route by defeating a combined British and Indian attack in 1780. From Cirker, *Dictionary of American Portraits,* Dover, 1967

Americans when the revolution ended in 1783, the British held on to its posts in the ceded area for another decade, poaching on both Spanish and American territory. But once the American settlers began pouring over the Alleghenies and pushing out the English, they seemed an even bigger threat. They pushed their settlements right up to the banks of the Mississippi. There was no longer a vast wilderness between these active, restless, energetic

Moses Austin, a wealthy merchant who revolutionized lead mining on the Missouri frontier, began colonizing Texas after the financial panic of 1819, but died shortly after. His son Stephen F. Austin followed him to Texas and became a leader in Texas' conflict with Mexico. From Cirker, *Dictionary of American Portraits,* Dover, 1967

Americans and the tranquil, laconic Spanish colony.

Since it seemed that Missouri could no longer be a desolate barrier between Spanish territory and that belonging to England on the north and the United States to the east, Spain decided to make it a refuge for those who were disgruntled with their mother countries. Like Britain and France, it became involved in various intrigues with American citizens to separate the western territories from the United States. Offering generous land grants, religious toleration, and a tax-free existence, Spain did manage to lure many Americans into Missouri and persuade them to become Spaniards. Spain also fostered various colonizing schemes. After the French Revolution, New Bourbon became a haven for French Royalists. The Spanish encouraged for a time the grandiose plans of Colonel George Morgan, who, disappointed with the U.S. Congress for refusing to back a land scheme, wanted to establish a semi-autonomous colony at New Madrid.

Nor did Spain neglect the Indians. As the Americans pushed the tribes westward, Spain granted them title to lands in Missouri. It gave asylum to Louis Lorimier, an Indian trader in the pay of the British who had led his Shawnee and Delaware friends on several raids of Kentucky villages. Providing land in southeast Missouri, Spain hoped Lorimier's Indian colony would serve not only as an additional bulwark to American aggression, but would also put a stop to Osage Indian raids along the Mississippi.

As the American Northwest grew, Spain became more agitated. Eager to create loyal subjects who would form a strong frontier against the United States and England, Spain finally undertook to recruit prominent Americans whom she hoped would become obedient subjects. For that purpose Spain hired a famous revolutionary war figure and intriguer named James Wilkinson, who seemed willing not only to act as Madrid's agent in enticing Kentuckians, but also to tempt Kentucky itself to break away and join the Spanish empire. Accepting even Protes-

tants who subscribed to a loyalty oath, Spain managed to attract such notables as Daniel Boone and Moses Austin, the latter who would revolutionize the lead mining industry in Missouri. Then in 1795 Spain signed a treaty which opened the Mississippi to American trade, and American immigration to Missouri became a flood.

They were attracted by Spain's two great assets: free land and no taxes. Even though most of them knew they were abandoning their nationality to become subjects of the Spanish monarch, they did not cease to be Americans any more than the Creoles had stopped being French a generation before. They shied away from villages and located on isolated farms. Compulsive doers, used to political talk, jury duty, and elections, they thought of the French not as charming and relaxed, but as supercilious and lazy. And regardless of their oaths, they rejected French values and institutions, especially the Catholic Church. Under the winking eyes of the Spanish authorities, the Americans continued to practice their more emotionally intense brand of Christianity. By the close of the century, they were in the majority. They still spoke the language of the American West. When Spain threatened to close the Mississippi and the port of New Orleans to American traffic, the American settlers were probably as ready as their relatives and friends back in Kentucky and Tennessee to go to war to keep the river trade flowing.

For a brief time, then, Missouri became the center of power politics, at the heart of the global struggle that had long defined her role in the world. In the area surrounding St. Louis, Spain contemplated making a stand against her European and New World rivals, seeking to refashion her own strength in two hemispheres. Soon, though, Madrid recognized that it had been no more successful in Missouri than had the French, despite all the time and money it had wasted in the effort. Once again Louisiana changed hands by secret treaty. Spain returned the whole region, including Missouri, to France in 1800. In the intervening years, France itself had changed much more than its col-

ony—undergoing a bitter and bloody revolution and the rise of Napoleon. Napoleon dreamed briefly of making Missouri the footstool for his empire, but he quickly changed his mind. Instead he sold it to Thomas Jefferson for $15 million.

Three years after they had bailed out of the New World, Spanish officials still ran New Orleans. No formal transfer of power had yet taken place when Spain abruptly closed New Orleans to Americans in 1802. American frontiersmen demanded that their president decide the matter of their chief highway once and for all, and Jefferson, fearing a conflict with France or Spain or both, dispatched envoys to Paris to prevent hotheads like Andrew Jackson from dispatching volunteers down the Mississippi. Jefferson's men were instructed to buy Florida and New Orleans, but they came back with a bigger deal. Missouri was only a part of the vast lands purchased by the United States in 1804, but it contained some 10,000 people—mostly American settlers and French merchants, but also nearly 1,500 black slaves and a large number of Indians that no one bothered to include in the count. None of them had made any ef-

fort to overthrow their monarch at any time, and no popular uprising had forced the Missouri region into the American fold. Since most Missourians, especially people like Auguste Chouteau, had lived under three flags, they probably watched with mixed feelings as Jefferson's emissaries replaced the flags of Spain and France with the Stars and Stripes on March 10, 1804.

Not long afterward, however, they were enthusiastically entertaining two of Jefferson's special emissaries—Meriwether Lewis and William Clark. Congress had accepted Jefferson's purchase, making the land it encompassed America's newest territory, and the president sent the two young men to discover just how much land the purchase did encompass. The town saw the two depart on their famous expedition in 1804, many of its residents fully believing that St. Louis marked the point of origin for the fabled Northwest Passage to the Pacific and the marvels of the Orient. Instead, with astonishing physical and emotional courage, Lewis and Clark would discover that Missouri stood as a gatekeeper to a new natural wealth of indescribable variety and abundance. And they would tell the world.

Far left: Famed frontiersman and Kentucky pioneer Daniel Boone was one of the well-known Americans attracted to Missouri by the Spanish. From Cirker, *Dictionary of American Portraits,* Dover, 1967

Left: James R. Wilkinson, a famous Revolutionary War hero and intriguer, was hired by Spain to entice prominent Americans to become Spanish subjects. Spain had hoped to check the westward expansion of American citizens. From Cirker, *Dictionary of American Portraits,* Dover, 1967

The Missouri State Capitol building dominated Jefferson City in 1850. Courtesy, Missouri Historical Society

The Missouri Compromise

Missouri, as a European colony, found itself at the center of a global struggle between those two great imperial world powers, England and France. As an American territory soon to become the 24th state, it found itself at the center of a national struggle between the fledgling country's two major regions, North and South—a struggle that would eventually lead to social disunion and bitter civil war.

The seeds of the struggle in Missouri had been sown in 1787 with the passage of the Northwest Ordinance, when slaveholders, and those who believed in slaveholding, were cut off from the rich lands of the Ohio Valley and the Old Northwest. They poured into the Louisiana territories purchased from Napoleon instead. From the very beginning, Missouri's ideological bent was to the South, although compared to states in the heart of Dixie, the actual number of slaves was small, and the number of plantations smaller yet.

Still, many of Missouri's wealthy and influential early settlers depended on slave labor. They objected bitterly when the federal government split the Louisiana Purchase lands in two, creating the Territory of Orleans and the District of Louisiana, and assigning administration of the latter to the Territory of Indiana, whose distant capital in Vincennes made it difficult for them to wield influence with the governor, Benjamin Harrison.

Worried that Indiana's laws did not fully protect the institution of slavery and that they would be unable to effectively press their claims to land granted them—

With the Chouteaus and others, Charles Gratiot, who owned this country house in 1790, would form what became known as the "St. Louis junto"—a group of wealthy businessmen who dominated the early affairs of the Louisiana Territory and pressed the United States government to recognize huge land grants they claimed to have received from the Spanish before the Louisiana Purchase. Courtesy, Pierre Chouteau Collection, Missouri Historical Society

often spuriously—by the Spanish government, they called a convention in St. Louis to protest the location of the seat of government in Indiana. They couched their worries in protests about new taxes, absentee officials, endless delays, and unfair treatment. In 1805 the United States Congress responded.

Congress renamed the district the Territory of Louisiana and located its capital at St. Louis. Because it was only a first-class territory, the area's inhabitants still had no direct voice in government, but then they never had. Used to dealing with officials appointed by distant authorities, men like Moses Austin, Auguste and Pierre Chouteau, Charles Gratiot, and Manual Lisa had achieved precisely what they were after when they led the protest. The slavery issue, they felt, had been laid to rest; U.S. officials, like the Europeans before them, would seek their advice and defer to their judgments. They could get on with the business of making fortunes off old land claims, continued control of the fur and mining trade, and their influence with the Indians.

These men would come to be known as

the "little junto," or the St. Louis junto, an established elite who would be opposed by a younger group of mostly St. Louis lawyers in their attempts to get the federal government to recognize Spanish land grants. The bitter feuds between these two groups for land titles dominated the politics of the early territorial government, and led to a growing resentment among "honest farmers" throughout the rest of the territory against the St. Louis clique and its special interests. As the territory attracted more and more land speculators and farmers, another issue also began to loom large: what to do with the Indians, who were growing increasingly hostile toward the land-greedy whites.

These were issues peculiar to the American West, just as slavery was peculiar to the South. Unlike any other territory or state, it was Missouri's misfortune to be injured equally by the divisive issues of both West and South.

When Lewis and Clark returned to St. Louis from their expedition in September of 1806, they were eagerly greeted and grandly entertained by Pierre and Auguste Chouteau. They had traveled nearly 8,000 miles, and though they could not report they had found the fabled Northwest Passage, the glowing descriptions they did give of the West proved a boon to the westward movement. That movement would later make St. Louis one of the world's great cities and make a number of other towns across Missouri wealthy.

The news they got from the Chouteaus, however, was not nearly as good. The new governor of the Louisiana Territory, whom Jefferson had appointed, probably at the urging of Vice President Aaron Burr, had turned out to be a disaster. A natural intriguer and secret traitor, James R. Wilkinson had gone from being an agent in the pay of the Spanish government to being a general and the top-ranked officer in the post-revolutionary army. Not only had he made the rivalries between the land-grant factions immeasurably worse upon his arrival in St. Louis, but he had also sent messages to the Spanish authorities in Santa Fe suggesting they arrest Lewis and Clark if they could track them down.

Perhaps the Chouteaus described for the two explorers Wilkinson's inauguration, a huge celebration, immensely enjoyed by St. Louis' citizens, at which Wilkinson revealed his great fondness for the bottle. The Chouteaus would surely have expressed their resentment at the general's attempts to elbow his way into their fur-trading business. They no doubt at least mentioned the dark talk, especially among English-speaking residents, of a Western Conspiracy—a plan Wilkinson had supposedly hatched to detach the West from the United States and make Aaron Burr its president.

Wilkinson was in fact deeply involved with Burr in some sort of scheme. Burr, who had killed Alexander Hamilton in a duel in New York and was quite popular in the anti-Federalist West, had spent two weeks in St. Louis in the fall of 1805 in consultation with the general. Not a few

Left: From one of St. Louis' first families, Jean Pierre Chouteau entertained Lewis and Clark when they returned from their expedition in 1806. From Cirker, *Dictionary of American Portraits,* Dover, 1967

inhabitants of Louisiana were rumored to be in on the plot. They included, for example, the cantankerous and notorious John Smith T, who had come to Louisiana from Tennessee, adding the "T" to the end of his name to distinguish himself from all other Smiths and hoping to take advantage of the lawless local conditions in the mining business created by disputed Spanish land claims.

Rumors of the Burr-Wilkinson plot reached the president in 1806, and when they got bad enough that Jefferson was forced to investigate, Wilkinson stayed

true to form and blamed the entire conspiracy on Burr. Burr claimed they had only planned to invade Mexico and declare Burr emperor, a proper enough dream in the Napoleonic Era. At any rate, there proved to be enough evidence to implicate Wilkinson in the plot and so much bitter opposition to him in St. Louis that Jefferson removed him from office on March 3, 1807. The president replaced Wilkinson with a very popular appointment—Meriwether Lewis.

If Wilkinson's governorship reveals the unsettled quality of the new territory—the country's still quite tenuous hold on its western lands and the difficult time even Missouri's best citizens had with questions of legality—Governor Lewis's term says much about the unrelenting hardness of frontier life. A well-educated, sophisticated, but mercurial man, Lewis appeared to feel deeply the responsibilities of his position. He tried, most successfully, to remain efficient and impartial, but he also worried incessantly about his inability to keep in touch with a faraway federal capital, and assumed personal blame for the troubles he had with the terri-

Far left: Small and unpretentious, Pierre Chouteau's St. Louis home in 1765 was only the first of several, much grander mansions he would build. Pierre and Auguste Chouteau had something of a monopoly on the Indian trade, especially with the Osage, and later became two of the territory's wealthiest men and largest landowners. Courtesy, Pierre Chouteau Collection, Missouri Historical Society

Aaron Burr was deeply involved with James Wilkinson, the territorial governor, in a plot allegedly designed to detach the West from the United States. He was later tried for treason and acquitted. From Cirker, *Dictionary of American Portraits,* Dover, 1967

tory's Indians.

Economic depression in the East had increased the already heavy flow of immigration into the territory. As white settlements pushed farther and farther into ancient hunting grounds, the cycle of raids, murders, and acts of revenge so common to America's Indian-white relations began yet again. In 1805 Lewis's co-explorer William Clark, who had been promoted to brigadier general and made Superintendent of Indian Affairs, concluded a treaty with a few drunken Sac and Fox warriors that greatly irritated the tribes' true chiefs, and time and again led to the spilling of blood. By 1808 even the Osage, Missouri's most powerful tribe, had begun making retaliatory raids and threatening open war.

From the beginning, Governor Lewis realized that trouble with the Indians was inevitable, and he reorganized the militia to prepare for the coming crisis on the frontier. He and Clark averted general hostilities with the Osage by promising to help fight the tribe's vicious Sac and Fox enemies in return for a goodly portion of Osage land in Missouri. Despite his foresight and his success in avoiding bloodshed, Lewis appeared to many of his fellow Missourians to be unsympathetic, even impatient, with traders, and overly delicate in his concern for Indian rights. Their

attacks and other harsh criticisms quite common to a territorial officeholder, such as the accusation that he was misappropriating public funds, took their toll on Lewis's sensitive soul. Always moody, he began to drink heavily.

When William Clark invited Lewis to come live with him and his new bride, the governor turned him down, choosing instead to take up residence with Auguste Chouteau. From there, in 1809, a despondent Lewis left for Washington, where he hoped to clear up the confusion over his personal expenditures for a new administration headed by James Madison. Somewhere along the way his melancholy overwhelmed him; in western Tennessee he apparently committed suicide.

Governor Lewis was not the only one to despair of the hard life on the edge of the country. Grim jokes about desolate frontier existence had long been an integral part of the territorial consciousness. By 1811 many in the territory had good reason to believe "Misery" a sobriquet for the entire area. To the settlers, it seemed a land beset by three great curses: Indians, land speculators, and a harsh mother nature.

For 1811 was the year in which the largest earthquake ever in the history of the United States struck New Madrid and all of southeast Missouri, with tremors stretching well into Latin America. Some 27 shocks wracked the earth before daylight on December 15, and several more hit the next day. Great chasms opened in the ground, trees toppled and split, the Mississippi roared into the crevices, and, as its banks crumbled, huge waves swept over land whose surfaces were already changing irrevocably. For a while the great river ran backwards. Present-day Pemiscot and New Madrid counties were devastated, mines washed away, homes destroyed, farms turned into swamps. Settlers fled the bootheel, either having lost everything or fearing for their lives.

Those who remained turned to Congress for relief. Aid came tardily four years later when the government offered to take back their farms in return for certificates they could use to buy public land

Far left: William Clark, together with Meriwether Lewis, explored the vast Louisiana Territory purchased from France in 1804. The two departed from St. Louis that same year, discovering that Missouri stood as gatekeeper to a land of indescribable variety and abundance. From Cirker, *Dictionary of American Portraits,* Dover, 1967

Left: Meriwether Lewis, Clark's co-explorer, was named governor of the Louisiana territory after James Wilkinson was removed. The rigors of territorial office weighed heavily on Lewis; his melancholy eventually overwhelmed him, and in western Tennessee he apparently committed suicide. From Cirker, *Dictionary of American Portraits,* Dover, 1967

elsewhere. In the meantime, many had simply given up, sold their property for a few dollars, and moved on. As always, the territory's ubiquitous and insatiable speculators were ready to take advantage. Playing on the honest farmers' misfortune, they defrauded the government by buying up farms for a song and turning them in for certificates to purchase other, more valuable acreage.

Also in 1811, the trouble Lewis had always feared with the Indians finally arrived. An Indian confederation headed by Tecumseh spread terror all along the frontier. Fighting broke out with the tribes of the upper Mississippi, and the new governor, Kentucky Congressman and soldier Benjamin Howard, called out the militia. The Indian War was under way in Missouri. The territorial skirmishes paled in significance compared to the holocaust Napoleon had been inflicting on Europe, but they were a prelude to conflict with England. When news reached St. Louis in July of 1812 that Congress had declared war against the British, the Indian threat suddenly seemed very serious.

As the War of 1812 began, Missouri could muster only 178 soldiers, and the federal government ignored requests for additional aid. Captain Nathan Boone, Daniel Boone's son, who had been fighting

Indians most of his life, patrolled the Missouri River with his band of mounted rangers, but the real fighting occurred at Portage des Sioux in St. Charles County. Elsewhere, occasional raids and the murder of isolated families kept settlers on edge, mostly because the feverish temper of the war magnified the threat. During the next two years, alarms and rumors spread fear and uncertainty throughout the territory. Matters would only get worse after Andrew Jackson defeated the British at New Orleans in 1814. For, regardless of Jackson's great victory, the War of 1812 was over, and America had lost.

The terms of the Treaty of Ghent of December 24, 1814, forbade all military activity on the frontier until the United States had concluded treaties with the "Indian allies of the English." That left the Indians free to roam the territory at will, while Missouri was hamstrung by international agreement—and the Indians knew it. William Clark, who had replaced Governor Howard when he was called to service during the war, could not officially fight back as Indian raids grew bolder in the six months following the signing of the treaty. The united tribes launched their most destructive attacks of the entire Indian War during that period—at Cote sans Dessein, Loutre Island, Cap au Gris,

Femme Osage, and the Boone's Lick Country. Finally, in July of 1815, Clark, Auguste Chouteau, and Ninian Edwards, serving as United States commissioners, managed to open treaty conferences at Portage des Sioux with some 19 tribes. The next year they signed treaties with 10 additional tribes in St. Louis. The War of 1812 had ended at last in Missouri.

Despite the country's less than sterling performance during the war, the conflict itself had helped to tie the West firmly to the young nation. The treaties that followed, on the whole, removed the Indian danger to westward migration. Settlers flocked to Missouri, speculation ran wild, and credit expanded, all causing the value of land to mushroom. William Clark would remain governor another six years, overseeing the last stages of territorial transition as Missouri boosters began enthusiastically to plat towns and organize counties. In 1818, confident that all their problems had been solved, the citizens of Missouri petitioned Congress for permission to frame a constitution and be admitted into the Union.

Missouri's request caused a national crisis. The area had gone through the three hierarchical stages of territorial government—statehood seemed the next nat-ural step, not much more than a matter of routine. But the simple act of asking created an outcry such as the nation had never heard before, and in the heated arguments that followed, many Americans actually felt for the first time the threat of disunion. On three occasions between 1818 and 1820, Congress met to consider the issue before finally agreeing to what became known as the Missouri Compromise, the name given the "solution" to one of America's most famous conflicts.

The Northern faction in Congress, particularly anxious to maintain the existing balance between free and slave states, never questioned that Missouri was ready for statehood, but instead raised the issue of whether human bondage should be allowed to move further into the Louisiana Purchase territory. Only when a part of Massachusetts known as Maine asked for admission as a free state did Congress find its way out of the dilemma. The South refused to accept Maine unless the North accepted Missouri, and a deal was struck. During the months of debate, some Southerners began to argue that slavery was in itself good. A few others began bold talk of somehow ridding the nation of slavery altogether. Exhausted by long, tense, bellicose sessions, representatives and senators in a fit of distraction decided that, except for Missouri itself, the state's southern border (the famed 36 degree-30 minute line) marked the division between slavery and freedom in the Louisiana Purchase territory.

During the crisis, the debate spread from Capitol Hill across the country. And as journalists, preachers, and keynote speakers both North and South discussed what Missouri's future meant to America, Missouri's citizens grew indignant. They felt that the Louisiana Purchase treaty on its merits alone allowed them the unconditional right to statehood and that the real motives of the state's opponents had more to do with their fears that Missouri's central location and potential wealth might give it, if admitted, a commanding position in the Union. Consequently, though Missouri swallowed the compromise Congress offered, the state legislature sent back a constitution forbidding free blacks to enter the new state. Congress took the act as a slap in the face, and its antislavery faction moved to delay statehood until Missouri accepted the gradual abolition of slavery.

The last minute intervention of Henry Clay saved the Missouri Compromise from being spoiled by a stubbornness that would become a hallmark of Missouri's inhabitants. With great ill-humor, they followed Clay's suggestion, agreeing to write a new state constitution that formally—and merely formally—forbade legislation depriving citizens from other states of rights bestowed by the U.S. Constitution. When the new constitution was approved, President Monroe proclaimed Missouri the 24th state on August 10, 1821. Shortly afterward, Missouri brazenly passed statutes once again blocking free blacks

Left: This was a typical young woman in St. Louis in 1818, when the city proudly claimed some 5,000 residents. Courtesy, Missouri Historical Society

from coming into the state.

Not only Missouri, but the whole country, had begged the question. Congress, congratulating itself on preserving the American experiment in democracy, had merely created by law a nation divided between liberty and bondage. The compromise lasted until 1854, when much the worse for wear, it collapsed. In the meantime, it opened the floodgates west for a restless population, which would totally transform the pugnacious little frontier territory turned defiant new state.

It was soon after statehood that Missouri truly became mother to the American West, as wave after wave of migrants took advantage of the state's elaborate waterways to transport themselves and their worldly goods to the point of departure for the more difficult overland trek to Oregon and California. But not all the travelers were merely passing through. In ever greater numbers, they stopped to farm the land or set up shop serving the great stream of traders and settlers going farther on. In the four decades following Missouri's admission to the Union, its population grew at a rate seven times that of the nation as a whole. In 1820 its population ranked 23rd among the 24 states; by 1860 it ranked 8th among 33 states. By

Far left: A boy in a beaver hat represents the typical young man in the St. Louis of 1818. Courtesy, Missouri Historical Society

Hart Benton to the United States Senate. Benton had the backing of many prominent citizens, but he took note of the growing resentment of Missouri's rural districts against the St. Louis clique of lawyers who had been in control of the territorial government.

That insight served him well in a state whose future lay with the farmer and small businessman. When the panic of 1819 reached Missouri, the state's inflated currency collapsed and both of its major banks, the Bank of St. Louis and the Bank of Missouri, failed. Missourians grew suspicious not only of banks, but of bank notes in general. To fight the panic, the legislature called a moratorium on all

Above: "St. Louis in the Olden Time," which was published in *Central Magazine* in 1873, depicts the city around 1820. By the time Missouri became a state, American settlers from the South and the Ohio Valley had become a majority in the territory. Unlike the earlier French settlers, the Americans shied away from communal property and village society, building their log cabins on individual farms and concentrating on private life. Courtesy, Missouri Historical Society

Right: The meeting of the mighty Missouri and Mississippi rivers is shown here in about 1850. Missouri's abundant waterways and the easy transport they provided bolstered the state's role as "Mother of the American West." This lithograph is by E. Sacher and Company. Courtesy, Missouri Historical Society

then its population had increased some 18 times.

As early as the first statewide election, the importance of Missouri's rapid growth to its political and social life was becoming clear to the astute observer. William Clark, whose close relationship with the Chouteaus and the little junto was well known, lost the governorship to Alexander McNair, who was backed by the state's "honest farmers." The state legislature elected David Barton, who had headed the constitutional convention, and Thomas

land debts in 1821 and established loan offices empowered to issue paper based on state credit. Eventually, the Supreme Court ruled both actions unconstitutional, but most officials and merchants had reached their own judgments long before and refused to accept the state-issued money. Distrust of the wealthy grew apace, and most of Missouri supported Andrew Jackson for president, as a Westerner who would teach Eastern bankers the evil of their ways. And there was no greater Jacksonian Democrat than

Thomas Hart Benton.

Throwing himself heartily into the fray on the side of the common man, Benton became a national spokesman for the American West and the country's most vociferous advocate of free land for the homesteader. Time and demographics were on Benton's side, and even as he began his 30-year reign as the foremost political figure in the state (and the region), prosperity gradually returned to the state. While the legislature wrangled with the problem of where to locate the state capital, the overland trade with Mexico started up in 1821, bringing both much needed specie and a new source of income. By the time Jefferson City had been chosen as the capital, regular steamboat traffic had been introduced on the Missouri River, lowering the costs of freighting and increasing the volume of trade. St. Louis' fur business, the most important in the state, expanded, pushing the western terminus of shipping from Franklin to Independence, and then on to the great bend in the river.

The overland trade and expanded shipping brought about the rapid settlement of western Missouri. A heavy surge of migration throughout the 1830s had already pushed settlements away from the original river corridors and opened up new areas. In 1836 the Indians relinquished the Platte country, a strip of land extending along the Missouri from present-day Platte County to the Iowa state line. The next year Missouri purchased the land, clearly in violation of the Missouri Compromise, and settlers swarmed into the territory. Within a decade they had firmly established their tobacco- and hemp-based economy, which thrived on slave labor. Elsewhere, self-sufficient farms were the rule, with corn the number-one crop, and wheat a close second. Most Missouri farmers also planted vegetables, cotton, and flax, all for home consumption. And they began to raise the famous Missouri mule.

St. Louis became a large and important manufacturing and merchandising center, not only supplying the westward movement and serving as a shipping port for the Mississippi, but also dramatically increas-

ing its industry by producing iron goods, such as plows, stoves, tools, furnaces, and pipes, as well as manufacturing furniture, clothing, barrels, and steamboats. As foreign-born Germans arrived in the 1840s, they brought with them their Old World techniques for making beer, and soon the city boasted some 40 active, thriving breweries. But St. Louis had no corner on the growing prosperity.

By the early 1840s wagon trains regularly left western Missouri for Oregon, and not long afterward for Utah and California. Santa Fe traders investigating trails for national expansion to the Southwest and fur traders exploring routes to California and the Northwest had opened the way for new towns like St. Joseph, Westport, and Kansas City to prosper as centers of trade for the westward traffic.

Not surprisingly, Missourians, especially in St. Louis and in the state legislature, became interested in railroads long before the roads themselves would be built. In 1836 a state convention in St. Louis recommended the immediate construction of two lines, but though 18 companies were incorporated to do the work, the economic downturn of 1837 scuttled the plans. In 1849 a national railroad convention met in the city, and Thomas Hart Benton called for a line from the banks of the Mississippi to San Francisco. The next year, Governor Austin A. King recommended that the state use its credit to supplement private capital, and Missouri

After Missouri became a state in 1820, the General Assembly agreed to locate the state government in St. Charles, shown here in 1850, where a building had been offered, but only temporarily. The assembly ultimately chose Jefferson City as the permanent capital. Courtesy, Missouri Historical Society

poured its money into transportation. But the railroad companies overextended themselves, many went bankrupt, and before the Civil War only one line, the Hannibal and St. Joseph, was built. The failures saddled the state with debt and helped spark the national panic of 1857, which in turn added to the volatility of sectional struggles pushing the country headlong into war.

Despite such ups and downs, economically the times were good for antebellum Missouri. The Gold Rush of 1849, silver mining in the West, and the cattle trade ensured that Missouri's interests lay for some time outside its boundaries. Not until after the Civil War, when the West had been broken into states and the frontier trails obliterated, did Missourians turn their attention mostly to their own territory.

Until about 1840, the vast majority of those migrating to Missouri had been from the South, some two-thirds tracing their roots back to Kentucky, North Carolina, Tennessee, or Virginia. Many of Missouri's 87,000 slaves had been a part of that migration, but by and large the white

settlers had been back-country farmers from the border states rather than plantation owners. From 1840 on, more and more of Missouri's immigrants came from the free states, and by the 1850s their numbers were increasing at a faster rate than that of the Southerners. In addition, many of the newest arrivals were foreign-born, mostly Germans fleeing the failed revolution of 1832-1833, though many also came from an Ireland devastated by the potato famine. By 1860 the immigrants were 160,000 strong, some 13.2 percent of the population.

These demographic changes had a profound impact on the new state. Whereas the traditional Anglo-American frontiersman, proudly independent, was suspicious of or even overtly hostile to organized religion, occasionally going so far as to participate in Bible burnings and drinking orgies that parodied the Lord's Supper, the incoming Yankees were a much more abstemious and God-fearing lot. Despite Missouri's frontier boast that "God would never cross the Mississippi," by 1820 not only had the Catholic Church been revitalized, but the Baptists, Methodists,

Presbyterians, Episcopalians, and Disciples of Christ had firmly established themselves. A decade later, they were joined by the Reformed Evangelical Church and the Saxon Lutherans.

The majority of the earlier settlers were almost as indifferent to education as they were to religion. Part of the problem was that frontiersmen and hardscrabble Southern farmers were simply not used to contributing financially to the support of public and social institutions—even schools, which took from them the children they needed to work the fields. Though the territorial laws had encouraged book learning and the Enabling Act of 1820 had set aside land for schools, it was not until 1839 that the state made its first important provisions for education, passing laws that created the office of State Superintendent of Common Schools, established school funds, and set up the state university.

As trade increased and Missouri's population burgeoned, several new institutions made their appearance. In 1837 the Bank of Missouri was chartered for 20 years, providing the state's first sound public banking facilities. In the next decade, libraries sprung up in St. Louis, St. Charles, Pike, Marion, Lafayette, Cooper, Cole, Clay, Boone, and Cape Girardeau counties. Debate clubs, like Hannibal's Down East Debating Society, formed, and one could even find a goodly number of gilt and velvet theaters.

For less refined tastes, circuses toured the state bringing exotic animals and awe-inspiring spectacles, while in the river towns showboats offered elaborate minstrel shows and melodramas. Touring troupes, magicians, spiritualists, ventriloquists, and fortune tellers traveled about entertaining the curious and gullible. And out in the sticks, farm folk met at church functions and summer camp meetings,

Independence became the Jackson County seat in 1826, and within a few short years developed into a major trade center supplying goods to immigrants headed west across the Great Plains. By 1844 many of its 700 residents owned or clerked in several general stores and saddle and harness shops, or worked as blacksmiths, wagonmakers, druggists, jewelers, hatters, gunsmiths, and tinners. But Independence declined in the late 1840s as Westport and Kansas City took over its trade. This Herman J. Meyer lithograph is of the courthouse in 1850. Courtesy, Missouri Historical Society

Colonel Stephen W. Kearny commanded the Army of the West during the Mexican War. Many—perhaps most—of the troops in the Army of the West came from Missouri. From Cirker, *Dictionary of American Portraits,* Dover, 1967

while young men from every community gathered each week for horseracing, cards, and shooting contests. Though duels, to which frontier Missouri was much addicted, had fallen out of fashion, whiskey, and, for the Germans, beer, remained the beverage of choice. It was quaffed not only at taverns, but at almost all social gatherings, from husking bees to camp meetings, adding generally to the passionate and sometimes brutal life.

The vast influx of new blood often contributed to the brutality as well as to the increased trade. In 1831 Mormon prophet Joseph Smith fixed on Independence, Missouri, as the Mormon Zion, and more than a thousand of his followers flooded the area. Mostly from the Northern states, vehemently opposed to slavery, and clannish and secretive, they came in such numbers and so quickly that they soon had taken political control of the city and surrounding county. As they began to acquire land as well, they aroused the anger and fear of their neighbors, who responded by driving them out and into Clay County within a few years. The violence escalated between the belligerent paramilitary organizations of the Mormons and armed vigilante groups, and in 1836 Smith's followers retreated yet again, into Davies and Caldwell counties. In 1838, during guerrilla fighting between "saints" and

settlers, Governor Lillburn W. Boggs came down hard on the side of "native" Missourians. He ordered the militia to exterminate the Mormons or drive them from the state, and by the spring of 1839 it had carried out his orders. The Mormons had moved to Nauvoo, in Illinois, where they set up what amounted to an armed state within the state. The episode was a harbinger of the civil disorder Missouri would experience when events once again raised the issue of slavery to a national level.

It was the war with Mexico that ultimately brought that issue to a head. Texas, which won its independence in 1836, had been something of a colony of Missouri, founded by Moses Austin's son, Stephen. A decade later, when the Army of the West was organized in response to Congress's declaration of war in April 1846, most of its troops came from Missouri. Under the command of Colonel Stephen W. Kearny, led by colonels A.W. Doniphan and Sterling Price, the army marched overland to Santa Fe—a route Missourians knew well—and occupied

New Mexico, where they put in office a fellow state citizen, Charles Bent. Doniphan then headed south, driving an incredible 3,600 miles without quartermaster, postmaster, commissary, uniforms, tents, or formal military discipline, to assist John C. Fremont hand California and New Mexico to the United States.

But it proved a Pyrrhic victory. Under Mexican law, the territories had been free, but now the South argued for extending the Missouri Compromise line, 36 degrees and 30 minutes, so that all lands south of it sanctioned slavery. In 1849 the Missouri legislature instructed its representatives to Congress to insist that the federal government had no right to decide the boundaries for either slavery or freedom, that only the territories themselves could settle the issue. By now it was becoming clear that conflict between the states was possible, and the so-called Jackson Resolutions indicated that Missouri would take its stand with the South. Thomas Hart Benton, completely devoted to the Union and national solidarity, rejected his state's instructions as the separatist blatherings of

Left: In one of the Mexican War's most incredible marches, Colonel Alexander W. Doniphan drove his troops 3,600 miles without quartermaster, postmaster, commissary, uniforms, tents, or formal military discipline to assist in handing California and New Mexico to the United States. From Cirker, *Dictionary of American Portraits,* Dover, 1967

a powerful minority. This split the Democratic party in Missouri and led to the end of Benton's long and distinguished career.

In 1850, Congress averted disaster by once again shuffling to delay the showdown. Under the Compromise of 1850, California was admitted as a free state. The other territories won from Mexico could organize for statehood, and the decision as to which should be slave, which free, would be made later. Slavery was banned from the District of Columbia. The fugitive slave laws were strengthened. But the battle was joined, and when Nebraska and Kansas applied for statehood in 1854, Congress threw up its hands, repealed the Missouri Compromise, and passed the Kansas-Nebraska Act, which left the question of slavery up to the individual states.

The Act spawned the Republican party and led Missouri Senator David R. Atchison, who had broken with Benton over slavery, to swear that he would let the territory "sink in hell" before allowing it to be organized as free soil. Clearly, Nebraska would opt for freedom, but Kansas was up for grabs. Abolitionists in the North organized the Emigrant Aid Society and financed free settlers in Kansas. New England authors like William Cullen Bryant and John Greenleaf Whittier organized one of history's great propaganda

Far left: The coming of the steamboat made St. Louis an inland port, and trade grew from 174,000 tons of goods passing through St. Louis docks in 1834 to some 716,000 in 1844, reaching around 1.5 million tons annually by the 1850s. This photo shows Nathaniel Phillips Piano Forte Music and Military Goods at 42 Market Street in 1843. Courtesy, Missouri Historical Society

In 1857, Dred Scott, a St. Louis slave, argued to the Supreme Court that because his owner had taken him north to a region closed to slavery, he was by law no longer a slave. The Court disagreed, and their decision made civil war inevitable. From Cirker, *Dictionary of American Portraits,* Dover, 1967

campaigns, soon aided by newspaperman Horace Greeley and correspondents sent by Eastern papers to report on the Kansas-Missouri "situation."

In response, fearing and hating the "Yankee slave-stealers" and egged on by Atchison, thousands of pro-slavery Missourians, mainly from the tobacco- and hemp-growing western counties, flooded into Kansas to vote illegally and then return home to their farms. Overwhelming the Kansas settlers, the majority of whom were probably free-soilers, they elected a territorial legislature that immediately legalized slavery and won official recognition from the federal government. Free-soilers poured in from Iowa to settle the land, formed their own legislature, set their capital up at Lawrence, and petitioned Congress for admission as a free state. Open warfare broke out along the Kansas-Missouri border.

Atchison resigned his seat in the Senate to lead the fight, organized a posse of Missourians, and, in the guise of answering a U.S. marshal's summons, raided Lawrence. Called "border ruffians" by Horace Greeley, the posse set fire to a hotel and a few houses, chopped up a printing press, arrested several free-state leaders, and killed three people in the process. A monomaniacal abolitionist named John Brown retaliated by murdering five pro-slavery settlers on the Pottawatomie Creek, then mutilating their bodies. Ideologically motivated assassination had begun. By the time the federal government could join with the governments of Missouri and Kansas to bring the guerrilla fighting in "Bleeding Kansas" more or less to an end in 1858, 200 people were dead and $2-million worth of property had gone up in smoke.

At the height of the bloodletting, the U.S. Supreme Court decided to enter the controversy. In 1857 it chose to speak to the question of congressional power over slavery in the territories. A St. Louis slave named Dred Scott had been trying to win his freedom through the courts. Once taken north by his owner into a region closed to slavery by the Missouri Compromise, Scott argued that he was by law no longer a slave. The Court disagreed. The majority held that Congress was powerless to exercise restrictions on property, and since it considered slaves to be property, the Dred Scott case implied that slavery was safe—and, according to the South's reading, should be protected—everywhere in the nation. The minority argued that slaves could not be considered property. The decision changed the terms of the debate and made civil war inevitable. From an argument over how the West should be settled it became a battle over the nature of property itself.

Though the much publicized border

war and the Dred Scott case made Missouri notorious as a lawless, slaveholding land, in fact by 1860 the average Missourian was for compromise and union. Slaves made up less than 10 percent of the population, and were owned by a mere 25,000 of the state's 1.2 million people. Half the slaves were in 12 counties, and some two-thirds of them along the Missouri River. Especially in St. Louis, Missouri's sizable number of Irish and German workers were opposed to slavery, and not merely because they had to compete with slave labor. Most Missourians were concerned about the excesses of the extremists in both North and South and would have been content to watch the fighting from the sidelines. But the politically powerful pro-Southern faction, who had cost them their beloved Senator Benton, forced them into a war where they had to make hard choices.

The struggle between the radical minorities for the heart and soul of a population with already acute differences in ethnic background, religious preference, and economic status entangled Missouri in the war years more thoroughly than any other state except Virginia and Tennessee. The deep schisms it created in even small towns and once-solid families would make the Civil War in Missouri especially hellish.

German-born lithographer Herman J. Meyer depicts St. Joseph in 1850. Meyer's peaceful romanticism belies the real bustle of Missouri towns like St. Joe. In the 1840s, Missouri's geographic position created a major business opportunity in the sale of cattle to Oregon, California, and Colorado, and St. Joseph became a center for the developing trade. In 1846 alone, some 38,000 head of cattle moved out of St. Joseph on the way to Oregon.

In 1860 St. Joe became the originating point for the short-lived Pony Express. Courtesy, Missouri Historical Society

CHAPTER III

A Savage Passage

The border states were vital to the Union cause at the start of the Civil War. Neither Kentucky, Maryland, nor Missouri had yet decided whether to secede or remain loyal. Their people's sympathies were split between North and South. Their governors, on the other hand, were already strongly committed to one side or the other. Kentucky and Missouri, with pro-slavery executives, rejected Abraham Lincoln's call for troops. Maryland's pro-Union head of state vacillated, sending men only to defend Washington, but not to fight in the South. Lincoln adopted vigorous policies to keep all three states in line, and in each case he proved, if barely, successful.

But in one important respect Missouri was different from the other border states: it engaged the North in battle long before the first shots were fired at Fort Sumter. For the most part, the warfare along the Kansas-Missouri border had abated by 1860. But on both sides of the line there were those who had not forgotten the destruction and slaughter of the late 1850s, those who longed for revenge, and those who sought in the outbreak of hostilities an excuse to resume the midnight raids, the bushwhacking, and the reign of terror.

Because Missouri never seceded from the Union, it escaped the harshest aspects of the military occupation visited on the South after the war during Reconstruction. But because of its lawless past, and the deep-seated hatreds of its divided population, it would spend most of the war itself under martial law, witnessing within its own borders a struggle that resembled nothing so much as the undeclared war America fought a century later in the jungles of Southeast Asia.

For that reason the Civil War was more destructive in loyal Missouri than in most of those states—except Tennessee and Virginia—that actually joined the rebellion, and the psychological scars the war left were as long in healing as any in the Deep South.

Governor Claiborne Fox Jackson was to be surprised often in the coming months, but probably never so much as by the results of the state convention he promoted in early February of 1861 to discuss Abraham Lincoln's election and Missouri's possible withdrawal from the Union. Author of the Jackson Resolutions of the late 1840s, which had called for the extension of slavery into the western territories, the governor hoped for vindication of his urge to secede and join six others—South Carolina, Georgia, Florida, Alabama, Mississippi, and Louisiana—who at that very moment were meeting in Montgomery, Alabama, to form the Confederate States of America. But Missourians were in no mood to humor him. The politically powerful pro-slavery faction had barely managed to put Jackson in office the year before against a virtually unknown moderate named Orr. Jackson's own legislature, while granting his request for a convention, had passed a resolution that stipulated secession could only be decided by a plebiscite.

As it turned out, the precaution was unnecessary. Not one pro-slavery delegate was elected to the convention, which was dominated by prominent St. Louis attorney and former Missouri Supreme Court justice Hamilton R. Gamble. A conservative ex-Whig, Gamble had come out of semi-retirement to seek a seat at the convention and argue the Union cause, which he did eloquently enough to return a majority of 80,000 votes for the Northern faction. The convention's report, written by Gamble, rejected secession and recommended equality among the states. Missourians, it seemed, though they disliked the Republican administration, did not

believe the presidential election itself sufficient cause to quit the Union.

Though frustrated for the moment by the electorate, Jackson had no intention of remaining neutral should war break out. In April, only weeks later, South Carolina hotheads fired on Fort Sumter, and Governor Jackson turned a deaf ear to Lincoln's request for 4,000 Missouri volunteers. As Texas, Tennessee, Arkansas, North Carolina, and Virginia one after the other joined the Confederacy, Jackson met covertly with the St. Louis militia to plan a takeover of the federal arsenal. He sent a secret message to Jefferson Davis requesting rebel arms and ammunition. The militia marched to the edge of St. Louis and formed Camp Jackson, a stone's throw from the armory.

Jackson's nemesis was Francis P. Blair, a close friend and confidant of Abraham Lincoln. Frank Blair had been authorized by the president to come to St. Louis and organize its pro-Union forces. Turning to the city's Germans, free-soilers to their very bones, he raised what he called the Home Guards. He was shocked by the developments in the city and appalled at the conciliatory attitude and lackadaisical preparations of the amiable commander of federal forces in the West, General William S. Harney. Blair prevailed on the president politely to recall Harney to Washington and temporarily replace him with Captain Nathaniel Lyon, a fiery-headed little New Englander and veteran of the 1850s border war who trusted almost no one in Missouri but Blair.

Jefferson Davis had responded readily enough to the governor's request for arms. Two days after Camp Jackson had been established, a shipment of boxes marked "marble Tamaroa" arrived downriver to await pickup by officers from the state militia. The goods inside had been liberated from the federal arsenal at Baton Rouge, and when the cases reached Camp Jackson they sat unopened so as not to arouse suspicion. But Lyon was a suspicious man, and the smuggling of what he was sure had to be Confederate guns and bullets convinced him that the camp posed a real threat. Already considering a preemptive strike, he disguised himself as Frank Blair's blind mother-in-law and took an afternoon ride in an open carriage through the camp to prove he was right.

That night, he told the Union Safety Committee, charged with protecting St. Louis, that he had seen small Confederate flags hanging from tent poles and two streets with handmade signs called "Davis" and "Beauregard." It was enough for Lyon and Blair, though not for the committee. Overriding the committee's objections, the next day, May 10, 1861, Lyon took some of his 10,000 troops, surrounded the camp, and demanded that the militia's commander, General Frost, surrender within half an hour. With only 800 or so men, Frost could only sputter that he had done nothing illegal—and comply. As the German Home Guards marched the militia under arrest to the arsenal, they drew a large crowd, some curious, some inebriated, some belligerent.

Amid cheers and curses for Jeff Davis, Abraham Lincoln, and the Germans themselves, a drunk who had been treated roughly by the troops drew his gun and fired. A federal soldier fell. The Home Guards stopped in place, raised their rifles, and let loose a volley over the heads of the crowd. Then something else went wrong, confusion reigned, and 28 people

were killed. William Tecumseh Sherman, out for a walk with his son, happened to be in the crowd. Perhaps like many caught in the turmoil, he failed to realize that the first shots of the Civil War had sounded in Missouri.

That was certainly not clear to General Harney, who, back from Washington, refused to declare martial law. Governor Jackson continued reorganizing his militia, now calling it the Missouri State Guard. Against his better judgment, he named the aging former governor and white-haired hero of the Mexican War, General Sterling Price, to head the pro-slavery volunteers. "Old Pap," as his fellow Missourians called him, persuaded Harney that his and Jackson's intentions were to keep Missouri aloof from the conflict, and Harney believed him. Even as Missouri grew into an armed camp, Harney issued a joint statement with Price, calling for a cooperative venture. Harney would look after St. Louis, it said, while Price maintained order in the rest of the state.

The Harney-Price communique was simply too much for Blair. He had the president permanently remove Harney and put the Department of the West, offi-

This *New York Illustrated News* picture from May 25, 1861, is called "Terrible Tragedy in St. Louis." When Democratic governor Claiborne Fox Jackson, a Southern sympathizer, refused to raise the 4,000 troops Abraham Lincoln had requested at the outbreak of the Civil War, Missouri Congressman Frank Blair returned to St. Louis and did so himself. Mostly German, Blair's Home Guards were commanded by General Nathaniel Lyon, who declared martial law in St. Louis and marched on Camp Jackson, near Grand and Olive streets, home of 800 of Jackson's state militia. The arrest of the militia drew a crowd, a drunk fired on federal troops, and 28 people were killed. War had come to Missouri. Courtesy, Missouri Historical Society

The Missouri State Guard, First Regiment, was stationed at Camp Lewis on the St. Louis Fairgrounds in 1860, just prior to the Civil War. The State Guard was often sympathetic to the Southern cause and would follow their governor, Claiborne Jackson, into the war. Courtesy, Missouri Historical Society

cially this time, in Lyon's hands. Bowing to moderates still hoping to avert conflict, Lyon, now a general, and Blair met with Jackson and Price at the Planter's House in St. Louis on June 11 to discuss the Union's right to raise Home Guards in the interior and station Union forces throughout the state. Lyon was in no mood to be trifled with. He knew Jackson was playing for time, and made his position perfectly clear: "Rather than concede to the State of Missouri for one single instant the right to dictate to my Government in any matter however unimportant, I would see you, and you, and you, and every man, woman, and child in the State, dead and buried."

Lyon stood up and continued. "This means war," he said. "In one hour my officers will call for you and conduct you out of my lines."

Jackson and Price did not wait for the escort. They fled by rail to Jefferson City, burning the bridges over the Gasconde and Osage rivers behind them. Once there, Jackson called out 50,000 state troops to "repel the invasion," and abandoned the capital. Before the day had passed, Lyon was in hot pursuit. Against the will of the vast majority of the voters, hostilities were under way in earnest. Nine months later, after a few significant skirmishes and a couple of major engagements, the Civil War was over—strategically—in Missouri.

Finding Jefferson City deserted, Lyon struck northwest and caught up with Jackson's State Guard a few days later on June 17, 1861, at Boonville. Price was ill, so Jackson took command of the ill-trained troops himself. Their field commander, understanding the predicament, refused to lead them into battle, but Jackson ordered them into a reckless headlong charge, which Lyon easily routed. As

Jackson ran, Lyon became an instant hero, and Hamilton Gamble was appointed the new governor of Missouri.

But the little general's glory was short-lived. Sterling Price's plan had been to lead the militia toward the Arkansas border, where he could join forces with the regular Confederate Army, raising volunteers as he went. From Jefferson City, Lyon detached the Home Guards under Colonel Franz Sigel to cut off the retreating Confederate troops. By the time Sigel came face to face with Price at Carthage on July 7, he was outnumbered four to one. When he charged anyway, Price brushed him aside and continued on his way. Meanwhile, Lyon was facing political problems, partly because of his high-handed declaration of war, and President Lincoln replaced him with John C. Fremont, the celebrated western adventurer.

While Fremont dallied in St. Louis, Lyon in the field had to deal with an Old Pap determined to gain control of the Missouri River and free the state from federal captivity. Price's confidence soared when he defeated Lyon at Wilson's Creek near Springfield on August 10, 1861. Lyon had desperately urged Fremont to send reinforcements, but Fremont ordered him instead to avoid the fight. With little love lost between the two Union officers, Lyon chose to ignore Fremont's orders, lost the battle, and died in the effort. Fremont, like many Northern commanders at the time, had been busy politicking, wrangling with Gamble and irritating the president. By the time Fremont finally decided to engage the enemy, Price was ready. Old Pap's subsequent victory at Lexington on September 13 cost Fremont his reputation.

But radicals like Blair and Lyon, and Jackson and Price, had always been one jump ahead of most Missourians, and when Jackson followed the victories with a general call to arms, few recruits appeared to rally to his cause. The call came after the pro-Southern members of the legislature had met in October in Neosho to pass an act of secession. Though Mis-souri was immediately accepted into the Confederacy, Jeff Davis, suspicious of Price because of his shenanigans with Yankee General Harney and possibly because of reservations conveyed to him via Claiborne Jackson, was reluctant to commit troops to help out. Price had no choice but to move south into Arkansas, where his forces were soundly defeated at the Battle of Pea Ridge on March 7 and 8 of 1862.

Price was transferred east of the Mississippi, and Jackson's government went into exile, first in Arkansas and then in Texas, by which time Jackson had died and been replaced by his lieutenant governor. After Pea Ridge, the Civil War in Missouri degenerated into the vengeful marauding of red-legged Jayhawkers and irregular guerrillas. But it was no less bloody and brutal because of that.

The first attacks came in the summer of 1861. John Brown was dead, but his spirit lived on in the bloodthirsty crew of Kansas killers and thieves led by men such as James Montgomery, Jim Lane, and Dr. Charles Jennison. Acting loosely as an advance guard for the Union army, a band under "Doc" Jennison sacked Harrison-

A political cartoon from June 1861 depicts the "Battle of Booneville," a skirmish that made Nathaniel Lyon, commander of the Union forces in Missouri, an instant hero. Shown here as a lion, the Federal general came face to face with the State Guard commanded by Governor Claiborne Jackson on June 17, 1861, in Boonville. Lyon easily routed Jackson's ill-trained troops when they made their first, reckless charge. Jackson is shown here in skirts, fleeing Lyon, with General Sterling Price, commander of the Confederate troops in the West. Courtesy, Missouri Historical Society

ville in July. There wasn't an enemy soldier in sight, and western Missourians knew the terror of the 1850s had returned.

They called these marauders Jayhawkers, or "Red Legs," for the red morocco leggings they wore, and decent Union officials protested their activities from the beginning. When the great western artist George Caleb Bingham, then state treasurer of the provisional government in Jefferson City, heard that Jennison had been charged with organizing the Seventh Kansas Cavalry, he wrote Missouri's congressmen protesting that "an outlaw, abhorred and avoided by honorable minds" should be allowed to become "an officer in the United States Army."

Even General Halleck, who had replaced the contentious Fremont, complained to Washington from St. Louis when he heard the rumor that Jim Lane had been made a brigadier general: "I cannot conceive of a more injudicious appointment. It will take 20,000 men to counteract its effect in this state, and, moreover, is offering a premium for rascality and robbing generally." Governor Gamble and his counterpart in Kansas both joined the chorus, expressing officially their concern that, after Lane's forces were organized, the border war would flare up again.

They saw their worst fears realized in the fall of 1861, when the Seventh Kansas Cavalry invaded Jackson County. The

troops occupied the county seat, then sacked and looted at will. They murdered all those they suspected of being Southern sympathizers and anyone else who dared to protest their actions or disobey their orders. On September 23, Price chased Lane back into Kansas, but the Jayhawkers returned the minute Old Pap moved his major forces to Lexington. Red Legs swept into the wealthy river port of Osceola, stole some million dollars worth of goods, and burned the city to the ground. Next they ravished Butler, then Parkville.

Not surprisingly, when a handsome young 24-year-old named William Clarke Quantrill gathered around him a few western Missouri toughs and struck back, he became a hero not just to the state's slaveholders and Southern sympathizers, but to the entire sullen, silent, and abused population. Quantrill's slight build, his boyish, wavy red hair, and his heavy-lidded pale eyes belied his ruthlessness. The son of a schoolmaster, an ex-schoolmaster himself, he had moved to Lawrence, Kansas, at the height of the border war, joining in several raids on Missouri, even freeing a few slaves. Now, he changed sides and led his band against Doc Jennison's raiders in mid-December as they looted a farm home in Jackson

County. Soon he was Missouri's most no-torious bushwhacker, for which he re-ceived a commission as captain in the Con-federate Army.

Quantrill was recruited by Major Gen-eral Thomas C. Hindman, commanding the CSA's District of Arkansas, under the Confederate Partisan Ranger Act of April 21, 1862. In addition to Quantrill, Hindman commissioned at least a dozen other Missouri officers early that summer to return to their respective areas and recruit both Confederate regulars and guerrillas who could be left behind. Men like William Anderson, George Todd, and Cole Younger joined with Quantrill to wreak havoc on the Kansas border patrols and Missouri's Union militia. In March of that year, Quantrill's Raiders sacked Au-brey, Kansas, and in October, they hit Olathe. Shooting down settlers "like so many hogs," Quantrill and his men proved to be enemies entirely worthy of a Jim Lane or a Doc Jennison.

As the deprivations mounted on both sides, Union General John Schofield, charged with pacifying the Missouri coun-tryside, mulled over a plan by his subordi-nate, General Thomas Ewing. Ewing's job was to guard the long boundary between Kansas and Missouri, and he had grown to distrust entirely the citizens he was bound to protect. He proposed to Scho-field that they try to control the guerrillas by mass evacuation, removing everyone known to have aided or abetted the guerrilla cause. Though reluctant, Scho-field approved the plan on August 14, 1862, with the provision that the evacua-tion be limited to the smallest number of people possible.

Ewing had already rounded up the wives, mothers, and sisters of suspected guerrillas and jailed them in a decrepit three-story brick building in Kansas City. The same day that Schofield approved his evacuation plan, the makeshift prison col-lapsed from overloading. Several of the women were severely injured. Five were killed, among them the sister of "Bloody Bill" Anderson, one of Quantrill's most ef-

Despite General Nathan-iel Lyon's early celebrity as commander for the Union's Department of the West, Missouri's conservatives soon be-gan to demand a more experienced soldier to lead their troops. When an attempt to detach Missouri and place it un-der General George B. McClellan's Department of the Ohio proved unwieldy, President Abraham Lincoln ap-pointed John Charles Fremont head of the western front. Fremont's bodyguard charges a detachment of Rebel forces in this drawing from *Frank Leslie's Illus-trated Weekly* dated November 23, 1861. Courtesy, Missouri His-torical Society

Missouri native Cole Younger took part in the "border ruffian" raids into Kansas and became a guerrilla leader under William Quantrill. After the war Younger formed a gang with his brother and Frank and Jesse James, continuing the violent life to which he was accustomed. From Cirker, *Dictionary of American Portraits,* Dover, 1967

fective guerrilla leaders. Immediately the rumor spread that Ewing had engineered the outrage from the start.

With 450 men, Quantrill took his revenge on Lawrence, Kansas. Riding all night, the raiders hit the sleepy town at dawn with Quantrill's order to "kill every man big enough to carry a gun" ringing in their ears. They did. Moving house by house, they murdered 150 men, often deliberately in front of their wives and children. Eighty widows and 250 orphans fled into the streets as Quantrill's men set ablaze over 185 buildings. While $2-million worth of property burned to the ground, Quantrill sat in the dining room of a Lawrence hotel, enjoying his breakfast and complaining that Jim Lane had escaped a Missouri hanging when he sprang from his bed in a nightshirt and hightailed off into the nearby cornfields.

As suddenly as they had appeared, the guerrillas vanished. They lost only one man, a drunk who had lingered long enough to be gunned down by an Indian. A bereaved mob dragged his dead body into the streets and tore it to pieces. Which is what everybody in Kansas—and, shortly thereafter, in the rest of the North—wanted to do with William Quantrill once the news had spread. Since Quantrill was unavailable, Jim Lane turned on those who were. He blamed Schofield. He blamed Gamble. He blamed the people of Missouri. They were too lax, or too soft-hearted, or too treasonous. Soon the radical press picked up Lane's complaint and lay the responsibility for the massacre at the feet of Governor Gamble. The *Missouri Democrat* even charged him with personally supporting Quantrill.

Schofield rushed to the border to take charge of the situation, but he was too late. Without waiting for his commander to arrive, Ewing instituted a general evacuation policy, one much harsher than Schofield had authorized. Vindictively placing Lane in command of the evacuation, Ewing proclaimed General Order Number 11—the most controversial of the war in Missouri. The edict ordered everyone in Jackson, Cass, Bates, and the north-

ern half of Vernon County, who lived beyond a mile's distance from a Union military post, to leave their homes within 15 days. Those who could prove their loyalty might remain at a post in the area. All other people would be forced to move completely out of the military district. The order also required them to take all grain and hay from their farms to the nearest military post. Their other crops and perishable goods would be destroyed.

Lane put the vicious Doc Jennison and his hated Kansas cavalry to work enforcing the order. Jennison ruthlessly drove the farmers off their hard-won homesteads, forcing many to leave without adequate clothing or transportation. The Kansas troops stole whatever furniture, household goods, and livestock they left behind. Everything else they put to the torch. For 100 miles around, the wind swept the fires across the prairie, leaving in their wake only smoke-stained chimneys, blackened stumps, and the scorched earth. Within two weeks much of the border area lay in ruins. For decades afterward, it was referred to acidly as the "Burnt District."

By mid-September, 5,000 refugees a week were crossing the Missouri River at Lexington. Of the 10,000 people who lived in Cass County when the war began, only 600 remained. Bates County was hit even harder. Governor Gamble had fallen ill, and Acting Governor Willard P. Hall pleaded with Schofield to rescind the order, but the general refused. He feared the hostile Kansans, who were still threatening revenge for Lawrence. One Union officer wrote home to his wife on September 10: "It is heartsickening to see what I have seen since I have been back here. A desolated country, and men and women and children, some of them almost naked. Some on foot and some in old wagons. Oh God."

Though less extreme, conditions were similar all over wartime Missouri. In November 1861, a *New York Herald* correspondent covering the first year of fighting in the state reported of his ride from Springfield to Rolla: "[I] found many houses deserted, or tenanted only by

HARPER'S WEEKLY.
A JOURNAL OF CIVILIZATION.

VOL. V.—No. 256.]   NEW YORK, SATURDAY, NOVEMBER 23, 1861.   [SINGLE COPIES SIX CENTS.
[$2 50 PER YEAR IN ADVANCE.

Entered according to Act of Congress, in the Year 1861, by Harper & Brothers, in the Clerk's Office of the District Court for the Southern District of New York.

Indian Scouts in Gen. Lane's Camp.

A group of Indian scouts visit General "Jim" Lane's camp near Humansville in this *Harper's Weekly* illustration from November 23, 1861. Senator James H. Lane and Dr. Charles R. Jennison, Kansas Jayhawkers who were veterans of the bitter border warfare of the 1850s, moved into western Missouri in the summer and fall of 1861, after months of periodic forays supposedly in pursuit of Quantrill's Raiders. Filling out his regiments with former slaves, General Lane taught his men that Missourians in general were traitors whose rights they were in no way obligated to respect. Lane and "Doc" Jennison looted and burned indiscriminately wherever they went in Missouri. Courtesy, Missouri Historical Society

women and children. Frequently the crops were standing, ungathered in the field. Fences were prostrated, and there was no effort to restore them." And at that point, the desolation was just beginning.

Union generals, whether battling Price's forces early in the war or hunting down guerrillas thereafter, were notoriously lax with their men, often allowing unlicensed and indiscriminate raiding and pillaging by the occupying forces. Like Major General John Pope, who patrolled northern Missouri, they would move into an area, set up committees of public safety in each county, and fully expect them to call out their citizenry as militia when trouble started. When the committees failed, the Union commander automatically assumed the failure was due to rebel sympathies. The county would be occupied by federal troops and countywide levies would be placed on local resources to sustain them. If county officials could not meet the levies, the general simply ordered his troops to take what they needed, regardless of the owners' political leanings.

While he was still alive, Governor Gamble protested the abuses the Union forces visited on Missouri's civilians, and when he was still in command General Halleck acknowledged the justness of Gamble's protest. Some of Halleck's successors even made a real effort to curb excesses, but the truth was that maintaining order in a bitterly divided state during the

middle of a civil war was no easy task. Honest differences of opinion that might once have caused little more than a heated debate now led almost inevitably to bloodshed. For example, even after the Union army began relying more heavily on the state militia, commanders found that militiamen often used their new power to settle old grudges, political or otherwise. And, as the twentieth century has amply demonstrated, sensitivity to the rights of citizens is not the long suit of military men facing a hostile civilian population under conditions of martial law.

Fremont had first imposed martial law in St. Louis on August 14, 1861, before extending it to the entire state two weeks later. From that moment, martial law flourished throughout the war and impinged on the life of every Missourian at virtually every point. Curfews were established, the sale of firearms forbidden, and newspapers censored. Passes were required for travel to and from an area, and citizens had to prove loyalty to secure them. Missourians using public transportation found their luggage subject to military inspection. Inspectors would visit hotels to check the bags of departing guests, then seal them and issue a permit, which soon led to a variety of permits and licenses being required for riverboats, railroads, and stagecoaches.

The military supervised the courts, setting up a system of provost marshals to police the state and handle cases of sedition. The mere suspicion of pro-Southern sympathies could land one in jail with a host of other political prisoners, army deserters, Confederate POWs, and hardened criminals. Those who criticized military policy publicly were subject to summary arrest. Since the cases were handled on a purely arbitrary basis by local officials, no one was safe. An argument with a relative, a dispute with a neighbor, a Sunday sermon, all could and did lead to cases being brought before the provosts.

In general, the average citizen in wartorn Missouri had a difficult time proving his or her loyalty. The provost marshals basically relied on test oaths and performance bonds. The provost could require

Guerrilla warfare on both sides, resulting largely from Missouri's deeply divided population and legacy of violence, made the Civil War in Missouri especially hellish. Courtesy, Missouri Historical Society

any hapless individual he suspected of disloyalty to post a bond of from $1,000 to $10,000. Thousands had to pay. In Liberty alone the provost forced some 612 men to cough up a total of $840,000 by the end of 1862. The Palmyra official boasted that he took more than $1 million from "several thousand traitors" during the same period. Sometimes those "known to be hostile" to the Union were also fined to cover various special activities, such as providing funds for the growing stream of refugees pouring into St. Louis. Protests had to be accompanied by proof of loyalty, and failure to pay on time could lead to additional penalties and, eventually, to the confiscation of property. By December 1862 the whole system had become so corrupt and fraudulent that Lincoln ordered the program suspended.

In the countryside, the abuses grew increasingly worse. Now a guerrilla, now a militiaman, now an army regular might show up at a farm with varying demands. None of them considered property sacrosanct any longer, and to say life was cheap would be an understatement. As pillage and assassination became commonplace, Missouri's refugee problem assumed major proportions. Because it was big and safe and well located, St. Louis turned into a mecca for Missouri's homeless masses,

Between William Quantrill and the Jim Lane-Charles Jennison raiders, western Missouri appeared on the brink of prolonged and bloody chaos. Calling it "the Dark Side of the War," *Frank Leslie's Illustrated Newspaper* **ran this drawing of Missouri refugees driven from their homes on February 1, 1862. Courtesy, Missouri Historical Society**

Lincoln's party urged the president to release his proclamation emancipating the slaves, the issue in Missouri was what to do about its human property and when. And behind that issue lay the struggle for political power in what everyone assumed would soon be postwar America.

Governor Gamble led the Moderates, who, like Lincoln, wanted to re-create after the war what they considered to be a tolerant society, one that did not rub salt into the wounds of the defeated slaveholders. To do so, they believed, required a calm, rational, and most of all slow process of emancipation. The Radicals were led by an enigmatic figure named Charles Drake, who before the war had been an undistinguished politician and competent

both black and white. The first wave came in the winter of 1861-1862 from the southwest. Many died on the way in the bitter cold. Those who did make it had often been robbed by various vigilante groups of the few possessions they managed to cart off from the homes burning behind them.

To care for these victims of the war, the women of St. Louis formed the Ladies' Union Aid Society to establish a number of refugee homes supported by voluntary contributions and compulsory assessments on Southern sympathizers. When Lincoln suspended the latter, the federal government underwrote the costs of the homes. By then, houses like those in St. Louis had sprung up in Pilot Knob, Rolla, Springfield, and Cape Girardeau. Agents of the Western Sanitary Commission, organized by Dr. William G. Eliot, supervised all of them.

But by 1863, in the darkest of the war years, a vast number of Missourians had simply decided to pull up stakes and head West. By the thousands, they joined wagon trains leaving for California and points in between—anywhere, just out of Missouri.

That same year the Union leaders in control of the wartime state government split into two factions, the Moderate and the Radical Republicans. As at the national level, where the radical wing of

speaker for the pro-slavery faction of the Democratic party. Evidently sensing opportunity in the chaos, Drake had changed his mind, his party, and his position, calling now for revenge upon disloyal citizens, a progressive business agenda for postwar Missouri, and an immediate end to slavery. For now the Moderates prevailed, engineering an act of emancipation through the legislature that called for the freeing of all slaves on July 4, 1870, except for those over 40 years of age, who would live on as the permanently indentured servants of their current masters.

But Gamble had been in ill health throughout the war. He died in mid-January of 1864, and Drake mustered his forces for the national elections to be held later in the year. And as those elections got into full swing in the fall, Old Pap Price, now something of a hero in the state, led one last invasion of Missouri. Accompanied by a colorful fellow Missourian, General Joseph O. Shelby, a cavalry leader who rode a Missouri mule, Price brought his troops up from Arkansas, through Pilot Knob, and cut a swath toward Kansas City. In preparation for his 1,500-mile march across the state, Price had sent orders to guerrilla leaders to attack north of the Missouri River in order to draw troops from St. Louis and the south.

Once again terror raged. Bloody Bill Anderson led the most effective of the bands, dashing here and there through central Missouri a step ahead of pursuing Union troops and militia. On Septem-

Left: Major-General John Charles Fremont and his staff inaugurated Camp Benton at St. Louis in the autumn of 1861, before starting for Lexington, Missouri. The small pro-Southern town on the Missouri River was held by the Union but under attack from Sterling Price. On September 14 the town fell, and so did Fremont's military reputation. Courtesy, Missouri Historical Society

A former Missouri governor and Mexican War hero, General Sterling Price was chosen to head the pro-slavery volunteers known as the Missouri State Guard. Called "Old Pap" by his fellow Missourians, Price led troops into battle against Union forces throughout the state during the war. Courtesy, Missouri Historical Society

manded they strip off their uniforms, and asked any officers to please step forward. One, a Sergeant Thomas Goodman of the Missouri Engineers, defiantly did so. Bloody Bill laughed and ordered him to move aside. Then he turned to Little Archie Clemens, his second in command, whose pathological grin played permanently on his lips. "Muster out the troops," Anderson told him. The shots came at point blank range, Clemens firing with a pistol in each hand, the others blasting away at will, murdering all 24 Union soldiers. Guerrilla leader Cole Younger's 15-year-old cousin, Jesse James, already an icy-blooded, blue-eyed killer, watched as Anderson told Goodman he was free to go on home and enjoy his furlough.

Price and Shelby reached Jackson County before they were defeated at Westport on October 23 in a three-day decisive battle, a kind of engagement rare in Missouri's war history. The Centralia Massacre was much more typical, and therefore a more fitting end—a futile and senseless slaughter in a war that had not counted strategically to North or South for nearly three years. After Price recognized he was beaten and scurried south across the Arkansas border, the irregular Confederate bands began to break up. But robbery and murder had become a way of life for them, the only vocation a goodly number would ever know. Many of them teenagers when the war started, they had lost their innocence in the 1,162 battles or skirmishes fought on Missouri soil, 11 percent of all the engagements in the Civil War, the third highest number in the entire nation—a savage passage to manhood.

They, and the other survivors among the 40,000 Confederate and 110,000 Union soldiers the state had produced, returned home often physically crippled, always mentally scarred. Some 27,000 of their friends and relatives had been killed. Whole counties had been burned out. Railroads, highways, bridges, churches, and courthouses had all, like them, been damaged, often beyond repair.

And as the first of them arrived home, they heard the news from Jefferson City.

ber 27, Anderson and 30 of his men rode into Centralia on the North Missouri Railroad. As they bullied and tortured Centralia's citizens, robbed its homes, and looted its stores, the Columbia stage rolled into town. On board was Missouri Congressman James S. Rollins. They pulled him from the stage, stuck a gun under his nose, and then let him go after he pledged his love to the rebellion. Hiding in a nearby attic, Rollins could hear the noonday whistle of a train coming from the east.

The raiders blocked the tracks with railroad ties, then hid from view till the train had stopped. They jerked helpless citizens from the cars and relieved them of their valuables. And then they came across 25 unarmed Union soldiers headed home to Iowa on furlough. Anderson lined them up on the station platform, de-

The Radical Republicans had swept the elections. Charles Drake was calling for a constitutional convention.

The Radical Republicans, for all their opportunism and vindictiveness, had put their finger on the moral pulse of America. The four-year carnage had to be about something, and for the clear majority of U.S. citizens it was about slavery. In Missouri, Drake's constitutional convention would abolish the peculiar institution immediately and unconditionally. Missouri, the only slave-holding state not to join the Confederacy, freed its slaves on January 11, 1865.

But that would not be enough for Charles Drake. He saw himself as Missouri's avenging angel, believing that past evils demanded a new righteousness. The convention had opened in January 1865, and by April, history gave a little boost to Drake's campaign to purify the state. News reached the delegates that Abraham Lincoln had been assassinated—by a Southerner—and that guerrilla raids had intensified in the countryside. Drake played so skillfully on the strained emotions of the delegates, and on Missouri's loyal and embittered citizens, that even the bravest dared not oppose him. The

convention turned into the apotheosis of hatred in Missouri's public affairs.

Having freed the slaves, Drake now moved to disenfranchise anyone who disagreed with him. Afraid that current officeholders in the state might try to undo the convention's work, Drake got the delegates to vote for the infamous "Ousting Ordinance." The edict declared that on May 1, 1865, three months hence, all incumbent judges, county clerks, circuit attorneys, sheriffs, and county recorders would lose their jobs. Drake's crony, Governor Thomas C. Fletcher, would appoint new men to complete their unexpired terms in office. After the ordinance had dislodged some 800 duly elected Union officials, Missouri's Supreme Court refused to be unseated and ruled the law unconstitutional. Drake's response was to remove the judges by force of arms.

But that was nothing compared to the

Above and far left: The Centralia Massacre was one of Civil War Missouri's most heinous atrocities, in which 24 unarmed Union soldiers were murdered on the railroad station platform. William "Bloody Bill" Anderson, above, one of Quantrill's most effective and brutal raiders, led the raid on Centralia. When Anderson ordered Little Archie Clemens, far left, to "muster out the troops," Clemens fired on the men, a pistol in each hand, at point blank range. Courtesy, Missouri Historical Society

Above: Missouri's United States Senator B. Gratz Brown was aligned with the Radical Republicans after the Civil War, but soon came to oppose the excesses of the movement. He helped to organize a liberal faction within the Republican Party, and as governor of Missouri led a reform movement that captured national attention. From Cirker, *Dictionary of American Portraits,* Dover, 1967

Right: The end of the war, the rise of the Radical Republicans, and Federal Reconstruction policies ushered in sweeping changes in Missouri and all across the nation. Large numbers of former slaves registered to vote, and many held public office. Courtesy, State Historical Society of Missouri

new constitution produced by the convention. It was called "Drake's constitution" because it aimed at making sure that no one who met with Drake's disapproval held public office, preached from a pulpit, or practiced his profession. It called for the administration of an "Ironclad Oath" to prospective voters, officeholders, clergymen, teachers, jurors, and attorneys. Each had to swear they were innocent of some 86 acts that Drake, who wrote the provision himself, considered disloyal. Even Governor Fletcher at first opposed the constitution. Edward Bates, whom Lincoln had made the U.S. attorney general, repudiated the document. And Missouri's German population turned its back on Drake, having seen this kind of thing hap-

pen all too often in the Europe they had fled.

Drake worked overtime to get the constitution approved, applying the oath to voters even before they could vote on the oath. Despite his success in drastically reducing the number of registered opponents, Missourians rejected the constitution by nearly 1,000 votes. At the last minute, Drake remembered the soldiers and arranged an absentee ballot. The veteran tally saved him, and the constitution squeaked to passage with less than a 2,000-vote margin. Soon Drake was arresting ministers, priests, and nuns who refused to take the oath, and throwing some of them in prison. Such acts led to accusations that Drake had begun a Robespierrelike "reign of terror," and throughout the state, opposition to his actions grew.

Missourians who had remained loyal during the conflict, however, saw no reign of terror in Drake's actions. Especially those who had suffered at the hands of the guerrillas very much resented the return of Confederate veterans and voted to keep the Radicals in power. In the general atmosphere of intolerance fostered by the war, by Drake, and by his associates, some communities made it clear that former rebels, no matter how penitent, were not welcome. In Jackson County, Radical-leaning grand juries indicted former guerrillas for war crimes even after President Johnson had granted them amnesty. Not a few of the accused took to the bush, and before long, word of a robbery here, a murder there, began to appear in the newspapers.

As the political agitation continued throughout the fall and winter months, a lawlessness very much like that which had plagued the state during the war broke out again in Missouri. In one among many such incidents, a group of armed men held up the Clay County Savings Association for $60,000 in February of 1866. They were led by an ex-guerrilla named Jesse James. Jesse, and his brother Frank, had launched their civilian careers.

Later in 1866 the United States Supreme Court joined the assault on Drake by declaring the test oath clause unconstitutional, but Drake nevertheless managed to capture Missouri's U.S. Senate seat in 1867 when B. Gratz Brown announced he would retire because of ill health. Brown was not too sick, however, to join Frank Blair and Carl Shurz in piecing together a liberal faction within the Republican party to check Radical excesses. In 1869, Shurz, a German immigrant who had lived in Missouri only for a few years, defeated the Radical Republican candidate for the other U.S. Senate seat, and the next year Brown won the statehouse. Senator Shurz and Governor Brown led a reform movement that captured national attention in the wake of the Grant administration scandals. On a joint state ticket with the revived Democratic party, the

Liberal Republicans won a complete victory over the Radicals in 1872. But with the Radical power broken, the Republican party in Missouri quickly disintegrated, and the Democrats took control.

The return of the Democratic party, which would dominate Missouri politics for nearly a century to come, was one legacy of the Civil War, born of the lingering resentment and bitterness of the majority of Missouri's citizens toward the federal government. There was another legacy: in the backwoods hollows and seedier city saloons of Missouri, Jesse James, with the help of Eastern publicists and dime novelists, was becoming a legend—and a folk hero.

Jesse W. James rode with William Quantrill and Bloody Bill Anderson as a teenage guerrilla during the Civil War, and remained a cold-blooded killer. In the postwar anarchy that swept the western part of Missouri, former raiders like James became lawless brutes, robbing, looting, and killing without conscience. They did so behind a facade of romantic terrorism, which led to a long-standing tradition of banditry in the Missouri breaks. Courtesy, Missouri Historical Society

From the earliest days of statehood, Missourians flocked to a number of traveling circuses, such as John Robinson's "10 Big Shows," which parades through Boonville in 1900. Courtesy, Missouri Historical Society

CHAPTER IV

Meet Me at the Fair

A fter the Democratic party victories of 1872, Missouri finally managed to secede and join the Confederate States of America, now called the Solid South. Throughout the region, Democratic leaders came forward to "redeem" their states from the carpetbaggers and to frame constitutions embodying a strong reaction against the meddlesome federal governments of Reconstruction. Missouri, never officially a "reconstructed" state, produced its ticket of admission in 1875. Like all the new constitutions of the Solid South, it was a laissez-faire tract, suspicious and distrustful of legislatures. The document placed hampering restrictions upon government, cut taxes severely, and starved tax-supported public services.

The last showdown between North and South came in the 1876 presidential campaigns of Samuel J. Tilden and Rutherford B. Hayes. The redeemers, crusading against the graft and greed of the Grant administration and its carpetbag rule, swung the South, and Missouri, behind Tilden and won the popular vote. The Republicans reversed the electoral tally of the three Southern states they still controlled under Reconstruction and stole the election. A deadlock resulted, followed by four months of wrangling and tension in which the nation had no president and civil war loomed once more. Hayes agreed never again to interfere in the politics of the South and ultimately became president, though even his close associates ever afterward called him "Your Fraudulency."

William Tecumseh Sherman was out for a walk with his son when hostilities broke out at Camp Jackson near St. Louis. The Union general returned to St. Louis after the Civil War, but became disillusioned with how the city had changed. He moved to New York in 1887. From Cirker, *Dictionary of American Portraits,* **Dover, 1967**

Allowed to go their own way, the Solid South Democrats, preferring to be called "Conservatives," proved every bit as corruptible as the Radical Republicans. Their new constitutions, like Missouri's, often touted by historians as signaling a return to Jeffersonian principles, merely allowed for a niggardly economy in public expenditure, a corrupt neglect of the responsibilities of government, and a laxity in public morals. The Civil War had destroyed the Southern planter, with whose slave-based wealth the Jeffersonians had never been comfortable. The planter's sole rival for power, the industrial entrepreneur, grew fully into his own after the rebellion failed, creating a new plutocracy based on industry and trade. The robber barons of the Gilded Age simply bought the "Conservative" redeemers—and their principles.

As the industrialists doled out "boodle" to state legislators and city officials, they appropriated for themselves the slogan that had traditionally belonged to Jeffersonian and Jacksonian radicals. "Laissez-faire," gussied up in a top hat and frock coat, now meant allowing men with economic power to have everything their own way. Under an imperious capitalism, Jefferson's basic philosophical and ethical concepts—democracy, liberty, equality, opportunity, individualism—suffered a strange political transformation. Rather than the popular watchwords of good government, Jefferson's hoary terms became the clarion calls of the new industrialists for virtually no government at all.

In Missouri, as elsewhere, the railroad was the engine of that transformation.

After the Civil War, General William Tecumseh Sherman moved back to the St. Louis he remembered fondly as a bustling town of honest and industrious people. But he found that conditions in the city and in the state had changed greatly during his absence. The frontier was gone, the old outfitting days over, the Santa Fe trade lost, the fur business and steamboat traffic both dying. St. Louis, grown fat on war supplies and railroads, sprawled in all directions and announced its ambition to become the new capital of the United States. In the interior, on the ruins of the great hemp and tobacco plantations, tenant farming had replaced slave labor. Lead mines in the southeast and lead and zinc mines in the southwest were expanding rapidly. And Kansas City was booming.

Obviously, the Civil War had smashed all the old barriers and opened up tremendous opportunities. The general's brother, U.S. Senator John Sherman, put it in perspective for him. "The truth is," he wrote William, "the close of the war with our resources unimpaired gives an elevation, a scope to the ideas of leading capitalism, far higher than anything undertaken in this country before. They talk of millions as confidently as they formerly talked of thousands."

Certainly talk of millions accompanied the incredible expansion of the railroads as they crisscrossed the state, tying together the strands of the new commerce and bringing with them hordes of new people and massive new debt. "Railroad through" was the ubiquitous cry on the lips of Sherman's fellow Missourians as the cowcatchers and smokestacks chugged into view and dominated the imagination, the politics, and the livelihood of the entire postwar generation. Rail mileage more than doubled in the 1860s and 1870s and increased another 50 percent in the 1880s. In 1852 Missouri had only five miles of track; by 1870 the state had some 2,000 miles.

The railroads diverted business from the old river towns, and once-flourishing ports such as LaGrange and Lexington declined as entirely new settlements sprang up along the right-of-way in places like Moberly and Sedalia. Because of the railroad, Joplin, which did not exist at the end of the Civil War, grew by leaps and bounds to become Missouri's fourth largest city and a major mining center by the end of the century. The railroad hubs—St. Louis, St. Joseph, and especially Kansas City—expanded dramatically. St. Joseph's population grew from 8,932 in 1860 to some 19,565 a decade later. During that same period Kansas City shot from 4,418, after having lost population during the war, to 32,260—second only to the giant, St. Louis.

In communities throughout the state, citizens eagerly promoted the coming of the railroad and the attendant increase in the value of their land, better communications, cheaper and faster transportation of goods, and development of new industries. The great debacle of railroad construction before the war had created a $25-million public lien against the private railway companies and had led the framers of the Drake constitution in 1865 to forbid the state government from providing public funds for railroad expansion. In the fol-

At the end of the Civil War, St. Louis had become the major city in the West, outstripped only by New York as a center of trade and culture. Something of the exuberance and the pretentions of the Gilded Age can be seen clearly in the elaborate and gaudy decoration of J.Y. Hart's Capitol Oyster Saloon and Restaurant at South Chestnut Street around 1865. Courtesy, Missouri Historical Society

lowing decade, local governments, not restricted by the law and lusting for the rail connection, promised huge sums of money to secure the services of the Iron Horse, some $17 million to private companies between 1866 and 1873.

Some county courts, at the instigation of railroad promoters, ordered the raising of funds through bonds without holding local elections to get public approval. Such

Logan U. Reavis, a historian and St. Louis newspaperman, wrote the quintessential booster's book about St. Louis, called *St. Louis, Future Great City of the World.* Courtesy, Missouri Historical Society

illegal debts created great turmoil when the railroad companies failed to construct lines as promised or economic depressions hit, like the one beginning in 1873, at which time county, city, and township governments would find it impossible to meet their bond obligations. The railroad fever reached such a pitch that Missouri's general assembly meekly surrendered the public's lien against the prewar companies, saddling the people rather than the rail companies with the old $25-million debt, and throwing into doubt the honesty of the state's elected officials. Amidst rumors of corruption and boodle, Missouri's legislators continued to mortgage an entire generation to the railroads, which already by then was proving to be a mixed blessing.

For one, the railroads helped fuel the rivalry between Missouri's various geo-graphical sections, pitting industrialized city against poor highlands and tenant farming areas, as well as the rivalry between its two urban giants on either side of the state. St. Louis, fast becoming an eastern metropolis, began to turn its back on the state entirely, and with the 1875 constitution, would opt for a "home rule" that made it virtually independent of the surrounding county. Kansas City, started as a speculative venture, embraced the West with open arms and later would try to annex itself to Kansas.

This fragmentation became clear in the 1870s, when Texas cattlemen began their great drives to Northern markets and immense wealth. They first tried the most direct route through Missouri to Sedalia, the nearest railroad terminus. But as the cattlemen entered the woods of southwest Missouri, local farmers and hooligans attacked them. The locals, raised in a tradition of lawlessness and vigilante justice, feared a recurrence of the Texas fever that had once before devastated their own livestock. They tied the cowboys to trees, whipped them with smoked hickory branches called "witches," and stole their herds. This episode added to Missouri's already considerable reputation for violence, and the cattlemen ever afterward stuck to the open prairie, coming up through Kansas to connect with the railroad and ship their beef to Chicago through Kansas City.

Kansas City, in turn, flourished as a western depot, its booming economy fed by slaughterhouses and meat-packing plants. Already having faced the fact that Chicago, not St. Louis, would become the continent's transportation center, Kansas City in 1866 built a bridge across the wide Missouri to connect with the Hannibal and St. Joseph line that led straight to the Windy City. That done, the West and the nation need no longer acknowledge St. Louis at all. By 1877, with seven railroads running through it, Kansas City was an economic fief of Chicago.

St. Louis, however, did not give up without a fight. Following the Civil War, the city had grown rapidly in wealth and population. New industries sprang up as older ones expanded, and the city swallowed wave after wave of foreign-born immigrants coming by railroad to Missouri to work in its factories and shops. St. Louisans liked to believe that their city ranked in population just behind New York and Philadelphia, though in fact there were only some 300,000 people rather than the half a million they imagined. Still, that was double the 160,000 living in St. Louis in 1860. Steamboats still lined the levee, but the glory days of the river were at an end, and the focus of trade had shifted from north and south to east and west, following the railroads.

The St. Louis of 1874 was a great manufacturing and trade center, stretching 18 miles along the Mississippi, facing Illinois. Iron and steel, meat packing, flour milling, shoe making, tobacco products, and foundry and machine-shop manufacturing were the chief industries. For some years local publicist L.U. Reavis had been calling St. Louis the "future great city of the world" and urging the nation to move its capital to the banks of the Mississippi. But the river itself had stood in the way. Then in 1874 Captain James B. Eads did what many thought impossible. He built one of the world's great bridges across one

of the widest points of the Mississippi, connecting St. Louis with the railroad center of East St. Louis, Illinois. Suddenly Reavis's dream seemed possible, and St. Louis began in earnest its struggle with Chicago for the championship title of "Gateway City to the West." When the Great Chicago Fire destroyed the latter in 1871, St. Louisans hailed it as a victory. But they were premature. The railroad speculation of the last decade sparked a nationwide depression in 1873, and as the panic spread to Missouri, St. Louis' postwar prosperity came to an abrupt end.

To most Missourians the decade of extravagant growth and outlandish promises by the railroads seemed a hoax. For only a modest rail system compared to other states, Missourians had watched railroad ownership go to remote out-of-state corporations who skillfully eluded the huge costs of building the system and failed to deliver the reasonable freight rates they had promised. Faced with rate-fixing and discrimination on the part of the railroads, and with a huge public debt cheerfully incurred by their local officials, some localities simply repudiated their indebtedness, causing a great uproar. The state debt itself would not be paid off until 1903; the

Above and below: In 1874 James Buchanan Eads, above, who had made his reputation as a builder of ironclad boats for the Union cause, did what seemed to many Missourians the impossible—he constructed a bridge across the Mississippi at St. Louis. Seen below under construction in December of 1873, the Eads Bridge immediately became a world wonder and a favorite symbol for promoting St. Louis. Courtesy, Missouri Historical Society

The Ohio and Mississippi Broad Gauge Railroad is shown here in about 1875. In the 1850s, Missouri succumbed to the national craze for railroads. Despite the fact that railroad companies, backed by state-issued bonds, incurred $25-million worth of debt by the Civil War, only one line—the Hannibal and St. Joseph—was completed. After the war, the state legislature transferred that debt to the public, and Missouri's communities and counties struggled until 1903 to pay it off. Courtesy, Missouri Historical Society

last of the local debts would be cleared only in 1940.

Railroad building would continue in America throughout the rest of the century in fits and starts, helping to create, and suffering from, the boom-and-bust cycles of rampant capitalist expansion. Even in Missouri, new tracks would be added, expanding from 2,000 miles completed by the panic of 1873 to some 6,200 in 1890, then nearly 10,000 during the first decade of the twentieth century. But the thrill was gone. After 1873 the debt haunted later generations of Missourians, helping to create a "show-me" skepticism that made it especially hard to raise public money for roads, education, and human services. The dream was over, and never again would Missouri command the powerful physical position in the Union that it had in the 1830s when water, not iron, was the transport medium of commerce.

As the living standards of workers and farmers plunged following the panic, popular anger at the railroads, banks, and corporations reached the high pitch that railroad fever once commanded. Western farmers, who had formed the National Grange of the Patrons of Husbandry in 1870, struck back at the railroads and banks, demanding an end to discriminatory freight rates, oppressive mortgages, and high interest on loans. The Grange or-

ganized the People's Party for the 1874 presidential election, and began using its state organizations to force "Granger Laws" through the state legislatures. Missouri's farmers responded warmly, creating some 2,000 local Granges, one of the highest numbers in the country. The Granges had an effect on the 1875 constitution, which included a provision calling for the regulation of railroads as well as one that once again forbade further state loans to private companies.

Despite the sop the Democrats gave the Grange, the party had no intention of taking on the railroads. In fact, because the underlying assumption of the Democrats was that the state should not meddle in any way with private enterprise, the document proved a boon not only to railroads, but also to utilities and industries, by lightening their tax burdens. After Rutherford B. Hayes took office the Grange movement declined, splintering into ephemeral parties with various kinds of anti-monopoly programs. The groups comprising the majority of Missourians—poor Irish and German immigrants, starving in the city, and hardscrabble dirt farmers and debt-ridden tenant-farm laborers outstate—suffered particularly from their elected officials' desire to let each care for his own, neglected by the state in the name of Jefferson and democracy.

Even after the compromise of the Hayes-Tilden election, when it became clear that conservative white leaders in the South were taking their stand with Northern industrialists against agrarian and labor radicalism, Missouri continued to suffer from anarchy in the countryside as a result of the "Recent Unpleasantness." In central and western Missouri, horse theft and bank robbery had become a way of life for former guerrillas. In the southeast the Ku Klux Klan had reared its masked head. As early as 1868, Klan leaders, calling themselves the Dead Men and wearing long black gowns with white stripes, began terrorizing Dunklin and Stoddard counties. In 1871 Governor Brown was forced to call out the militia, but the Klan simply moved its activities to nearby Butler and Ripley counties.

Outlaws and hoodlums sometimes donned Klan outfits, and time and again throughout the next two decades, outraged citizens demanded the protection of state militia. Some formed vigilante posses to run down horse thieves and robbers, but the vigilantes themselves, like the infamous Bald Knobbers, occasionally

turned to marauding. The Democratic administration seemed to many singularly uninterested in maintaining law and order, and in truth throughout Missouri there were a good number of former Confederates, including some in the state legislature, who sympathized with the Klansmen and ex-guerrillas. In 1873 Governor Silas Woodson offered a $2,000 reward for the arrest of Frank and Jesse James, but nothing came of it.

Little could be done, of course, as long as the violence served a purpose: the more-or-less official policy of disenfranchising Missouri's recently freed black people and terrorizing any who might be tempted to sympathize with them. Emancipation had brought no miraculous reversal of the degradation blacks suffered under slavery, and especially in central and southern Missouri their lot continually grew harsher. Lynchings became widespread and common through the rest of the century and into the 1930s. Many fled to the cities, where they could at least find work, if not respect. The 1875 constitution called for dual education of the races. Though it stipulated that 25 percent of public rev-

By the turn of the century, Missouri had its network of railroads—at a great cost to its citizens and too late to bring the kind of economic prosperity the railroads had afforded Chicago and the Midwest. Here, a passenger train leaves St. Louis' new Union Station, built in 1904. Courtesy, Missouri Historical Society

enues would go to Missouri's schools, there were actually precious few public revenues, and pitifully little for black schools. Outstate, segregation became the rule. Even as St. Louis' black schools were being called a model for the country by W.E.B. Du Bois, when the city moved to control its venereal disease epidemic and established a hospital for diseased prostitutes, it confined black women separately in the basement.

Not until the race problem was "solved" —and the train robberies started —did Missouri get serious about its lawlessness. The first train holdup came at Gatt's Hill in Wayne County in 1874, and proved so lucrative that a series of hijackings followed over the next seven years. Whether the James gang actually committed all of them or not, it was blamed for most. When four men took control of a train in Winston in 1881, robbed the passengers and crew, and murdered both the conductor and an uncooperative passenger, the days of the James brothers were numbered. Governor T.T. Critteden took immediate action, offering a $5,000 reward for the arrest and another $5,000 for the conviction of Frank and Jesse. Working behind the scenes with the railroad companies, local citizens, and gang members themselves, the governor managed to destroy the band. Within a year its ringleaders were dead or in jail, and Jesse James had been shot in the back by two fellow travelers while dusting a picture in his home in St. Joseph. Frank James surrendered to the governor, though he was acquitted in the murder trial that followed.

If ridding Missouri of its outlaws was an afterthought for the early postwar Democratic governments, the potential for another kind of violence was centermost in their minds: Missouri's cities, especially St. Louis, threatened to erupt in class war.

Farmers had not been the only ones to feel the crushing blows of the most serious and prolonged economic crisis up to that point in the country's history. The distress of the industrial workingman had been growing

Above: Frank James, riding with his brother Jesse and the Younger brothers in the notorious James gang, terrorized the Missouri countryside in the 1870s and 1880s. Frank surrendered to the governor in 1882 and was acquitted in the murder trial that followed. He returned to his farm near Excelsior Springs, where he died quietly in 1915. From Cirker, *Dictionary of American Portraits,* Dover, 1967

Far left: The legend came to an end on April 3, 1882, when the Ford brothers, seeking to collect reward money, shot John Howard, a.k.a. Jesse James, in the back at his house in St. Joseph, as shown in this engraving from a *Harper's Weekly* drawing. Courtesy, Missouri Historical Society

Right: The hatmaker Keevil's giant top hat dominates an 1876 view of Broadway south of Carr in St. Louis. Throughout the early postwar decades the city fought hard with Chicago for its position as the West's major urban center. In 1870 Logan U. Reavis called St. Louis "the Future Great City of the World." William T. Harris had made it an intellectual mecca for Hegelian philosophy and organized the city's fine education system. Joseph Pulitzer created one of the country's great newspapers, the *Post-Dispatch.* Courtesy, Missouri Historical Society

Above: Joseph Pulitzer combined the *St. Louis Post* with the *St. Louis Dispatch* in 1880 to form the *Post-Dispatch.* His newspaper quickly became a success, attacking high tariffs and corruption. After profits declined following a scandal, Pulitzer moved to New York, bought the *New York World,* and helped launch "yellow journalism." From Cirker, *Dictionary of American Portraits,* Dover, 1967

exponentially in the four years of depression since the panic of 1873. The panic itself had been caused by wild speculation and a series of ruinous rate wars between railroad tycoons, which benefited no one as much as John D. Rockefeller and his Standard Oil Company, the first of the big trusts. The corporations made up their losses by shoddy operating practices and wage cut after wage cut. The workers went on strike, only to have it broken by the Pinkertons. By July 1877 the series of wage cuts and abortive strikes resulted in a wave of social insurrections that rocked America from coast to coast. Spreading spontaneously like an electrical charge along two-thirds of the country's railroad tracks, the strike exploded in Philadelphia, Harrisburg, Reading, Scranton, Buffalo, Toledo, Chicago, San Francisco—and St. Louis.

The first great industrial conflict in American history caught the new president napping. Without a set policy, urged on by the hysterical fears of four state governors, Hayes took the fateful step and sent in federal troops. While the strike in

St. Louis caused none of the bloodshed and little of the property damage that marked the riots in other cities, it was in many ways more alarming to businessmen and property owners than any of the others. Only in St. Louis did the original railroad strike expand systematically and completely into a general strike. And only in St. Louis, with its huge population of German workers and their proud socialist traditions, did an American city come close to being run by a workers' council— what we today would call a soviet and what the newspapers of 1877, with the Paris Commune of 1871 fresh in their memories, called "the Commune."

St. Louis itself was never quite the same again. In the summer of 1877 St. Louisans had yet managed to ignore the signs of decay highlighted by the long depression. When challenged in their claim that St. Louis should become the new capital of the United States, they pointed out that they had faced adversity before. In 1850 the city had overcome a disastrous fire on its waterfront and a savage invasion of Asiatic cholera to become the cultural mecca of the Midwest. William T. Harris still ran his center for Hegelian studies in St. Louis, they argued, making it America's philosophical headquarters. They had the best city school system in the country, also organized by Harris. Joseph Pulitzer's *Post-Dispatch* had became one of the country's finest newspapers. The Planter's House, where the highball had been invented, was still the best hotel in the West, and the house drink, Planter's Punch, the best drink anywhere, except perhaps for a few of the city's German beers.

Why, St. Louis was home to the nation's second-oldest symphony, and a professional theater had been flourishing since 1835. Its Mercantile Library had assembled one of the nation's greatest collection of books and periodicals. If Kansas City had its George Caleb Bingham, who painted Missouri's settlers, courthouse crowds, and Civil War outrages, St. Louis had its Carl Wimar, who painted Indian life and frontier scenes. And St. Louis had been listening to opera before Chicago even existed! For that matter, what about baseball? All Americans loved baseball, and the St. Louis Browns just last year joined the National League.

But disillusion came swiftly. First there was the strike itself, with rowdy workers—German, Irish, and black—crowding the streets and calling the shots for nearly an entire week. For the first time, it seems, St. Louisans took real notice of the factories and the slums with which they had surrounded their city. St. Louis had always bragged about its fine business offices, its grand hotels and shops, and its fashionable restaurants and amusement parks at the center of the city close to the river. After the strike, the areas beyond that core commanded attention. The Cross Keys, Clabber Alley, Wild Cat Chute, and Castle Thunder, the picturesque names of dirty alleys and dilapidated apartment buildings, found mention the way Grand Avenue, with its wealthy homes on the upper ridge, once had—mention not only in the local press but in the national press as well.

Then, fast on the heels of the strike

William T. Harris, a prominent educator, writer, editor, and philosopher, became the public school superintendent of St. Louis in 1868. In 1889 he was appointed U.S. commissioner of education. From Cirker, *Dictionary of American Portraits,* Dover, 1967

came the cruel 1880 census, which confirmed St. Louis' worst suspicions: the detested Chicago had surpassed it in wealth and size. Now, instead of the hubbub and bustle, the hurrying crowds, or the showy, modern, metropolitan storefronts with plate glass windows and iron faces five and six stories high, local citizens and visitors alike were apt to notice the general unkemptness, the filth, the smoke, the wretched sewer system, the liquid mud some called drinking water, and the amazing number of brothels.

After 1880 the exodus of the great and mighty began. William T. Harris headed for greener pastures in the East, and not far behind him was Joseph Pulitzer. Chiding the city for its precipitous fall from grace, Pulitzer stormed into New York, where he opened the *New York World,* created yellow journalism, and helped launch America on its road to empire. Carl Shurz, Missouri's former U.S. senator, also moved to New York in 1881 after serving as Hayes' secretary of the interior. There he continued to preach reform as the country's foremost mugwump jour-

The Famous Cowboy Band of Dodge City, Kansas, performed at the first National Convention of Cattlemen, which met in St. Louis in 1884. From *Frank Leslie's Illustrated Weekly,* December 6, 1884, courtesy, Missouri Historical Society

George Caleb Bingham, a celebrated Kansas City artist, is shown here in a self-portrait. Bingham is famous for his paintings of river scenes, settlers, court-house crowds, and Civil War outrages. From Cirker, *Dictionary of American Portraits,* Dover, 1967

nalist and author. Gen. William T. Sherman also left St. Louis for New York in 1887. Replacing the Old Guard was a new generation of business leaders who were pragmatic and cautious, giving St. Louis its reputation as a conservative town where little happened.

Between 1870 and 1900 nationwide, business booms led to wild speculation, which in turn led to financial panics and a new round of strikes that brought out federal troops. To the cities, the cost of crushing labor was corruption, and the city machine dominated politics, while the boss dominated the machine. In New York it was "Honest" John Kelley and Richard Croker, in Philadelphia "King" Jim McManes, in Boston "Czar" Martin Lomansey, and in St. Louis the city boss was "Colonel" Ed Butler.

Butler, a blacksmith become millionaire politician, put together a machine called the Combine, which controlled a two-thirds majority in each of the two houses of the municipal assembly. This was enough to override any major's veto. The Combine, in a systematic, business-like way, set the standards for bribery in the city. For the right amount, Combine members could ensure a measure's passage or defeat. Whether one wanted to relocate a railroad switch or buy an entire railroad franchise, one checked first with the Com-

bine. Blackmail, payroll padding, and profiteering on public works and city contracts all became second nature to Combine members.

But a vocal group of citizens, as well as the city's three daily newspapers, didn't like what Butler was doing to the city. They elected David Francis as mayor in 1885. Francis, president of the Merchants' Exchange and a man of great integrity, ran the city well without boodle, and he did so without making too many enemies. By letting out honest contracts, he lowered the city debt, cut the budget, built via-ducts, began a street-paving programs, and initiated the Chain of Rocks water-works, which would bring St. Louis clean water. He was elected governor in 1888, but his greatest coup was in organizing the 1904 Louisiana Purchase Exposition. Francis' successor as mayor was a Butler man and City Hall returned to the old practices of lining politicians' pockets until reformer Rolla Wells became mayor in 1901.

Missouri's farmers traditionally had lit-tle good to say about St. Louis. Especially since 1875, when St. Louis had taken ad-vantage of the "home rule" clause to de-clare its virtual independence from the state, rivalry, resentment, and even fear of the city had grown apace. To those good, God-fearing, sober folk who had swelled the ranks of the Baptists, Methodists, and Campbellites (Disciples of Christ) in ever increasing numbers after the Civil War, St. Louis seemed the embodiment of sin and corruption. Even the St. Louis Browns, one thing farmers probably liked about the city, got themselves booted out of the National League the year after they joined for throwing baseball games. Until the Cardinals organized in the National League in 1899, and a rejuvenated Browns' club joined the American League three years later, only the University of Missouri football team could really brighten a hard-won day off.

But in truth, the forces that were tear-ing the city apart were also at work de-stroying the cherished ideals of Missouri's farmers. The Civil War had destroyed much of Missouri's agriculture. After the war the use of new machinery helped agriculture make a remarkable recovery through increased productivity. To the improved plows, disk harrows, reapers, and staddle-row cultivators available before 1860, the farmers now added sulky plows with wheels and a seat for the driver, corn planters, end gate seeders, spring tooth rakes, binders, threshing machines, hay balers, hoisting forks, and corn shellers. Whereas self-sufficiency had once been the rule, now not only did the farmer produce for market, but the increased yields and rapid development of transportation broke forever his isolation and tied him to the swings and fortunes of the business and price cycle.

But the farmer faced something even worse. The revolution in communications and transportation had created a worldwide market, one in which the farmer was forced to compete without protection or control over output. He could not see the abstract market itself, but he could watch as productivity increased and prices for his commodity dropped. And he could feel the unfairness of it all: the more he grew, the less he earned. And as he became ever poorer, his expenses mounted. With the gap between income and expenses constantly growing, farmers found themselves forced to mortgage their land or borrow money to cover debts. Not surprisingly, the 1880 census held no more good cheer for the farming community of Missouri than it had for St. Louis. The census

In the early days, cotton was grown by farmers aiming mostly to produce fiber for their housewives to weave into textiles. But after the Civil War, the cotton trade was stimulated by the reclamation of Missouri's bootheel area. In the first decade of the new century, Missouri was producing some 60,000 bales annually. Courtesy, F.A. Behymer Collection, Missouri Historical Society

Right: Two women take a stroll around the grounds of the Boonville Reform School, circa 1900, dominated by the superintendent's house on the hill behind them. Photo by Dr. Chas Swap, courtesy, Missouri Historical Society

Facing page: A group of Missourians relax on the houseboat "Nadine" in Boonville around 1903. Photo by Max Schmidt, courtesy, Missouri Historical Society

Below: These convicts are breaking rocks in the Boonville Jail, or calaboose, as Missourians called it in 1900. According to notations left by photographer Chas Swap, they were probably serving time for drunkenness. Courtesy, Missouri Historical Society

revealed that the number of tenant farmers had risen in Missouri above the national average, grave news for a state that worshiped the truly Jeffersonian ideal of a land dominated by independent farmers.

Throughout the 1880s and the early 1890s, halls of government everywhere rang with the voice of the farmers' complaints. If sometimes their protests seemed a bit disjointed, one should remember that their enemies had stolen the very words with which they had once defined themselves, and they were forced to look beyond their old Jeffersonian vocabulary. Feeling (to quote Thomas E. Watson of Georgia, who would head the Populist Party) "like victims of some horrid nightmare," they proposed some of the most radical political and economic changes of the late nineteenth century: government ownership of the railroads and utilities, a graduated income tax, the secret ballot, women's suffrage, prohibition, and most of all the creation of inflation through manipulation of the money system, or as they called it, "the free coinage of silver."

They were the first to insist that laissez-faire economics was not the final solution to all industrial problems and that the government had some responsibility for social well-being. And they scared people, especially Eastern capitalists.

The unions and alliances went by a number of different names, starting with the old People's Party created by the Grangers in 1874. From 1876-1878 they called themselves the Greenback Party, then the Greenback Labor Party in 1880, 1882, and 1884, then the Union Labor Party in 1888, and then the Farmers' and Laborers' Union in 1890. Though they were never powerful enough to control Missouri's government or win many national offices, they did manage to force the Democrats to take up one of their major issues. U.S. Representative Richard P. Bland became Missouri's prophet of the free and unlimited coinage of silver. "Silver Dick," as he became known, introduced a free silver bill into Congress in

A circus parade, complete with camels, proceeds down the boulevard in Boonville in this 1900 photograph. Circuses brought to the state's landlocked towns the kind of excitement river showboats offered its port cities. Courtesy, Missouri Historical Society

1877, which passed, but was later much modified and then repealed in 1893.

The year before, on February 22, 1892, the most radical third party yet to appear on the American scene had been formed in St. Louis—the new People's Party, which became better known as the Populist Party. Farmers had reached the lowest point ever in their history. Their National Alliance dominated the huge Confederation of Industrial Organizations meeting attended by delegates from the Knights of Labor, the Nationalists, Single-Taxers, Greenbackers, Prohibitionists, and a dozen other assorted reform groups. The new party called for a national convention to nominate a candidate for president in 1892, which it did in Omaha on July the Fourth.

The Populist candidates lost the election to the Democratic nominee, Grover Cleveland, but that hardly mattered. The Populists' main service was to usher in a long-delayed period of reform. They bridged the gaps betweens parties, sections, races, and classes that had kept reformers apart in the past, reviving the old agrarian alliance between the South and West and creating a new one between farmers and labor. And what gave them the edge was the worst depression yet. The panic of 1893 began when the Philadelphia & Reading Railroad went bankrupt, shaking the New York Stock Exchange into the biggest selling spree on record. Banks called in their loans. Credit dried up. The Erie, the Northern Pacific, the Union Pacific, and the Santa Fe failed, one after another. Mills, factories, furnaces, and mines everywhere shut down. By the time it was over, 500 banks and 1,500 firms went down in bankruptcy.

The year before the Populists had said "we meet in the midst of a nation brought to the verge of moral, political, and material ruin. Corruption dominates the ballot box, the legislatures, the Congress, and touches even the ermine bench. The people are demoralized . . . The fruits of the toil of millions are boldly stolen to build up the colossal fortunes of a few . . ." What had seemed like wild rhetoric suddenly appeared more reasonable, and the

Richard P. "Silver Dick" Bland, a U.S. congressman from Missouri, became the state's prophet of "the free and unlimited coinage of silver." Bland was an important leader of Missouri's populist movement. From Cirker, *Dictionary of American Portraits,* Dover, 1967

outlandish Populist demands, from an income tax to the franchise for women, seemed, if not entirely acceptable, at least thinkable. Masses poured into the party. When President Cleveland, as conservative a Democrat as one could find, proved predictably truculent, "Silver Dick" Bland saw his chance. He forced a split in the Democratic party over free silver, overthrew the conservatives, and forged an alliance with the Populists.

But the 1896 presidential nomination, which Bland had assumed was his, got snatched from his grasp during a deadlocked convention by the brilliant young orator William Jennings Bryan, who had electrified the convention with his famous "Cross of Gold" speech. McKinley would soundly defeat the joint Populist-Democratic ticket, and his war with Spain and his empire building would spell the end of the Populist party, but its reforms were on the national agenda. In a few short years, due to an assassin's bullet, Theodore Roosevelt would be president and the process of writing the Populists' demands into law would be under way.

It was Mark Twain who first called the period between the close of the Civil War and the rise of Progressive reform "The Gilded Age." And he was Missouri's most precious gift to that age. Christened

Samuel Langhorne Clemens, from Hanni-bal, he embodied in his writings and his life the inner tensions and cross-purposes of post-Civil War America. A pure prod-uct of Missouri, he was a child of the fron-tier, who, like his entire country, was born on the farm but moved to the city, to para-phrase Richard Hofstader. A provincial cast into a strange new world, Twain captured in his books, especially in *The Adventures of Huckleberry Finn,* the nos-talgia for the past and hatred for the corruptions of the present that most Americans, and particularly Missourians, felt. They had retained their rural ways of life and habits of mind even as technology advanced around them. But they lacked Twain's savage irony, the knowledge that the past, too, is corrupt, so they read their greatest satirist as a writer of boys' adven-ture stories, and loved him.

Twain's genteel audience inherited from the hayseed anarchists and hick communists of the Populist party the re-formist concepts with which to correct the excesses of the Gilded Age. Respectable, middle-class, and most of all moral, Pro-gressivism increased the demand for change at home, particularly after Mis-sourians had duly contributed to the suc-

cess of the Spanish-American War. They had listened to a succession of governors warn against the menace of uncurbed big business, and they watched as nothing was done about it. Then, in 1900, the St. Louis streetcar workers went on strike.

Thugs, hired as strikebreakers, attacked the protesting workers, and the violence got ugly indeed. Before it was over, 15 men had been killed and many others injured, but city officials refused to investigate and merely shrugged their shoulders. William Marion Reedy, famous editor of the city's *Mirror,* wrote: "The disgrace, the tragedy, the horror of the situation in St. Louis is all due to politics." In that year's election, reformers went after Republican Mayor Henry Ziegenhein with a vengeance, adopting the slogan, "No more Ziegen-heinism."

Boss Butler thought it prudent to run a "reform" ticket against the mayor. He persuaded a young Tennessee-born St. Louis lawyer named Joseph W. Folk to join as circuit attorney. Folk finally ac-cepted, saying simply: "If elected, I will do my duty." Ed Butler had heard it all before. But Folk meant what he said, and once elected he began an investigation that uncovered the fact that the Com-bine's "boodling" city officials had ac-cepted bribes to grant some $50-million worth of city franchises and other munici-pal privileges for a tenth of their value. Combine members regularly earned $25,000 a year in bribes, and a few had managed to garner as much as $50,000 for a single vote. Most daring of all, Folk revealed that many of the city's leading businessmen, from wealthy, respected families, had been involved in schemes to defraud the city.

On the basis of Folk's evidence, 39 men were indicted and even Boss Butler was convicted of bribery. Several leading members of the Combine jumped bail and headed for Mexico. Butler stuck it out, and the Missouri Supreme Court reversed his conviction on a technicality. Undaunt-ed, Folk then followed the trail of corrup-tion to state government.

With St. Louis' growing reputa-tion as America's worst-governed city,

Left: This is the reputed home of Huck Finn, boyhood chum of Tom Sawyer, in Hannibal. As Mark Twain, Samuel Clemens created both characters. Courtesy, Missouri Historical Society

Below: Samuel Clemens lived in this Hannibal house as a boy. As Mark Twain, he wrote the book that gave the name to his times—*The Gilded Age*—and created the perfect image of an 1870s Missouri booster in Colonel Beriah Sellers, a fast-talking and delightful rascal. Courtesy, Missouri Historical Society

Above: By the turn of the century, St. Louis was well into its decline. It became the first town to be attacked by one of America's foremost muckrakers, Lincoln Steffens. In his book, *Shame of the Cities,* Steffens made St. Louis famous for its tenements, filth, violence, and corruption. Courtesy, Baumhoff Collection, Missouri Historical Society

Left: These strikebreakers were probably at work during the streetcar operators' strike of 1900. Courtesy, Missouri Historical Society

Facing page: As if to underscore St. Louis' growing reputation as America's worst governed city, the streetcar operators' strike turned ugly indeed. Fifteen men were killed and hundreds injured, while city officials shrugged helplessly. Courtesy, Baumhoff Collection, Missouri Historical Society

McClure's Magazine sent in 1902 its best muckraker, Lincoln Steffens, to find out what was going on. Steffens made the courageous young attorney a national hero as he wrote about the case and claimed that "the whole machinery of justice broke down under the strain of the boodle pull." Furious that the people of St. Louis did not immediately destroy the Butler political machine, Steffens gave the city the unusual honor of a second blast of his con-

tempt. He made St. Louis the star of his book, *Shame of the Cities.* But it was no use. Butler remained an important power in city politics, regularly consulted by Republican and Democratic leaders alike.

In the midst of all the turmoil, St. Louis was preparing to celebrate the centennial of the Louisiana Purchase. Outraged by the loss of the Colombian Exposition to Chicago in 1892, the city had taken steps as early as 1898 to create its own world's

fair. Determined to make the exposition bigger and glitzier than the Chicago World's Fair, the city set aside an area twice the size of the Windy City fairgrounds, some 1,240 acres, in Forest Park. Both the city and state government matched the $5 million raised from private donations, and the fair opened in 1904 to the tune of:

Meet me in St. Louie, Louie

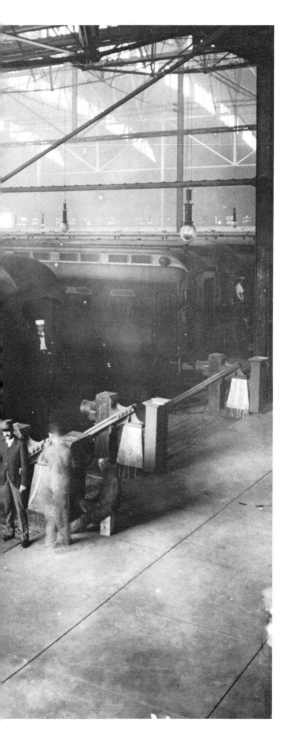

Meet me at the Fair,
Don't tell me the lights are shining
Any place but there.

We'll dance the hootchie-kootchie,
You'll be my tootsie-wootsie,
If you'll meet me in St. Louie, Louie
Meet me at the Fair.

Some 100,000 people a day jammed the streets of the fair and the city, marveling at such wonders as Palaces of Electricity, Education, Transportation, Agriculture, Mines, Machinery, and Manufacturers, a full-scale Filipino village (America had recently annexed the Philippines) and ex-

Above and left: St. Louis' proud new Union Station opened in 1904, the same year the city hosted the fair. The inside of St. Louis' Union Station is shown at left in about 1907. Courtesy, Missouri Historical Society

Facing page: In 1902 *McClure's Magazine* sent Lincoln Steffens to report on the political corruption in St. Louis. From Cirker, *Dictionary of American Portraits*, Dover, 1967

otic Japanese garden (Teddy Roosevelt was playing shuttle diplomacy between the Russians and the Japanese), priceless art collections, a colossal floral clock, totem poles, and, of course, the latest locomotives. Visitors could stroll through a six-acre rose garden, the home of a Chinese mandarin, or the streets of a German village in the Tyrolean Alps. They could ride in a Venetian gondola or a 16-horsepower Swift Rambler. They could listen to the Victor Talking Machine or the president of Princeton University, Woodrow Wilson. After 184 days, almost 20 million tourists had spent nearly $50 million, and the fair closed.

The fair was a smashing success, an event Missourians would never forget. Meanwhile, they had elected Joseph W. Folk their new governor. The Gilded Age was over.

Perhaps a few of the visitors to the fair took the time to wander into the less reputable parts of the city, maybe to visit one of St. Louis' much-touted brothels. If they had, they might well have heard a strange, new, haunting kind of music, with intricate rhythms and odd, twisting notes. Young black men, one named Scott Joplin, another Tom Turpin, played piano music of their own composition with titles like the "Maple Leaf Rag" or the "Harlem Rag." They would say they played the music "ragtime." If the adventurous visitors were especially lucky, they might run across an older black man named W.C. Handy, who had compiled a collection of blues from melodies he had heard on the wharves and in the cotton fields as he wandered about.

If Handy was in the mood, he could play a tune that caught the very soul of the city behind the fair, a song called "The St. Louis Blues."

Above: The Corn Pagoda of Missouri stood proudly in the Palace of Agriculture at the 1904 World's Fair. Courtesy, Missouri Historical Society

Left: More properly called the Louisiana Purchase Universal Exposition, the 1904 World's Fair grew out of civic anger in St. Louis at losing the chance to hold the great Columbian Exposition to Chicago in 1893. The fair, shown here from Art Hill across Cascade Gardens, proved to be St. Louis' most successful attempt to capture the country's attention. Courtesy, Missouri Historical Society

Facing page: The Ferris wheel became famous at the 1904 World's Fair. Courtesy, Missouri Historical Society

The first equal suffrage headquarters in St. Louis is shown here in 1912. Courtesy, Missouri Historical Society

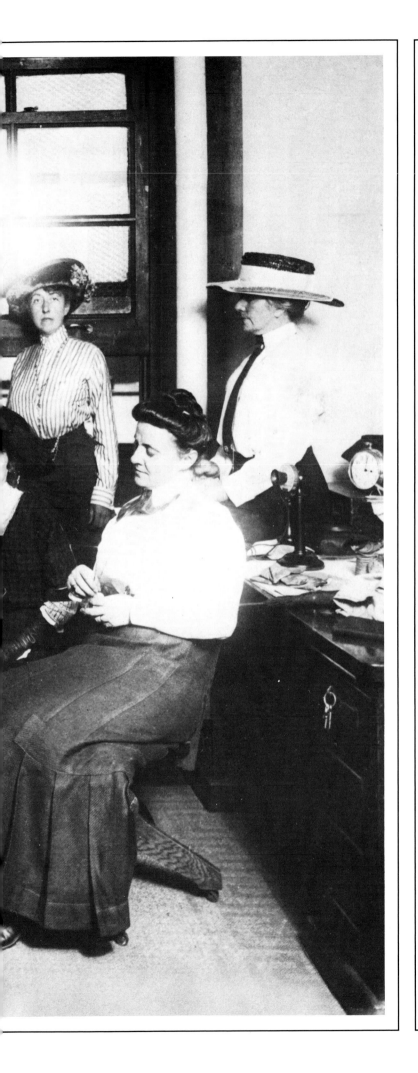

CHAPTER V

Uncle Tom's Cabin

The Progressives who came to power at the dawn of the twentieth century in Missouri were part of a national political movement that transcended party but not class. Born of the decay of Populism, the sensational writings of muckraking journalists, and the involvement of America's churches in social issues, Progressives reacted to the growing power of organized labor, the revolutionary demands of America's new intellectual radicals, and the changing racial and ethnic composition of America's cities with a moral "uplift" program of reform intended to check the excesses of capitalism while preserving it.

The Progressives spoke largely for upper- and middle-class reformers and developers, business and religious leaders, and the more successful newspapers. Interested in economic growth and clean government, they talked in lofty terms of "progress," "civic reform," and "modernization." They attacked politicians, particularly those elected officials more interested in patronage than patriotism, in political power than honest government, in vote-getting than moral decay. Their crusade for "good government" called for the initiative and referendum, public control of the railroads and utilities, a certain amount of trust-busting, primary elections, the popular election of senators, female suffrage, and prohibition.

They did not, however, speak for the urban poor, or racial and ethnic minorities, or labor radicals, all of whom they tended to view as morally decadent at best, viciously criminal at worst. From their country clubs, comfortable homes, and churches they reached out to destroy the saloons and brothels where the working-man relaxed and talked politics. They created the first great "red scare" to purge the intellectuals who took up the cause of the oppressed. They used World War I as an excuse to attack ethnic cultures and homogenize as much as possible America's white population. And the merit system with which they hoped to replace the spoils system excluded blacks from local, state, and federal government.

Not suprisingly, during the "progressive era," Missouri's urban poor, its Irish and German immigrants, its unorganized workingmen, and its separate and unequal

blacks turned to the politicians of the city machines, who, for a vote, could offer them food when they were hungry, rent and clothing when they were down and out, legal help when they were in trouble, cool jazz to cheer them up, cold beer to help them forget, and now and then a good job to get them on their feet. So even while Missouri's Progressives came to power in the first two decades of the new century, its city machines grew stronger, especially in Kansas City. There, Jim Pendergast had put together a muscular political alliance that before long, under the able leadership of his brother Tom, would spread throughout Jackson County and then the state itself. By 1930 the capitol building in Jefferson City had become known as

These gentlemen are shooting craps on the New Franklin Ferry in 1900. Courtesy, Missouri Historical Society

"Uncle Tom's Cabin."

It would take the Great Depression, and the desperate search for solutions it engendered, to meld together the Progressive longing for honesty and decency in government with the otherwise corrupt machine's human warmth and constructive genius. These groups would be united under the New Deal offered by Franklin Delano Roosevelt and symbolized in Missouri by its favorite son, Harry S. Truman.

In 1904 Missouri astounded the nation: for the first time in living memory, it bolted the Solid South and instructed its electors to cast their ballots for the Republican candidate for president, that irrepressible "Rough Rider," Teddy Roosevelt. Along with sending T.R. to the White House, Missourians placed Joseph W. Folk, young hero of the muckrakers, in the statehouse. That year, Folk, touting his "Missouri Idea" (the simple notion that even elected officials should obey the law), was the only Democrat honored by the state's electorate with a state office. But because the new governor was considered a Progressive and an honest Democrat, he got along with the reform-minded Republican legislature. Together they passed a statewide primary law; forbade lobbies, trusts, and child labor; mandated inspections for public utilities and factories; established maximum freight and passenger rates for the railroads (at two cents a mile); and adopted the initiative and referendum.

Folk was lucky in that the previous administration under Alexander M. Dockery had managed at last to retire Missouri's railroad debt. Citizens did not seem overly worried about the increased costs of the reforms to state government, though Missouri's entrenched politicos complained bitterly. Dismissing their carping, Folk considered himself of the stature of a La Follette in Wisconsin or a Charles Evan Hughes in New York. But his own party did not. Big-city Democrats had hooted at him in the primaries as "Saint Joe" or "Holy Joe." When he began upholding statutes banning the operation of saloons and the running of dog

Despite the best efforts of Charles Drake and other Radical Republicans to ensure blacks, and sometimes women, the right to vote and the benefits of citizenship, Missouri—like other Southern states—managed to gut the reforms born of the Civil War and reduce its black population, like this 1900 laundrywoman, to either penury or idleness. Courtesy, Missouri Historical Society

races on Sunday, even those Democrats who once supported him remembered the catcalls and nodded their heads in agreement. Though a good stump speaker, Folk was a cold fish and a lousy politician. During his term in office, he couldn't bring himself to get chummy with the Democratic leadership, and the party refused his request for nomination to the U.S. Senate.

The voters, however, did not give up on reform and sent yet another Progressive to the statehouse in 1908, this time Herbert S. Hadley, a Republican. Hadley made his reputation trust-busting as Folk's attorney general, which, like the secretary of state's office and a number of other administrative posts, was an elected position in Missouri. Having taken on and beaten the Standard Oil Company and other trusts in violation of the new state laws, Hadley found himself in a good position as governor to foster better roads, wider education, penal reforms, and new industry for the state. With such impeccable reform credentials, Hadley was put forward as a compromise candidate at the Republican National Convention in 1912. The grumbling Progressives, egged on by Teddy Roosevelt, wanted to dump the portly, complacent President Taft. But when T.R. himself decided to become the Progressive champion, Hadley threw his support to Taft, destroying his own chances.

That same year another Missourian figured prominently in the Democratic National Convention. Champ Clark, having served nine terms in Congress, eight of those as Speaker of the House, came very close to capturing the nomination before William Jennings Bryan withdrew his support at the last moment and backed the dark-horse candidate, Woodrow Wilson, the former president of Princeton University. Wilson, the governor of New Jersey, was mildly reformist, but had the backing of Eastern capital and big-city bosses nevertheless. Teddy Roosevelt did Wilson the favor of forming a third party, the Bull Moose party, which drained Progressive support from the Republicans and landed Wilson in the White House. Bryan became his secretary of state.

Wilson brought the Democrats back to power in Missouri, though voters still put a Republican in the governor's chair—the state's third Progressive head of state, Elliott Woolfolk Major. Major, like Hadley, had been attorney general and had made his reputation trust-busting. He did manage to get some Progressive legislation passed, most notably the establishment of a state public service commission and the abolition of an ancient and corrupt convict labor system. But Major spent much of his term in office in a frustrating battle with the Democrat-controlled state legislature for the funds he needed to pay for Progressive programs.

Missourians simply did not like taxes, even those that paid for honest, responsible government. It was all well and good when the Progressives promised the popular election of senators, and when Woodrow Wilson floated a constitutional amendment to that effect in 1913, it passed in Missouri as it did everywhere else. They might even go along with a graduated income tax, an inheritance tax, and a corporate franchise tax, all of which seemed to be aimed at the rich, and the first of which was finally legalized at the national level also in 1913. But they had been bamboozled too many times by the bankers and the railroads to put up with deficit spending by state government, and the Progressives had already run Missou-

ri's public debt up to some $2 million.

The writing was on the wall when Democrat Frederick D. Gardner rode Wilson's shirttails into the governor's office in 1916. He immediately secured the necessary revenue measures—state income, inheritance, and corporate taxes, plus a few minor levies—to pay off the deficit, and then demanded that henceforth the state government live within its means. He went so far as to veto a bill approving pensions for the blind and a home for neglected children when the legislature refused to pass additional taxes to pay for them. And there were other signs that Missouri had grown weary of reforms and disenchanted with the Progressives. One was the rise of Tom Pendergast after 1910 in Kansas City. Another was the not unrelated elec-

Above: Champ Clark served nine terms in Congress as a Missouri representative, eight as speaker of the house. From Cirker, *Dictionary of American Portraits*, Dover, 1967

Facing page: Missouri Governor Joseph W. Folk took control of the Democratic Party on a reform platform he called "the Missouri Idea," which stated that all the state needed was honest leaders who fearlessly enforced simple laws. Courtesy, Missouri Historical Society

tion of that city's ex-mayor, James Reed, to the U.S. Senate in 1911.

At the beginning of the Progressive era, Kansas City boasted the most famous advocate for reform in the state, if not the country: William Rockhill Nelson, owner of the Kansas City *Star.* Nelson had come to Kansas City in 1880 from Fort Wayne, Indiana, where he managed a newspaper once owned by his father. Cofounding the *Star* with Samuel K. Morss, Nelson expanded it rapidly by selling it cheap, borrowing money, and practicing to perfection the art of the exposé. In addition to fighting election fraud and utility franchises, the *Star* came out in support of workers' compensation, the initiative and referendum, and the commission form of city government. Associating himself locally with Folk, Hadley, and Roosevelt, Nelson became the representative Progressive reformer. As journalist Mark Sullivan wrote: "The liberal and progressive movement which arose in the Middle West . . . centered largely around the Kansas City *Star* and the other forces of public opinion which took their leadership from the *Star.*"

Four years before Nelson arrived in the city, a 20-year-old Irish workingman from Ohio via St. Joseph came to Kansas City looking for a job. Friendly, competent, popular, and lucky, Jim Pendergast saved enough from his jobs at a packinghouse and a couple of iron foundries to place a hefty bet on a horse named Climax. Pendergast named the saloon he bought with his winnings "The Climax," and his career was launched. He prospered, made friends everywhere, bought other saloons, made more friends, and soon found himself building a political machine in Kansas City's first ward that led to a position on the city council. At first Nelson's *Star* hailed Alderman Pendergast as a reformer, and his biggest rival was another Irish ward heeler named Joseph Shannon. But by 1898, the *Star* was calling Pendergast "A New Democratic Boss in the City." By 1902, having backed James Reed as prosecuting attorney, then as a two-term mayor, and with powerful friends in the statehouse, Pendergast controlled about

half the Democratic vote in the city and was unchallengeable anywhere in Jackson County.

But the Pendergast machine did not really take off until Jim Pendergast, in failing health, slowly turned the organization, called the Jackson County Democratic Club, over to his brother Tom beginning in 1910. Tom Pendergast had been groomed for the job as a deputy constable in the First Ward, then deputy marshal, then marshal, then superintendent of streets, appointed by James Reed. When he ran for alderman in 1910, he had more than just the backing of the city's Irish. Joe Damacio, the "King of Little Italy," gave speeches for him in Italian. The Heims, a brewing family in Kansas City, distributed free beer in German neighborhoods in his support. And the *Call,* a local black and usually Republican newspaper, strongly backed him because of the unusually fair treatment he had given black prisoners as county marshal. Once he had completely picked up the reins from his brother, Tom Pendergast resigned as alderman to concentrate on his career as a political mechanic, at which he was something of a genius. A chagrined Nelson watched as Jim Pendergast's little brother took the first steps toward becoming, outside Chicago's Richard Daley, the greatest political boss of the twentieth century.

James Reed had been known in Kansas City as a reform mayor, despite the help he received from the Pendergast machine and his personal friendship with both Jim and Tom Pendergast. That reputation did not follow him to the U.S. Senate, where he became known as the irascible and implacable foe of both prohibition and women's suffrage, two Progressive reforms yet to succeed by the time Woodrow Wilson began his inexorable march toward the war he had been reelected to avoid.

As early as 1867 the Missouri legislature had been asked to grant women the franchise, and two years later suffragettes held a national convention in St. Louis. At various times the Populists, the Farmers' Alliance, the Missouri State Teachers Associations, and others had supported women in their attempt to claim the basic right of American citizenship. When the Christian Women's Temperance League was formed in the 1880s, it seemed natural enough for the two movements, led by women on behalf of women, to work together. Though early feminists had a much broader sense of purpose, the creation of the Anti-Saloon League in 1893, with its dynamic leaders, abundant financing, and strong backing from Protestant churches, made suffrage and attendant feminist issues more or less an appendage of prohibition. Despite the fact that several western states had already given women the right to vote, in Missouri women's suffrage had been forced to ally itself with the temperance movement and the Anti-Saloon League in order to get on the ballot in 1914. Fewer than 20 percent of the all-male voters favored suffrage.

The battle over prohibition was more heated. The League carried on a nationwide propaganda campaign against the evils of liquor, stressing alcohol's potential to destroy productive lives, corrupt youth, and lead to suicide, jail, poverty, insanity, and death. But the main focus, before the First World War, was on the economic damage to Missouri itself. Ignoring the fact that Missouri had a local option law since 1887, that some 96 of its counties

were already dry while only 19 were wet, by 1912 the League began contrasting dry Kansas with wet Missouri. Kansas had a higher per capita income. Kansas appropriated more money to education. Kansans made higher wages. Kansans owned more automobiles.

The League no doubt thought it had an iron-clad case, but Missouri's voters, their ranks swelled by the machine's hard-drinking Irish-Americans and beer-loving German-Americans, rejected a proposal to make the entire state dry in 1910 by some 218,000 votes. And even in 1916, with Wilson in his second term and Progressive government clearly the order of the day, Reed's forces defeated the same proposal by 122,000 votes. It would be Wilson's "war to end all wars" that gave the League a powerful, new, even more

At the turn of the century, Missouri—like much of rural America—was being swept by Progressive reform, including prohibition. Here, a young Ozark girl poses under a sign that makes abundantly clear the moral rectitude of its authors. Courtesy, F.A. Behymer Collection, Missouri Historical Society

THE USE OF INTOXICATING LIQUOR, TOBACCO, PROFANITY and VULGARITY, ABSOLUTELY FORBIDDEN IN THIS CITY UNDER PENALTY

Above: This old man tended an Ozark ferry in 1904. Courtesy, F.A. Behymer Collection, Missouri Historical Society

Right: This 1904 view depicts Main Street in the Ozark settlement of Three Sands. Courtesy, F.A. Behymer Collection, Missouri Historical Society

Left: Ozark residents were not known for their friendly, trusting ways, especially to outsiders. In 1904 Stella Carter, called locally Queen of the Barge, and her daughter sized up photographer F.A. Behymer. Courtesy, F.A. Behymer Collection, Missouri Historical Society

Below: Never prospering in much more than native beauty and the call of the wild, the Ozark area had been shorn of its forests and devastated by the early mining enterprises. Its thin soil was threatened by erosion from farmers who could barely scratch out a living on land ill-suited for agriculture like this truck patch in 1904. Courtesy, F.A. Behymer Collection, Missouri Historical Society

"Shall we be more tender with our dollars than with the Lives of our sons"

W.G. McAdoo
Secretary of the Treasury

Buy a United States Government Bond of the
2nd **LIBERTY LOAN**
of 1917

Posters like this one, emphasizing the need to sacrifice, were put up all over the state during World War I. Courtesy,

wary people into this "Great War," trying desperately to convince himself, his ethnic minorities, and his embittered intellectuals that he had the best of intentions, the holiest of purposes. But the senior senator from Missouri remained unconvinced. As chairman of the Senate Committee on Foreign Relations, William J. Stone made himself infamous for denouncing Wilson's desire to join the battle. Earlier Stone had led 11 other senators against the president's request to arm America's merchant marine, and now, despite Wilson's increasingly shrill invectives, he urged the nation to resist war.

But it was a lost cause. In April of 1917, Stone was one of only six senators to reject Wilson's request for a declaration of war against Germany. Four of Missouri's congressmen, however, joined Stone in trying to block what sounded suspiciously like yet another Progressive crusade, this time to provide the entire world with "good government." Champ Clark and James Reed added their voices to Stone's when the senator raised doubts about military conscription under a selective service bill written by another Missourian—Enoch H. Crowder, who held the highest position in the army's legal department.

Stone and the others dropped their public opposition when hostilities began, like most of those faced with the hysterical patriotism Wilson whipped up with his massive propaganda machine, called the Committee on Public Information. Headed by ex-Kansas City editor and Denver newspaperman George Creel, the committee's task was to foment war fever in America with pamphlets, posters, newspaper reports, and silent movies. Creel supposedly documented the atrocities committed by the dreaded Hun and the patriotic sacrifices made by American troops at the front and ordinary citizens back home. As Creel freely admitted later, most of the stories were fabricated, but they were nevertheless quite effective. Not surprisingly, many of the Creel committee's writers and artists went into the booming advertising business after the war.

In addition, the administration cen-

shamefully spurious argument that pandered to the worst in the reform temperament—its latent racism and nativist hysteria—and allowed the drys finally to triumph in the last great spasm of Progressive uplift.

In 1917 the world found itself still at war. Very little had been accomplished by the four-year carnage but the invention of a new and disenchanting "weapon": the trench. Europe had machine-gunned and gassed itself to a standstill. Woodrow Wilson wanted to drag his anxious and still

sored, intimidated, or incarcerated critics of the war—sundry intellectuals, socialist workingmen, conscientious objectors, and card-carrying communists—and turned a blind eye to the mistreatment of German-American citizens. In outstate Missouri, efforts were made to discourage the use of the German language during church services, and in St. Louis there was talk of segregating the German-American population entirely. Berlin Avenue was renamed after General John J. Pershing, the Missouri veteran of the Spanish-American War who led the American Expeditionary Forces in France and became a war hero. Everywhere German-American Missourians learned to fear their neighbors, who spied on them, threatened them, forced them to buy Liberty Bonds to prove their loyalty, and sometimes physically attacked them. The anti-German hysteria created by Wilson's wartime government seemed complete when the Anti-Saloon League took up the argument that "German brewers in this country have rendered thousands of men inefficient and are thus crippling the republic in its war on Prussian militarism . . . The brewers are helping the enemy."

By the time Congress proposed the 18th Amendment to the United States Constitution in 1917, German brewers, their very livelihoods at stake, had braved the hostile wartime atmosphere and formed the German-American Alliance to counteract League propaganda. In Missouri, brewers came together in the Association

Against the Prohibition Amendment, published a paper called the *Minute Men,* and even commissioned a play, which told the sappy, heartrending story of a good, fun-loving German saloonkeeper whose business was ruined by the drys. Even at the height of the war hysteria in 1918, the wets—brewers, saloonkeepers, distributors, and the working class of St. Louis and Kansas City—managed to defeat yet again a statewide prohibition referendum by some 73,000 votes. But when the constitutional amendment came before the Missouri legislature in January 1919, the

Above: When World War I broke out, the citizens of St. Louis (and every Missouri city and town) became addicted to parades and other patriotic displays. Courtesy, Missouri Historical Society

Left: Mules were the state's finest contribution to agriculture before machinery pushed them aside. At the turn of the century, they were still being used—as here in 1904—in the primitive agriculture of the Ozark highlands. Their finest moment, however, would come in World War I, when they were especially cherished along Europe's western front as dependable and imperturbable. Even in 1922, some 440,000 mules were still hard at work on Missouri farms. Courtesy, Missouri Historical Society

By the 1910s women's suffrage was once again on the agenda of Progressive reform, after having earlier been pushed aside by the Temperance Movement. Courtesy, Missouri Historical Society

rural-dominated body ratified it by 22 to 10 votes in the senate and 104 to 34 votes in the house. That same year Missouri became the 11th state to ratify the 19th Amendment to the U.S. Constitution, calling for women's suffrage. By 1920 women anywhere in America could vote, and no one could legally celebrate that milestone with a drink and a toast.

Meanwhile, as the First World War came to a close, U.S. Senator James Reed had begun to fight anew. If Wilson and the Progressives had thought his stand against suffrage and Prohibition a mite vigorous, they must have been astounded by the single-minded passion with which he castigated Wilson's attempt to establish the League of Nations. The battle was a mean and bitter one. It broke Wilson's health and created many enemies for Reed

among his fellow Democrats in Missouri, who began to form "Rid us of Reed" clubs all over the state. Nevertheless, Americans seemed to be coming out of their war stupor as if awakening from a long, disturbing dream. They rejected Wilson's idealistic hopes for the future, and handily returned Reed to the Senate in 1922.

A recession immediately followed the war, and while Missouri's rural areas were hit hard, it suffered less trouble with its industry than other states, partly because it failed to grow as fast during the war as others had. Farm values were depressed, and a number of rural banks failed. Missouri mules had been at a premium during the war, but the demand had vanished on the 11th hour of the 11th day of the 11th month of 1918, and mule-breeding went into an irreversible decline. Monsanto, the St. Louis chemical company, was forced to slash its work force and go into receivership to a New York City bank when its German competitors began to undersell its products in order to break back into the market. But even more important to St. Louis, one of its major industries, brewing, had been crippled by Prohibition.

Reed's splintering of the Democratic party and the postwar recession left an opening for the Republicans in 1920. The 43-year-old Arthur M. Hyde, a small-town lawyer, automobile dealer, banker, and insurance agent, became governor. Hyde was a member of the GOP's Progressive faction, having bolted the party in 1912 to support Teddy Roosevelt. Like other reformers, Hyde found the Missouri statehouse a frustrating place to hang his hat for four years. Though most of the actions he tried to foist on the state met with failure, he did manage to get some $60 million in road bonds authorized, with which he planned to "pull Missouri out of the mud."

The move proved prescient. The automobile was quickly becoming a fact of life for Missourians. In 1915 there had been only 76,000 cars in the state. By 1920 Missouri residents owned some 297,000 motor vehicles. But outside the larger cities and

the business districts of a few towns, every street, alley, and highway in the state was a dirt road. The contemporary Missouri author Homer Croy has one of his Junction City characters proclaim in *West of the Watch Tower:* "These people raise corn for the whole country. They work hard and yet they are virtual prisoners. The roads are our jailers."

The United States Post Office's decision to operate a system of rural free delivery made the development of hard-surface roads, passable in all kinds of weather and in the gloom of night, more important, but the move to pave highways would have come anyway. The automobile was everyone's ticket to freedom, and two-lane blacktops, like the railways before them, seemed capable of making or breaking a community. Good roads became a passion in the twenties. Nearly all state capital expenditures, though not local ones, went to highways at great cost to everything else, including education. And the number of cars traveling those roads increased at an amazing rate: 640,000 by 1925; 762,000 by 1930.

In 1921 radio stations in Jefferson City, Kansas City, St. Louis, and Columbia began broadcasting their programs across

The Liberty Memorial, built to commemorate those lost during the Great War, was dedicated in 1926. President Calvin Coolidge spoke and the American Legion, which grew out of that war, cheered. Courtesy, Liberty Memorial Museum

the state. Within a few years, too, almost every Missouri hamlet had at least one, usually two, motion picture theaters. Broadcast radio and the movies added to the immense changes brought about by the automobile in the life of the individual Missouri farmer and the small-town resident, breaking down the isolation of rural life and dispelling the claustrophobic atmosphere of Main Street culture. Through the radio the siren call of the saxophone beckoned the young in the back parlors and the cafes to jump in their roadsters and head for a speakeasy or blind pig in St. Louis or Kansas City. On the silver screen, Gloria Swanson, Clara Bow, Rudolph Valentino, and Douglas Fairbanks showed them how to act once they got there. In doing so, they accelerated trends already under way—the decline of small towns and the depopulation of the rural countryside. By 1930, for the first time, more Missourians would live in urban than rural areas. And even for those who stayed behind, there was no escaping the fast times and glamorous dreams of the 1920s.

Missouri's artists and writers, of course, were as deeply affected by the changes as were her farmers and Main Street denizens. Most of the major

Missouri-born talents—Sara Teasdale, Marianne Moore, T.S. Eliot, Langston Hughes—found their hometowns a bore, and middle-class Midwestern life narrow and stifling. They rejected the state and broke away, like a whole generation of their readers, defining their existence by strict aesthetic codes or inner experience or ethnic origin. Others, even when they left for New York to make a living, made farm and small-town life the central literary theme of their work, like Rose Wilder Lane in *Hill-Billy*, Harold Bell Wright in *The Shepherd of the Hill*, or Homer Croy, a farmer turned novelist, in all his work. Thomas Hart Benton, son of a congressman and great-nephew of Missouri's most prominent pre-Civil War senator, reversed the trend by breaking from his New York City crowd and Parisian modernism in art to search for a usable past in the small-town rural life that was his family's heritage.

Others reacted with fear to the modern world and its faith in science, its revolt against the family, and its overturning of old sexual mores, all prompted by a vogue for the teachings of Sigmund Freud. The evangelical religions, with their almost sensual fervor, enjoyed a heyday. A general hostility to the teaching of evolutionary theory led to several attacks on Missouri's already beleaguered schools. When a University of Missouri graduate student working with the respected psychologist Max F. Meyer distributed a questionnaire on the economic status of women, the sexual code, and the family, it created a major scandal. Hounded by charges from his own university president, Stratton D. Brooks, that he was practicing "sewer sociology," Meyer was driven from the classroom and ultimately from the university. Brooks lost his own job when the board discovered he had misrepresented the facts, but an unappeased Meyer was not welcomed back.

Not only did Missourians reluctantly part with tax dollars for their schools, attack them as dens of sedition and iniquity, and go to almost any lengths to make sure they remained segregated, they showed a marked preference for the old one-room

These purebred Herefords were fattened up in Carroll County in 1926. Missouri's reputation as a mostly agricultural state dominated by small farms and flanked by two decaying cities had become fixed by the early decades of the twentieth century. Courtesy, Missouri Historical Society

City, the Klan had some 50,000 to 100,000 members. They lynched a black man in Columbia in 1923. They bombed a black realtor in Kansas City in 1924. Later that same year they defeated a young judge in Jackson County, who was backed by the racially and religiously tolerant Pendergast machine. It was the only time Harry Truman would be defeated for political office in his life.

The Klan's attack on Catholics, Jews, and blacks was the dark side of Missouri's dislike for the way America was heading, which was straight down its new highways in its new cars to the big city and surrounding suburbs. Prohibition, with which Missourians had hoped to tame the city, had forced it into a wild, corrupt, fun-loving, and heedless period called variously the Roaring Twenties and the Jazz Age.

For it was in the big cities, in St. Louis and Kansas City, that Missourians could find the world they had heard about on the radio and seen at the movies. In St. Louis they could see the Cardinals, who, with the help of the farm team system they had invented (much to the amusement of the rest of professional baseball), were quickly becoming a powerhouse in the National

Far left: St. Louis Cardinal Stan Musial was king of the home run. Courtesy, Missouri Historical Society

schoolhouses that continued to flourish while they fought modern consolidation and centralization. No wonder an outside agency, the Sage Foundation, ranked the system 34th in the nation, and the state's own subsequent survey could raise it no higher than 32nd.

Many Missourians reacted to the changes, especially urban demographic changes, with seething racial hatred and religious bigotry. From the beginning of the century, blacks migrated from the Deep South, Jews from Russia and Middle Europe, and Italians from Lombardy and Sicily, primarily to Missouri's big cities. At the same time, the native-born, white, Protestant American population declined, relative to other states. The Ku Klux Klan reemerged in Missouri, as it had throughout the South before the war, and it flourished in the 1920s. By 1924, when it held its "klonvocation" in Kansas

Left: Leroy Robert "Satchel" Paige pitched for the Kansas City Monarchs of the Negro Baseball League. After the National League's color barrier was broken, Paige pitched for the St. Louis Browns from 1951 to 1953. In 1971 he was inducted into the National Baseball Hall of Fame. Courtesy, William J. Curtis Collection

League. If one had a hankering to root for the underdog, St. Louis also offered the spectacle of the hapless American League Browns, for, like only Boston, New York, Philadelphia, and Chicago, the city had two major league teams. The Browns became so famous for losing season after season that St. Louisans began to boast of their city as "first in booze, first in shoes, and last in the American League." In 1920 the Negro Baseball League was formed in Kansas City, and Missouri boasted two black baseball teams, the St. Louis Stars and the Kansas City Monarchs. Whites seldom saw the black players, who became heroes in the cities' black communities.

For more highbrow visitors St. Louis offered the nation's first outdoor theater, the Municipal Opera Theatre in Forest Park, where fans could view productions on a soft summer night or listen to one of the many public concerts given by the St. Louis symphony orchestra during the 1920s to help reverse its flagging fortunes. Not far away was the new St. Louis Zoo, which gained an international reputation during the decade under the direction of George Vierheller. But most people, especially the young, did not drive into the city to see a concert or visit the zoo. They came looking for fun, a night of bootleg booze and some of the jazz music that had given their "age" its name.

St. Louis jazz, much influenced by New Orleans greats like King Oliver and Louis Armstrong, who traveled up the river by showboat, had a dominant rhythm of two beats to the bar. A number of good bands played this "Dixieland" sound in the 1920s, but one of the best was the Missourians, which included among its members Cab and Blanche Calloway, Jack Teagarden, Pee Wee Russell, Frankie Trumbauer, and Bix Beiderbecke. Kansas City jazz, on the other hand, was heavily influenced by the blues, folk songs, and ragtime, with a heavy 4/4 beat. Ma Rainey and Bessie Smith sang in the city, and the leading figure in the early years, Bennie Martin, had been a ragtime piano player.

To the parents and grandparents back

home, the music and glamour that attracted their children to the city seemed based entirely on demon alcohol served by loose-living men and women in sleazy speakeasies and glitzy nightclubs belonging to violence-prone gangsters; jazz and sin seemed synonymous. And they were dead right.

From the moment the 18th Amendment passed, America became a nation of lawbreakers. Folks in the ethnic neighborhoods of St. Louis and Kansas City, neighborhoods that had opposed overwhelmingly the various state referendums to outlaw liquor, began immediately to brew and bootleg bathtub gin and moonshine, often with the encouragement of their friends and neighbors. Contemptuous of a law they hated, determined themselves to continue drinking, and looking to make a buck as well, these neighborhood bootleggers had the support of their local grocers, who supplied the necessary raw materials, and of their local former saloonkeepers, restaurant owners, and ice cream and soft drink parlor operators, who helped distribute their products. Neighborhood policemen looked the other way. Friends warned one another about raids. Even the Reverend W.C. Schupp, superintendent of the Anti-Saloon League

in St. Louis, got caught in 1923 using his influence to secure an alcohol permit for his son's firm, the Druggists Cooperative Company, in order to sell it to bootleggers. Evidently, Schupp also arranged raids on his clients' competitors.

The Italian-American neighborhood on "the Hill" in southeast St. Louis was a good example of a local haven for bootleggers, though the pattern repeated itself elsewhere among the Germans and the Irish and in Kansas City as well as St. Louis. Italians from Lombardy, and later Sicily, had been settling on the Hill since the 1880s. Though they stopped coming during the First World War, they arrived in record numbers in 1920 and continued to pour into St. Louis until 1924, when the country shut off further mass immigration from Europe. Prohibition drew the Lombards and Sicilians together in a common enterprise. With their profits from illegal liquor sales, many of the Hill's Italian-Americans built new homes, improving their standard of living and the neighborhood. Volstead's Act had offered them a golden opportunity to move up the socioeconomic ladder.

But the business was risky. Raids did occur. People were punished. Some even lost their citizenships. And lured by the

Left: Charlie "Yard Bird" Parker, jazz musician and composer, was heavily influenced by the Kansas City sound. He moved on to New York, where he was one of the inventors of the "beebop" style, which emphasized listening over dancing. Courtesy, *Kansas City Call Collection,* Jackson County Historical Society

Facing page: This view of Kansas City's "Petticoat Lane" is from the mid-1920s. Courtesy, Missouri Historical Society

In the 1920s, inside one of the 50 or more jazz clubs between 12th and 18th streets, Count Basie and his "Kansas City Seven" could be found playing a new kind of jazz that influenced musicians worldwide. Kansas City jazz reached new heights as the "jam" became that city's specialty. Courtesy, *Kansas City Call Collection,* Jackson County Historical Society

Meerscham pipes were in the making in Franklin County, which became a center of the corn-cob pipe industry. By 1926, Franklin was producing some 125,000 pipes daily. Courtesy, Missouri Historical Society

dered mobsters.

The mainstream press, pandering to its nativist, middle-class audience, tried to make an ethnic issue of the crime wave created by Prohibition and blame it all on the Italians. Almost weekly, headlines announced still another Sicilian gang war or the discovery of another still on the Hill. The Kansas City *Star* treated Little Italy even worse. Meanwhile the mobsters, protected by their big-city politicos, poured their profits into clubs to play jazz over the rat-tat-tat in the background. As one wide-eyed observer of St. Louis noted in 1926: "Prohibition is probably more completely forgotten there than in any other American town." He had obviously never been to Kansas City.

For there, in 1925, Tom Pendergast had taken over the entire city council under a new reform charter that he had supported to the reformers' surprise. He appointed his own man, Henry F. McElroy, as city manager, who in turn picked a very agreeable police chief. The town was wide open, and though some local citizens may have gritted their teeth at the phrase, to the city's chamber of commerce, hotel owners, and many small businessmen, the words sounded like sweet music. National magazines and eastern papers ran feature articles on Tom Pendergast and the Kansas City nightlife, which went on around the clock in gangster-owned night spots like the Sunset Club, the Reno Club, and the Subway Club. All were protected by the police for a cut of the action.

Journalists were fascinated by the new kind of jazz being nurtured there, and Kansas City jazz reached new heights, with the "jam" becoming a Kansas City specialty. Inside the Reno, the Sunset, or the Subway, or in one of the 50 or more clubs between 12th and 18th streets, Count Basie and his "Kansas City Seven" played while a young Charlie Parker sat enrapt. At the Yellow Front Saloon, the great blues singer Julia Lee mesmerized customers who came from their homes in the city, or farms out in Jackson County, or rooms in the convention hotels.

When they were done listening to Paul Banks, Jay McShann, Andy Kirk, or

chance for big profits, the underworld moved in. The gangsters, like those they preyed on, were immigrants. Crime simply offered a convenient, alluring, and quick way up the ladder of success, and bright, ruthless, upwardly mobile immigrant youths, convinced that other means to wealth and personal happiness were cut off to them, turned to it as a profession. Such men tended to be at home with violence, and neighborhood bootlegging looked like a good, easy mark.

The mobsters began terrorizing the illegal traffic, extorting protection money, and brutalizing the uncooperative. Gangs, like the Cuckoos, the Green Ones, Egan's Rats, the Bergers, and the Sheltons in St. Louis, began battling each other for control, using sawed-off shotguns and Thompson machine guns to make their points and establish their monopolies. In Kansas City, gambler Solly Weissmann and Little Italy's John Lazia seemed to come out on top, for a while at least. In St. Louie, everybody was afraid of gunman Blackie Armes. Between 1919 and 1932, the bootleg wars resulted in some 60 killings, and the fighting got so fierce in the late-1920s that Archbishop John J. Glennon refused to grant last rites to mur-

George E. Lee, they could stumble down the block to play poker and roulette or feed slot machines in the gambling dens peeking out among the jazz clubs. Whores tempted strolling men along 13th and 14th streets as they checked out the bawdy houses. Not far away was the Chesterfield Club, where businessmen and out-of-towners gulped down meals while strippers did their bump-and-grinds up top. The waitresses at the Chesterfield, according to Julia Lee, "wore nothin', if yo' overlook the slippers n' a cellophane apron."

At election time a few never-say-die reformers complained about the corrupt police and the illicit goings-on, but the chamber of commerce merely pointed to the U.S. Department of Justice's statistics, which gave Kansas City the lowest crime rate of any city in its class. Later, in Chicago, Tom Pendergast would boast: "Ours is a fine, clean, well-ordered town."

The twenties were not just flush times for a few gamblers and gang leaders. As did the rest of America, Missouri experienced nearly a decade of urban growth, industrial development, and business prosperity, all built upon credit, extravagant speculation, and reckless installment buying. Though Missouri did not grow in population as rapidly as other states, some cities, like Springfield and Kansas City, boomed. And though St. Louis proper grew more slowly than any other major city but Boston, its suburbs swelled as the metropolitan area continued to attract Missourians from outstate and a growing number of southern blacks. Missouri underwent constant industrial growth during the 1920s, ranking 10th in the nation in total value of products manufactured, while wages steadily increased from 1919 to 1929.

Aviation, centered mostly in St. Louis, became the state's newest industry. When regular airmail was instituted in the twenties, Robertson Aircraft Corporation won the franchise between St. Louis and Chicago, making it one of the first to offer such a service. Robertson built the city's first commercial airport in Forest Park between 1919-1920 to handle the mail

flights, but when the service fell victim to President Harding's economy drive a year after it started, pharmaceutical manufacturer Albert Bond Lambert began to develop a more adequate all-purpose flying field northwest of the city. But it was Charles Lindbergh's famous flight across the Atlantic in 1927 that really gave a boost to aviation in Missouri and brought commercial flying to Lambert Field. Transcontinental Air Transport hired Lindbergh and set up its national headquarters in St. Louis in 1928. A year later, TAT, which eventually became TWA, inaugurated coast-to-coast airmail service through St. Louis with the Pennsylvania and Santa Fe Railroads.

But it was only two short years between the soaring optimism of Lindbergh's *Spirit of St. Louis* and the despair engendered by Black Monday, in October

The Air Terminal Building at the new St. Louis Airport was dedicated in the 1930s. Courtesy, Missouri Historical Society

Above: A Works Progress Administration soup kitchen provides meals in 1940. Courtesy, Missouri Historical Society

Right: The poor and the jobless, both black and white, protest the social conditions of Depression-era Missouri in this 1931 march. Courtesy, Missouri Historical Society

way, the president of the United States gave Pendergast complete control of all federal programs in Missouri.

Control of federal patronage became one of the most powerful weapons in Pendergast's political arsenal. Throughout the 1930s he was able to carry his city, county, and statewide tickets with overwhelming majorities. He no longer ran just Kansas City or Jackson County; he ran Missouri. Whoever he wanted to be governor was governor, and he put Guy B. Park in office. In 1934, when he needed a loyal candidate for the U.S. Senate, he turned to Harry S. Truman, who ran things in Jackson County for him and whom he once called his "office boy." Thousands of Missourians survived the Great Depression with the help of the New Deal as administered by the Pendergast machine. Though Kansas City clearly benefited more than the rest of the state, and Pendergast's own pre-mixed concrete company made plenty of money off the deal, most men and women, black and white, were cared for with few of the racial discrimination and seniority problems that plagued the federal programs in other states. Pendergast was, after all, a topnotch ward heeler, and the New Deal had made the entire state his ward.

At the same time, Pendergast continued to practice the petty corruptions that are almost second nature to a big-city political boss: bribery, election fraud, and payoffs. These were made worse by a com-

1929, when the New York Stock Market crashed and sent the country spinning into the Great Depression. Farmers, already suffering from the prolonged agricultural recession following World War I, were devastated by the wave of bank failures and bankruptcies that followed the crash. As their loans were called in, their mortgages foreclosed, and their farms put up for auction, they began to pour into Missouri's cities to join the throngs of urban workers thrown out of jobs as unemployment raged ever higher. Then came year after year of blistering drought that scorched crops and created huge dust storms, destroying more farms and helping to populate the "Hoovervilles" cropping up on the outskirts of the big cities. Finally came the locusts. Before it was over, one out of every 10 people in Missouri would be on relief.

At the 1932 Democratic National Convention, Tom Pendergast wanted to back Franklin Delano Roosevelt for the nomination. The only thing that stood in his way was his crusty old friend James Reed, who wanted to be president. Pendergast would not desert Reed outright, but he arranged it so that on each ballot, a few more of Missouri's delegates would change their votes to FDR. Most of the big-city bosses had come out for Al Smith, and Roosevelt would not forget Pendergast's help when he became president in 1933 after having carried Missouri by some 460,000 votes, the largest popular plurality in the state's history. When the New Deal got under

pulsive gambling habit that he later admitted led him to look for ever greater sources of income, legal and otherwise. In 1933 "Pretty Boy" Floyd, Adam Richetti, and another gunman, trying to free a fellow bank robber, shot down an FBI agent, two Kansas City policemen, an Oklahoma police chief, and the robber himself in Union Station. Johnny Lazia helped plan the event and recommended the third gunman. Lazia was one of Pendergast's chief lieutenants, head of the North Side Democratic Club, and "king" of Little Italy. He had made Kansas City a haven for gangsters and outlaws on the run. In 1934 the dapper Lazia was assassinated, and his close friend Big Charley Carollo became head of the Kansas City mob.

Incidents such as the "Union Station Massacre" and the machine-gun killing of Johnny Lazia tended to make Pendergast something of an embarrassment to the Roosevelt administration. And Pendergast, while powerful, was not invincible.

Champ Clark's son, Bennett, had made it to the U.S. Senate despite opposition from the machine. In fact, that was why Tom Pendergast had needed Truman there, to counterbalance Clark's growing power in the Missouri Democratic party. Now an ambitious Lloyd Stark, whom Pendergast had put in the statehouse, was angling for favor with FDR. Blessed by Senator Clark, the governor joined forces with U.S. District Attorney Maurice Milligan to go after Pendergast and his machine for election fraud. When Milligan came up for reappointment, Truman tried to help his friend by attacking Milligan's qualifications on the floor of the Senate, but without FDR's backing he got nowhere. Before the show was over, more than 100 members of the Jackson County Democratic Club had been convicted of vote fraud, and Pendergast's power was destroyed. In 1939 Tom Pendergast himself pleaded guilty to income tax evasion and went to jail.

Not all Works Progress Administration work was as glamorous as producing a state guide. In 1940 these black workers had been hired to dig ditches. Courtesy, Missouri Historical Society

Joplin's Fiesta Days Parade brightened the intersection of Sixth and Main on April 24, 1940, led by this high school band. Courtesy, Baird Studios

CHAPTER VI

Give 'em Hell, Harry

While Pendergast fell from power, FDR was preparing to lead his nation into the great European war. Most of the country was still slowly recovering from the Depression. But while production and employment had reached higher levels than in the hard times of the thirties, in Missouri as elsewhere, the economy had not bounced back to the levels of 1929. Watching yet another president who had promised to keep them out of war tippy-toe to its brink, Missourians were not much more eager to fight Hitler's Nazis or the legions from the Land of the Rising Sun than were their Midwestern neighbors.

When the inevitable happened, Missourians plunged into the battle with the best of them. Omar Bradley proved an able and humane leader of the troops in Europe, called by Ernie Pyle the "G.I.'s General." General Maxwell Taylor, too, came from Missouri, along with some 450,000 other combatants. Hardly anything however matched the contribution of the small town of Lamar, population 3,000. Rear Admiral Charles A. Lockwood, Jr., commander of the submarine fleet in the Pacific, came from Lamar, as did his friend Rear Admiral Freeland A. Daubin, who commanded the Atlantic submarine fleet. Lieutenant Commander Dorothy C. Stratton of Lamar served as director of the SPARs, and Lamar boasted yet a third rear admiral: Selby Combs. And Harry Truman, though he made Independence his hometown, was born in Lamar.

Above: Bess Wallace married Harry S. Truman shortly after he returned from active duty during World War I. The 35-year-old Truman proposed to Wallace some 27 years after they first met. From Cirker, *Dictionary of American Portraits,* Dover, 1967

Far right: Harry S. Truman, the 33rd president of the United States, was born in Lamar and grew up on a farm in Independence. He rose through the Pendergast machine in Kansas City, and gained national fame as head of the Truman Committee, a senate committee that investigated inefficiency and fraud by government contractors. Much loved and respected for his honesty and feistiness, Truman retired to Missouri after his presidency. He died in Kansas City in 1972. From Cirker, *Dictionary of American Portraits,* Dover, 1967

Truman's emergence toward the end of the war as FDR's vice president, and then as the nation's chief executive after Roosevelt's death, overshadowed in Missouri even the profound changes prompted in America by World War II. Race relations at home shifted dramatically, and the impact of the federal government on the economy and on American life grew ever stronger. Science and technology revolutionized postwar society. The Cold War and the threat of an atomic armageddon reshaped national and state politics. As these changes swept through the country and the state, Missouri tended to focus on its native son in the White House, who seemed so typical a product of Missouri. Truman's rise was truly one of the most spectacular, and telling, events in Missouri's history.

Truman retired to Missouri in 1953 to watch his native state struggle through the difficult decades following the Korean War and America's engagement in Vietnam, with the attendant polarization of the body politic into extreme right and left along racial and generational lines. After his death in 1972, Truman became an American folk hero, while Missouri itself was left to face the legacies of the New Deal and the Cold War he had left behind.

The year after Tom Pendergast went to jail, Harry Truman had to face reelection in Missouri. Both of the men who had engineered Pendergast's fall from grace, Governor Stark and District Attorney Milligan, ran against Truman in the Democratic primaries. Though both made political hay out of their crusade against big-city corruption, neither ever directly accused Truman of illegal or unethical behavior. In fact, Milligan was careful to state that "at no time did the finger of suspicion ever point in the direction of Senator Truman." But in the way of all political campaigns, semi-official rumors abounded, and Truman felt called upon to respond. "Tom Pendergast never asked me to do a dishonest deed," Truman declared. "He knew I wouldn't do it if he asked."

The image of Truman as a tool of the

Pendergast machine persisted, however, and it would haunt Truman throughout his career. Truman did not help matters by remaining steadfastly loyal to his one-time benefactor: "Pendergast has been my friend when I needed it. I am not one to desert a ship when it starts to go down." Years later, even as president, and while under attack in the national press for his risque political connections in Missouri, Truman would attend Tom Pendergast's funeral against the advice of his closest associates.

Both the scrupulous honesty in public affairs and the unbending loyalty for even flawed friends was typical of Truman, part of his Missouri heritage and much admired long after the heat of the political moment had passed. Truman's forebears had come to Jackson County, Missouri, in the 1840s from Kentucky, bringing with them their slaves and taking up agriculture with an occasional foray into trade and land speculation. Both Truman's grandfathers were prominent figures in southern Jackson County who sympathized with the Confederate cause in the Civil War. His father, John Truman, was a farmer, a real estate salesman, and a strong Democrat. When his first son was born on May 8, 1884, he planted a pine tree to commemorate the event and christened the boy Harry.

After his father, who in addition to farming had gone into trading and the raising of mules, lost it all speculating on grain futures, the family moved about quite a bit. John Truman finally settled in Independence, Missouri, where Harry attended public schools and became an avid reader. John Truman's financial reverses made it impossible to send Harry to college, and the bespectacled, bookish bachelor failed to get into West Point or Annapolis because of his eyesight. Young Harry went to work, moving through a series of jobs as a railroad construction timekeeper, a mail-room worker at the Kansas City *Star,* and a bank employee, living in a sedate boardinghouse the typical life of a young Missouri country boy trying to start out in the big city. He had a sweetheart, Bess Wallace, and he spent most weekends visiting his aging parents who now lived in Clinton. He spent some years as a farmer, but when the First World

War came along, Harry Truman jumped at the chance to enlist.

The Kansas City boys of Battery F, most of them Irish, elected Truman lieutenant in 1917, and when the unit reached Fort Still, Oklahoma, he and a Jackson County crony named Eddie Jacobson set up a canteen, assessing each of the new soldiers two dollars apiece to buy goods for the enterprise. Within six months, they turned a profit of $15,000, which they split with their shareholders. The fun ended in March of 1918, when Truman shipped out for France. There, as part of the 35th Division, Harry saw his share of action, coming under fire in August when the division had been assigned to the front in Alsace.

After the war, the 35-year-old Truman finally proposed to Bess Wallace, some 27 years after they first met. Bess had no desire to be a farm wife, and Truman, much changed by the war, had little taste left for farming himself. He went into the haberdashery business in Kansas City with his old war buddy, Eddie Jacobson, but this time they failed to make a profit. A bank-

At the waterworks by the Missouri River near Sugar Creek, a young Harry Truman was photographed with, from left to right, Will Rugg, Nell Rugg, Frank Wallace, May Southern, Julia Rugg, and Bess Wallace in October 1913. Courtesy, Harry S. Truman Library

rupt newlywed veteran, Harry Truman entered Missouri politics.

Truman got a break when one of his fellow officers in World War I, James Pendergast, old Jim Pendergast's son, recommended Harry to his uncle, Tom. The Kansas City boss backed Truman for judge of a rural eastern district on the government body that managed county affairs, the Jackson County Court. Truman won, of course, but when he refused to join many of his friends in the Ku Klux Klan, who despised Tom Pendergast, they made sure that he failed to be reelected to a second term, which only strengthened his ties to Pendergast's Jackson County Democratic Club. In 1926, backed by the machine, Truman became presiding judge of Jackson County and the political leader of the county.

Though Pendergast insisted on controlling county patronage, he did not otherwise meddle in Truman's affairs, and the new judge was brilliantly successful. He stressed honest government, provided efficient service, and built durable and desperately needed roads. Securing a bond issue authorizing some $20 million in highway funds, Truman put bipartisan engineers to work planning and overseeing the road projects. In total he spent some $60 million while in county office, and not a breath of scandal attached to him.

In 1934 when the U.S. Senate seat in Missouri fell open, Pendergast was anxious to cement his budding relationship with FDR. He saw the advantages of controlling the federal dole during the Depression and hoped to use it to expand his power base in the state. "You can't beat

five million dollars," he told his boys in Kansas City. From the beginning Truman had been a rabid fan of the Roosevelts, and he had proved his loyalty. After two other party favorites declined to run, Truman became Tom Pendergast's choice for the job. Truman would have preferred the House of Representatives, but Pendergast had given him the nod, and Pendergast was the boss.

Truman ran on his record as county administrator against accusations that he was a Pendergast lackey. The sizzling summer of 1934 found Truman stumping the state, developing the neighborly campaign style he would never abandon, noted for its candor and homespun wit. He knew from firsthand experience the plight of the farmers, he spoke their language, and he saw the world as they did, divided into good guys and bad guys. As one newspaper pointed out, he drew a surprising amount of support from "the creek forks and the grass roots." That, and thousands of fraudulent votes provided by Tom Pendergast, won him a narrow victory.

Tom was no longer around in 1940, and the voting rolls of Jackson County had been purged of all its friendly "ghosts." Now, with no established organization of his own and no money to finance his campaign for reelection in 1940, Truman found himself facing not only Pendergast's enemies Stark and Milligan, but every major big-city newspaper in the state, with the sole exception of the Kansas City *Journal*. The *Journal* was still friendly to the much-diminished Jackson County Democratic Club run by Pendergast's nephew and Truman's war buddy, James.

Truman's record in the Senate during his first term was remarkable only for his slavish devotion to the president, whom he even backed in the ill-starred attempt to pack the Supreme Court. Running a campaign staffed by volunteers and funded by a few private contributions, Truman stressed his solid support of the New Deal, touted his close friendship with labor, and talked good old down-home Missouri Democrat politics: simple government, how the wealthy always took advantage of the farmer and the laborer, and the need to be suspicious of power and size in high places. He was renominated by some 8,000 votes. In November he regained his Senate seat. Close elections would become a Truman hallmark.

While Truman was still an obscure senator from Missouri in his second term, the war started. He managed to secure for himself the chairmanship of a congressional committee examining the honesty and efficiency of the national defense programs contracted to America's corporate giants. In time the group became known as the Truman Committee, which gained its chairman national fame as it denounced again and again the fraud and waste visited upon the American people by

the industrial and commercial world. Truman reputedly saved the taxpayers billions of dollars by exposing the corrupt practices of banks and big industry in a time of national peril. His activities also allowed him to send a few defense dollars Missouri's way.

Truman's high profile brought him to the attention of the more conservative New Dealers and Democrats who were looking for somebody to replace FDR's vice president, Henry Wallace, who they considered a wild-eyed radical.

Those Missourians who did not march off to war or to the U.S. Congress found themselves nevertheless caught up in the

Above: The look of military parades had changed in St. Louis by World War II. Here tanks, instead of uniformed men and women, lead the Navy Day Parade, October 24, 1942. Courtesy, Missouri Historical Society

Below: During World War II, air power became a vital concern, sparking Missouri's aviation industry and bringing women out of the home and into the factory to work on assembly lines. Courtesy, Missouri Historical Society

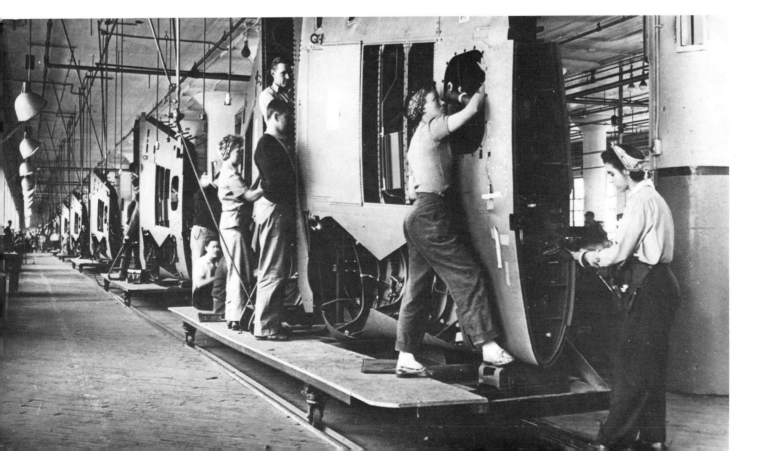

war effort. The government rationed automobile tires, cars, shoes, farm machines, gasoline, sugar, and meat, among other commodities. It established a point system for canned goods, allowing only 50 points per month per person when a can of tomatoes cost 20 points. Almost no one could afford steak or pork chops, so St. Louis butchers offered unrationed shark meat at 45 cents a pound. All over the state, in vacant lots and backyards, Missourians planted "victory gardens" to supplement their diet. Highway patriots honked their horns at speeders, since the government had set a 35 mile-per-hour limit to conserve gas and tires: three short blasts and a long one, Morse code for "V." Salesmen joined car pools. Women went to work in factories. Grandmothers and grandfathers volunteered for the Civilian Defense Corps. And many teenagers turned to vandalism and sexual delinquency.

Farmers found themselves short of labor. Not only had too many volunteered for the armed services, or been drafted, but also thousands had left for the well-paying war plant jobs in the city. They would never come back. To compensate for the losses, farmers turned to new sources of labor. Mothers and children replaced hired hands. Grandmothers and nine-year-olds drove tractors. Urban kids picked crops during summer vacation. Even small-town businessmen closed their shops to help in the fields during peak seasons. As a result of the war, Missouri farmers increased their productivity by improving their habits, using limestone and commercial fertilizers, proper crop rotation, terracing, contouring, hybrid seed, and by constructing deep ponds and grass waterways.

The war also stimulated Missouri's sluggish industry. St. Louis, the hub of the country's most populous ordinance district, manufactured 95 percent of the military ammunition and explosives used by American forces. St. Louis firms also manufactured prefabricated railway bridges, blasting machines, portable machine repair shops, airplanes, and gliders. Lambert Pharmaceuticals supplied a lotion called M-5 to protect against blister

gas. Monsanto produced classified chemicals, experimental rocket motors, and chemical propellants. The new McDonnell Aircraft Corporation became the largest supplier of airplane parts in the city and began working on its own aircraft designs, including the jet fighter for the navy, the Phantom, which was ready for production in 1945.

Even the older industries got in on the act, outfitting the American warrior from head to toe. St. Louis manufacturers provided steel helmets, its shoe factories combat boots. Kansas City clothiers supplied the rest. In Kansas City the American Royal Arena was converted into an assembly line for the manufacture of training gliders. North American Aviation built two of every three Mitchell bombers flown in the war. Twenty-five percent of the walnut gunstocks in American rifles came from K.C. Its stockyards supplied tons of beef for the armed service messes. Gasoline trains, trucks, and semi-trailers delivered products for shipping overseas from 394 Kansas City plants.

Out of it all, Missouri's place in the postwar boom was beginning to take shape. The state passed a new constitution in 1945. Given Missouri's tradition of regional conflict, a tradition almost dictated by geography, the delegates at the constitutional convention that began meeting in 1943 were certain that any innovative document—one that increased the franchise, or integrated the schools, or provided needed tax revenues—would be doomed. They carefully steered away from issues that might increase the bitterness between Missouri's two major cities and the countryside. Once again, the 1945 constitution made sure that Missouri, in the words of one historian, "did not have an effective political system, capable of moving successfully against its problems, including a rather weak educational system, decay and decline in St. Louis, and racial discrimination."

Meanwhile, Harry Truman had become vice president. Four months later, Franklin Delano Roosevelt died. At last Missouri had a man in the White House.

Not since Lincoln was assassinated, however, had anyone come into the chief executive's office under such unfavorable conditions. The war in Europe was winding down, but Japan seemed far from surrender. Truman, who said Stalin reminded him of a Kansas City politico, believed the Russian leader was lusting for the spoils of war and an empire. Churchill hated and mistrusted Stalin, perhaps even wanted to go to war with him. After the war, the boys in uniform wanted to disband immediately and go home, despite the fact that a precipitous withdrawal would scuttle any hopes for real peace. Labor was up in arms, and the huge CIO-led wave of strikes had already begun. Inflation was raging out of control. The country faced a major housing shortage. Racial tensions were high, and some riots had already broken out. And despite these problems, the new president was calling

himself just a simple country boy.

It was hard for the country to adjust to Truman's Missouri style. As president he was never far from the farm and the small town. In Washington he surrounded himself with Missourians—John W. Snyder, Robert Hannegan, Charlie Ross, Commodore Vardiman, Major General Harry H. Vaughn, Stuart Symington—and on weekends, whenever he got the chance, he flew home in a plane called "Independence." There, in the days before we shot our presidents, he relaxed with morning strolls through the old neighborhood and long talks with folks he had known all his life.

On the domestic front he wanted to take the New Deal a step further and repeal the Taft-Hartley Act despised by labor, establish a Fair Employment Practices Commission to stamp out racial discrimination, and build T.V.A.-like projects all

A Wabash streamliner, *The City of St. Louis*, was inaugurated on June 2, 1946. Here it passes through Forest Park. Courtesy, Missouri Historical Society

over the country, especially on the Missouri River. He was for farm subsidies, national health insurance, universal military training, and federal aid to public schools. Truman never seemed to have the slightest doubt that he was right. And he explained it all to the American people as if he were talking to a friend on his front porch. The enemy—all the powerful interests which threatened the farmers and the working stiffs and the regular guys of America— was sinful, and one did not bargain with the devil; one exorcised him. His was a homespun call to take sides with the oppressed against the privileged few, and he was the last of the small-town presidents.

The newspapers ridiculed him. They called his entourage the "Missouri Gang" and sneered at them as country bumpkins. They made fun of Truman's village habits and small-town ways, of his spicy dirt-farmer's language and his simplistic explanations of complex issues and ideas. They thought him weak, intellectually inferior, out of his league.

When it was all over, Truman had not gotten far with his domestic programs. Postwar America witnessed a boom in babies and business, and America turned sharply to the right, returning Truman a truculent Republican Congress in 1950. He simply could not shake the bad odor left from his close association with Tom Pendergast. The accusations grew worse after the 1948 election, when Truman astounded everyone by beating Thomas Dewey in a close contest. The issue took on sensational dimensions in 1950, when Charles Binaggio, the head of organized crime in Kansas City, and his bodyguard, Charles Gargotta, were killed in the Kansas City Democratic clubhouse . . . beneath a large photograph of a smiling Harry Truman.

But Truman did more, perhaps, than any other single human being to shape the nature of the postwar world, and not only because he decided to deploy the atomic bomb. Truman was responsible for national defense policies that called for "containment" of communist governments and maintenance of "first-strike"

capability in America's nuclear weaponry. Whether good or bad, these policies influenced America's entire postwar history. The Berlin Airlift, the Korean War, the Cuban Missile Crisis, and the Vietnam tragedy all flowed directly from the fundamental principles Truman first declared. The good guys and the bad guys, Us against Them: just the responses one would expect from a Missouri boy who grew up in a small town and cut his political teeth on a big-city machine. Not to belittle that heritage—it made Truman a great president.

In March 1946 Truman made a visit back to Missouri and invited Winston Churchill to tag along with him to Westminster College in Fulton. "This is a wonderful school in my home state," he wrote. "Hope you can do it. I'll introduce you." The speech that Churchill gave following Harry's introduction announced that "From Stettin in the Baltic to Trieste in the Adriatic, an iron curtain has descended across the continent." Harry Truman's Cold War with Russia had begun. In 1953, Truman, retiring from that war, made his final trip back home to Missouri, this time to stay.

Truman admired Missouri, and said so every chance he got while he was president. In his eyes, as in the eyes of all Missouri boosters, its greatest strength was its diversity. "It's the only state in the Union around which you can put a fence and it will survive," he said. "It has got everything it needs."

From the very beginning Truman had endorsed the old myth of Missouri's manifest destiny, rampant during the 1840s, and asserted ever more shrilly thereafter. As historians Lyle and Mary Dorsett wrote: "Full of energy, optimism, idealism and a bit of romanticism, Missourians dreamed child-like dreams of grandeur and success. Nothing, absolutely nothing could stand in the way of Missouri becoming the hub of the nation—indeed the hub of the world."

But clearly something had stood in the way, and Truman was clearly disappointed with Missouri's development when he returned. Back in the 1930s, he

Farms in northern Missouri, like
this one near Clarksville, still
thrive. Courtesy, Missouri
Division of Tourism

Above: St. Charles has kept its 18th century charm while offering tourists 21st century shops and restaurants. Courtesy, Missouri Division of Tourism

Table Rock Lake in the Missouri Ozarks is one of the most beautiful areas in the state. Courtesy, Missouri Division of Tourism

The Amish community in Jamesport maintains the old ways. Courtesy, Missouri Division of Tourism

Opposite page bottom: Missouri artist Thomas Hart Benton painted this mural depicting Missouri's history in the Harry S. Truman Library in Independence. Courtesy, Missouri Division of Tourism

Opposite page top: The Twain house and museum in Hannibal draw visitors from around the world. Courtesy, Missouri Division of Tourism

Above: Missouri's geology fascinates spelunkers and rockhounds. This is part of the Meramec Cavern in Stanton. Courtesy, Missouri Division of Tourism.

Opposite page, top left: The Common Pleas Courthouse in Cape Girardeau reflects the area's southern heritage. Courtesy, Missouri Division of Tourism

Opposite page, top right: The restored Iron Mountain train in Jackson keeps alive the era of steam railroading. Courtesy, Missouri Division of Tourism

Opposite page, bottom: This was the last home of Laura Ingalls Wilder, author of the much-loved "Little House" books. Located in Mansfield, it is now a museum. Courtesy, Missouri Division of Tourism

This remarkable monument at the University of Missouri-Rolla was copied from Stonehenge in southern Britain and made of 160 tons of granite. Courtesy, Missouri Division of Tourism

Above: The Pettis County Courthouse in Sedalia advertises the region's love of liberty. Courtesy, Missouri Division of Tourism

Left: The Current is one of Missouri's many rivers where residents enjoy floating. Courtesy, Missouri Division of Tourism

Opposite page top: The Scout looks out over Kansas City as it has for more than half a century. Courtesy, Missouri Division of Tourism

Opposite page bottom: Civil War enthusiasts reenact the battle of Wilson's Creek near Springfield. A cemetery in Springfield holds the remains of the thousands killed in the 1861 battle. Courtesy, Missouri Division of Tourism

The dramatic sky stations on
Bartle Hall add distinction to
Kansas City's nighttime skyline.
Courtesy, Missouri Division of
Tourism

The Kwanza celebration at
Missouri Botanical Garden
recalls the African heritage of
many Missourians. Courtesy,
Missouri Botanical Garden

Above: A dancer performs during the colorful Fiesta Hispana in Kansas City. Courtesy, Missouri Division of Tourism

Above right: Crown Center in downtown Kansas City turns into a pumpkin patch every October. Courtesy, Missouri Division of Tourism

Right: Youngsters inspired by Tom Sawyer race to finish whitewashing a fence in Hannibal. Courtesy, Missouri Division of Tourism

Above: Ponies stand patiently in their traces while being judged at the Missouri State Fair in Sedalia. Courtesy, Missouri Division of Tourism

Below: Farmers show off their livestock at the Missouri State Fair in Sedalia. Courtesy, Missouri Division of Tourism

Above: The Kansas City Chiefs play the St. Louis Rams in front of a sell-out crowd. The long-standing rivalry between the two cities is played out in the yearly Cardinals/Royals baseball game as well. Courtesy, Missouri Division of Tourism

Below: The Edward Jones Dome in St. Louis is home to the Rams, Super Bowl XXXIV champions. Courtesy, Missouri Division of Tourism

Above: Jazz may have been born along the Mississippi River, but it grew up at 18th and Vine in Kansas City, where Charlie "Bird" Parker and other greats had jam sessions that lasted until the sun rose. The yearly festival draws thousands of fans. Courtesy, Missouri Division of Tourism

Right: Missouri's several theme parks are favorite spots for summer fun. This is Oceans of Fun in Kansas City. Courtesy, Missouri Division of Tourism

Left: Ragtime composer Scott Joplin has inspired an annual festival each June in Sedalia, where he lived between 1895 and 1900. Ragtime is a combination of American folk tunes, African rhythms, and Creole accents. Missouri Department of Tourism

Below: Mardi Gras in Soulard, the old French quarter of St. Louis, gives everyone a reason to celebrate. Courtesy, Missouri Division of Tourism

Left: The yearly Jour de Fete in Ste. Genevieve celebrates the state's French heritage. Courtesy, Missouri Division of Tourism

Above: The St. Louis metropolitan area stretches from the Mississippi River west to Franklin County and south into Jefferson County. Framed by the Arch is the Old Courthouse where the Dred Scott case was heard before the Civil War. Courtesy, U.S. Army Corps of Engineers

Above: Grapes are cultivated in Missouri's wine-growing region. Courtesy, Missouri Division of Tourism

Right: Picknickers enjoy the summer at Mount Pleasant Winery in Augusta. Courtesy, Missouri Division of Tourism

had explained Missouri's problems away by criticizing the discrimination corporate executives practiced against the state, especially the railroads. It was an old populists' tune, one dear to the hearts of Missouri's farmers. When he headed up the Truman Committee, he tended to place the blame on government officials who granted contracts to the corporate giants, but ignored a needy Missouri. Now, he struck out at Kansas farmers who tried to block the implementation of the TVA-like project he had created for the Missouri River.

It may be that, as historian Richard S. Kirkendall has written, "only help from Washington on a scale comparable to that received by Tennessee or California would have enabled Missouri to fulfill its destiny." Kirkendall continues, "Or perhaps Missourians should have done for themselves." As he points out, that was the possibility that Truman and other Missourians before and since, have refused to admit.

Truman shared the low-tax mentality of Missouri's leaders and, although he did not share the hostility toward modernization present in the Ozarks and elsewhere, he understood it. With only a high school education himself, he passed over the state's defective educational system. And though he had been a strong advocate of black civil rights as president, he did not speak out much about the state's refusal to change its old, ingrained racism nor did he give encouragement to the few who dared to buck the system.

In 1944, a black serviceman asked to be served at a Woolworth's lunch counter in downtown St. Louis. He was refused. Instead of shuffling off, he enlisted the aid of friends, including those in the NAACP, Urban League, and Citizens Committee on Civil Rights. Months of lunchroom sit-ins followed at drugstores, department stores, and restaurants, with the only result being that the City Hall lunchroom was integrated a few years later.

All attempts at social interaction between the races in the postwar years were met with stiff resistance from whites. When St. Louis parks were integrated in the early 1950s, violence followed, and passions were as high as at any time since the Civil War. For a time, the public swimming pools were closed to avoid conflict.

Labor unrest in Missouri in the late 1940s was closely tied to racial unrest. Labor unions insisted on remaining all-white and grievances relating to racial discrimination mounted. After the boom in well-paid jobs during World War II, blacks were not willing to return to low-paying, dead-end service jobs. A state-wide Human Rights Commission was formed in the mid-1950s to implement fair employment practice, and Governor James T. Blair, Jr., showed strong leadership in ensuring civil rights for all residents. In 1963 a long boycott of St. Louis stores and banks that practiced discrimination brought national attention to the city and forced open doors that had seemed permanently closed.

The history of the integration of education is not a proud one. In 1940 a black journalist was refused admittance to the University of Missouri School of Journalism, a decision upheld by the Missouri Supreme Court. The state's public schools were rigidly segregated then, and the all-black Lincoln University and Stowe Teachers College were considered sufficient for Negro higher education. Saint Louis University opened its doors to blacks in 1944.

In 1947, Archbishop Joseph Ritter ordered the Catholic schools of St. Louis integrated. Some of the state's schools were desegregated in 1954 in accordance with the U.S. Supreme Court decision. The bootheel lagged far behind, and residential segregation in Kansas City and St. Louis frustrated efforts there. Eventually, the federal courts ordered busing, the creation of "magnet" schools to get around the limitations of neighborhood schools, the merging of suburban and urban districts, and pupil exchange policies. The proposals met public disapproval at every turn. In 1980 federal judge James H. Meredith ruled that the state of Missouri was in part responsible for the racial isolation of St. Louis students and called for a comprehensive plan for integrating

Marching peaceably and quietly, St. Louis blacks asked Carter Carburetor Company in the mid 1940s, "Why Can't We Work Here?" Carter had several lucrative defense contracts and sought new workers, white only. Western Historical Manuscripts Collection, University of Missouri-St. Louis.

St. Louis City and St. Louis County schools. While this is still being implemented, real integration has been stymied because of continuing residential segregation.

A hundred years after it had so proudly proclaimed its independent status in 1876, St. Louis was being strangled by that autonomy. Ringed by some 100 incorporated communities that did not and would not contribute to the city budget, St. Louis consistently lost its population to the suburbs after World War II. Mostly middle-class whites moved out, leaving the black and the poor to contend with the decaying metropolis. In western Missouri, Kansas suburbs benefited from the middle-class exodus, leaving Kansas City struggling to find new sources of revenue.

The 1960s witnessed a brave attempt at revitalization in both cities. In St. Louis, bond issues met with approval, an earnings tax produced new revenues, and the National Park Service cooperated in rehabilitating the St. Louis riverfront. Following a plan developed by Luther Ely Smith, train tracks were rerouted underground, decaying warehouses were leveled, and a park was created alongside the Mississippi to commemorate the vision of Thomas Jefferson. The stunning Saarinen Gateway Arch rose, an engineering marvel that

reinvigorated civic pride. A new baseball stadium was built, and a refurbished Union Station was turned into a popular entertainment-shopping center.

An enormous low-income housing development, the Pruitt-Igoe project, opened to much fanfare in 1955. By 1975, most of its 33 buildings stood empty, a desolate stretch of "urban renewal" testifying to the error in its concept and design. Reluctantly, the city leveled the eyesore, as wealthy Missourians looked on from St. Louis County, shaking their heads.

Kansas City, too, was adjusting to changes in its economy and population. When Truman died in 1972, Kansas City was no longer a meatpacking center; its stockyards were rarely full, its downtown stores either closed or falling apart, and its Union Station a place of eerie silence and looming shadows. In 1968 ghetto riots came to K.C., and whole portions of the city went up in flames as the sound of breaking glass and gunshots alternated in the night. St. Louis missed the general racial violence of the year because of the hard work of black and white leaders who were dedicated to peacemaking and bridge-building.

In rural areas of the state, the number of abandoned farmhouses increased as family farms succumbed to the pressures of financing expensive equipment with decreasing revenues. Young people were reluctant to make a commitment to the land. By the 1980s, the cities had been pulling people off the farms for nearly 40 years. The trend was not reversible.

The spread of television after World War II did more to homogenize the state than automobiles, radios, and the movies had done after World War I. At the same time, differences in background and culture could still be divisive. Two candidates who emerged during the 1980s typified the divergence of political views in this "land of contrasts." Harriett Woods, a liberal Democrat from St. Louis served as lieutenant governor and was narrowly defeated for higher office. She spoke for blacks, women, and other minorities, especially the disabled and elderly. John Ashcroft, a Republican from rural Springfield, waved the conservative banner. An outspoken Christian fundamentalist, he served as both governor and U.S. Senator. In 2001, President George W. Bush appointed him U.S. Attorney General.

The free flow of information, the waning importance of geographic divides, and the wearing away of sharp cultural differences, all had their effect on Missouri, as on every other state. In such a world, education became no longer a choice, but a necessity, and the popular growth of the community college found no state more ready-made for its appeal than Missouri. These were institutions that, with their open-access policies, took learning directly to the people.

In the 1960s, two-year state colleges sprang up Kansas City, St. Louis, Jefferson County, Neosho, Joplin, St. Joseph, Potosi,

Moberly, Trenton, Union, Sedalia, and Poplar Bluff. The University of Missouri itself expanded, establishing branches in Kansas City and St. Louis in addition to the traditional campuses at Columbia and Rolla. Private schools grew as well—from prestigious Washington University in St. Louis to small religious colleges, such as Evangel in Springfield and William Jewell in Liberty.

Along with the technological transformation of work and education came longevity and free time. Missouri's low taxes and diverse landscape, combined with its generally pleasant climate and ample recreational facilities to give Missouri the reputation of an excellent retirement haven and vacation attraction, a reputation that the state government was quick to act upon and promote.

In 1965, thousands of St. Louisans craned their necks to watch the topping out of the Arch, an incredible engineering feat. In this photo, the last piece is being hoisted into place. Courtesy, Jefferson National Expansion Memorial.

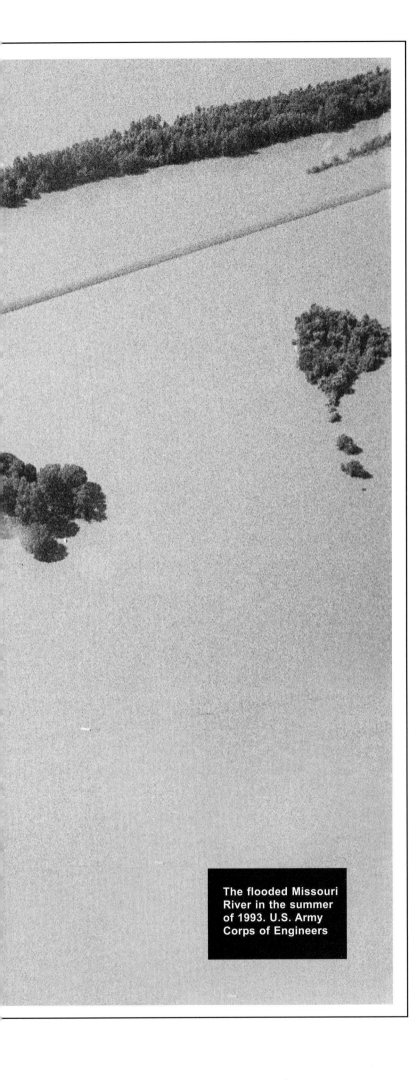

The flooded Missouri River in the summer of 1993. U.S. Army Corps of Engineers

Rollin' on the Rivers

The summer of 1993 brought one of the nation's greatest natural disasters to the Midwest. For Missouri—"the land where the rivers run"—it was a statewide catastrophe, a 500-year flood, maybe even a 1,000-year flood. Nearly 150 rivers and tributaries were affected throughout the Midwest—not merely the Missouri and Mississippi Rivers—and seventy-five entire towns were submerged. Fifty-two people died; some 74,000 residents were forced from their homes.

In Missouri, three-fourths of the state was affected. The damage to commercial property in the state was $662 million; to residential property, almost $400 million; to agricultural lands, $535 million. The psychological costs were not measurable, but in many cases, the trauma was long lasting, as residents watched the work of a lifetime wash away.

Flood conditions lasted for more than six months, an unprecedented length of time, and the Father of Waters itself was above flood stage for 80 unheard of days. It began simply enough, with an especially snowy winter throughout the north central states. Creeks and streams overflowed with the March thaw, and heavy spring rains increased the flow. By early May the ground was saturated. And then the serious rains began. Throughout May, June, July, and August, rainfall broke records for both amounts and intensity—one storm dumped eight inches of rain in only a few hours in northern Missouri.

Missouri could have handled its own rainfall without much of a problem, but in the upper Midwest, it was also raining heavily. Creeks and streams rose there, emptying into rising tributaries that led to the already full Mississippi and Missouri Rivers.

Farmers paced the floors and fretted. May was too wet to plant, so was June. By June 10, the grain markets reacted, and investors got worried as they watched soybean prices rise. In early July, the USDA predicted crop losses would be around $1 billion throughout the Mississippi and Missouri River basins. That figure did not include damage to farmland, which would not be known until the waters receded. By mid-July, 8 million farm acres in the Midwest were under water and countless farm buildings had been washed away. Forage and silage were destroyed. Hundreds of animals and fowl drowned. Rescue missions in pontoon boats saved as many animals as they could, but were at a loss as to where to put them until the water went down.

Hunting and fishing aficionados tried to rescue the eggs of waterfowl from sub-merged nests for later hatching. The loss of trees and brush forced wildlife from their native habitats into cities and towns, where they were lost and confused. The good news was that fish were thriving.

In late June the port of St. Louis was closed to barges, because the water was too high to risk docking. On June 28, the Army Corps of Engineers closed the Mississippi above St. Louis to all watercraft. The Missouri River was closed shortly thereafter. About 2,000 grain barges and hundreds of barges filled with coal, fertilizer and cement were stranded. Soon, barge operations were losing $3 million a day.

On the first of July, parts of Minnesota, Wisconsin, South Dakota, and Iowa were declared disaster areas. Forewarned, Missourians hunkered down for the fight to come, ordering hundreds of thousands of sandbags and building levees with whatever was at hand. Residents asked each other incessantly, "When will it crest? How high will it get?" The National Weather Service predicted that the Mississippi would crest in St. Louis on July 7 at 40 feet. It was off by a month and 10 feet.

The flood quickly became a transportation nightmare. Levees crumbled in northwest Missouri, flooding Interstate highways. The massive re-routing of trains began, as tracks threatened to wash out. All the bridges on the Missouri River between St. Joseph and St. Charles were closed, except the I-70 bridge at Rocheport. Most of the bridges between Missouri and Illinois were impassable, and some were extensively damaged. When the Glasgow railroad bridge collapsed, "the rails were left hanging in the air like clotheslines," a reporter wrote. Getting to work was a trial for those who had to commute. One example: the four-mile route from New Franklin to Boonville became impassable. An alternate circuitous 35-mile route averaged an hour drive time. Getting in and out of Jefferson City was so difficult that only bus traffic was allowed.

The immediate response to the flood was heroic, as residents fought to save their homes and those of their neighbors

Water crept up the flood wall in St. Louis, but didn't go over the top because levees collapsed in Illinois, reducing the pressure. The riverbank is normally to the right of the tree. Courtesy, U.S. Army Corps of Engineers

from the rising waters. Thousands of volunteers from far beyond the rivers' borders joined the National Guard to do the backbreaking work of filling and stacking sandbags with temperatures in the high 90s and humidity to match. As conditions worsened, they worked around the clock. The Red Cross, Salvation Army (Operation Noah's Ark), Scouts, church groups, unions, inmates from correctional facilities, and whoever else was inspired to join the fight donated time, energy, muscle, money, sympathy, food, clothes, and household goods. Neighbors buoyed each other up and reinforced a sense of community not seen since the early days of settlement. Some looting of abandoned property occurred here and there, but the flood brought out the best in people—their generosity, good humor and esprit de corps. In Howard County, expensive farm equipment was towed to high ground and left beside the road. No one touched it.

Early in July the evacuation of homes began along the Missouri. Four hundred families near St. Charles, where the Missouri meets the Mississippi, were told to pack their valuables and move out. Nearly 4,000 sites in St. Charles County would be abandoned before it was over.

A week after Independence Day— when celebrations were cancelled in most river towns—the flood was recognized as a national disaster. Hordes of journalists, along with TV crews, descended on St. Louis. Led by Missouri governor Mel Carnahan, President Bill Clinton and Vice President Al Gore—as well as senators, representatives, department heads, and cabinet officials—showed up to lend their support, while FEMA set up offices in a dozen river towns.

There was growing concern about whether or not the water supplies and sewage systems along the rivers would become polluted. On July 24, St. Joseph lost its water plant. Despite 4,000 sandbags and countless barricades, taps in that city were dry. The racing river was full of debris—tanks, camper shells, trailer homes, dead animals, uprooted trees, furniture, and thousands of tires. Oil, sewage, and chemicals made the floodwaters a serious hazard to both wildlife and people. Boil-water orders were issued in many communities.

Amazingly, the levee at Hannibal held. Across the Mississippi, in Illinois, levees were collapsing like dominoes as sand boils erupted. Flood walls kept water out of the St. Louis business district, but the river licked at the legs of the Arch.

Barges in Kansas City broke loose and damaged bridge piers. The *Goldenrod* showboat in St. Charles was ripped from

Built on a bluff overlooking the Missouri River, the state capitol was never in danger from the flood, but the surrounding area was. Emergency generators were brought in, just in case the city lost power. Courtesy, Army Corps of Engineers

her mooring. A World War II minesweeper, the U.S.S. *Inaugural*, and the floating Burger King broke free in St. Louis and crashed into the Poplar Street Bridge.

In central Missouri, the small towns of Dutzow, Marthasville, and Treloar faced extensive damage. Bonnots Mill Historic District lost approximately one-fifth of the community's buildings. In what many saw as the greatest insult, 600 caskets were unearthed and swept into the Missouri River at Hardin.

In community after community, residents had to take a hard look at their future. Was it worth it to try to rebuild? They'd already lost so much that was irreplaceable. Cedar City, a suburb of Jefferson City, was so badly damaged that residents agreed to a federal-state buyout. In September 1994, the town's remaining buildings were bulldozed.

Ste. Genevieve on the Mississippi fought for its life. A major portion of its revenue came from tourists who enjoyed wandering through this restored eighteenth-century French settlement 50 miles south of St. Louis. Despite their best efforts, more than 40 historic buildings were damaged by floodwaters, including the Green Tree Tavern, Amoreaux House and Bequette-Ribault House.

On August 8 the flood crested at Cape Girardeau at 48.49 feet, four feet above the old record, and Missouri's Great

Flood of 1993 was history. Residents were too exhausted to cheer.

By now the water was filthy, saturated with herbicides and other potentially dangerous chemicals. After floodwaters began to recede came the long, tedious process of coping with soggy carpets, mud-coated furniture, ruined appliances, decaying vegetation, shaky infrastructures and endless insurance forms to fill out. Farmers were left with acres of sand, silt, rotting brush, and sewage to clear. The losses to small businesses—beauty shops, restaurants, corner groceries, hardware stores, and pharmacies—were so great than many owners lost heart and gave up. Flood insurance was a luxury many residents hadn't considered.

But many more saw the flood as an opportunity (with state, federal and insurance help) to modernize and come back stronger than ever. Then cleanup efforts were stalled by more rain and a disheartening flood in early fall. Nonetheless, by 1996, Missouri could say it was recovered and ready to take part in the economic boom of the late 1990s.

The temporary paralysis caused by the flood underscored the state's investment in tourism. For almost one year, vacationers avoided Missouri, and the loss of revenue hurt. Tourists are attracted to the state by the long list of "Things to Do" in guidebooks. In urban areas there are museums, theaters, concerts, theme parks, and specialized exhibits, such as the recovered steamboat *Arabia* in Kansas City. Missouri's rolling terrain and abundant greenery invite lovers of the outdoors, who camp, hunt, fish, and navigate its rivers. Enterprising Missourians have made it their business to welcome visitors.

The blossoming of the Branson area in southwest Missouri as a major recreational spot has been the lynchpin of the state's tourism economy. Branson's role as a vacation center began more than 100 years ago, when an ailing minister named Harold Bell Wright traveled into the Ozark hills, looking for a healthful climate. He got as far as the railroad could take him and then continued on horseback, alighting at Mutton Hollow near the White River. While recuperating, Wright wrote *Shepherd of the Hills*, a simple story of the faith of Ozark families. When it appeared in 1907, it became a best-seller. Many of its admiring readers traveled to the Ozarks to find "Matt's cabin" and the other landmarks that Wright described. The Branson community staged a play based on the book each summer, bringing in more tourists, who stayed to fish, go boating, and enjoy the scenery.

Isolated for years by its geography, residents of the Ozarks preserved their Anglo-Saxon heritage in their language, music, storytelling, and crafts. Hardscrabble farms in the rock-covered hills forced them into self-sufficiency. These Ozark dwellers became a source of laughter and embarrassment to their urban cousins. Now they've had the last laugh. From being the most "backward" and poorest area in the state, the Ozark region has become the richest, "the engine that drives the state's economy," as Missouri's Department of Economic Development states. Tourist dollars have overflowed from Branson into Springfield and Joplin.

Branson's innovations in entertainment—some 60 family shows are offered—have made it an international travel destination. Shows begin as early as 8:30 a.m., and the last ones end late at night. The scope of their variety seems to be a throwback to the exhilarating days of vaudeville, with acrobats, jug-

Craftsman at Silver Dollar City near Branson keeps alive nineteenth-century skills. What was once work has become fun. Courtesy, Missouri Division of Tourism

A crowd-pleasing production number at the Lawrence Welk Champagne Theater in Branson. Courtesy, Missouri Division of Tourism

The *Aztar* at Caruthersville, one of 11 floating casinos in the state. Courtesy, Missouri Division of Tourism

of 4,000, where rodeos and other entertainments are held, pulling in visitors from Memphis.

Competitive sports give Missourians something to cheer about, from Little League and high school swim teams to the Super Bowl. Professional sports events draw thousands of fans to St. Louis and Kansas City. In 1985 a unique "I-70" World Series pitted the Kansas City Royals against the St. Louis Cardinals. Kansas City won, spurred on by the amazing George Brett. During the 1980s Kansas Citians watched Brett become a baseball legend at third base, and cheered as he was tapped for 13 All-Star games. The Royals reached the World Series in 1980, the same year he achieved a .400 batting average. He retired in 1993 with a lifetime record of 3,154 hits and was inducted into the Baseball Hall of Fame in 1999.

One of the Cardinals' favorite players during the 1980s was the always-cheerful Ozzie Smith, the back-flipping shortstop who won 13 Gold Glove awards during his career and was voted into the Baseball Hall of Fame in 2002. In 1998 another Cardinal became a St. Louis hero when Mark McGwire hit an incredible 70

glers, musicians, dancers, trained animals, and comedians in fright wigs. Audiences eat up the mixture of glitz, glamour, down home country music, cornball humor, gospel music, and flag-waving. Veteran stars, such as Andy Williams and Glen Campbell, along with other performers, including singer Pam Tillis and violinist Shoji Tabuchi, entertain in shows that elicit a "Wow!" from audiences.

Shops and restaurants have sprung up alongside or inside the theaters. Environmentalists complain that the crowds are spoiling the Ozark wilderness areas with exhaust fumes and footprints, but local boosters aren't listening. In the pull between economics and unspoiled beauty, economics (along with one of the lowest unemployment rates in the state) wins.

After state residents overwhelmingly approved riverboat gambling in 1994, floating casinos appeared. Eleven riverboat casinos are now scattered across the state in Kansas City, St. Joseph, St. Charles, St. Louis, Caruthersville, La Grange and Boonville. All are profitable. Many have elaborate adjacent hotels and restaurants. On board the boats, slot machines, roulette wheels, card games, and video poker draw players from all over the Midwest. Harrah's, one of the largest employers in Kansas City, offers Las Vegas-style musical entertainment. In the bootheel, the floating casino *Aztar* at Caruthersville has a huge arena with a seating capacity

Kansas City Royals baseball legend, George Brett, retired in 1993. Courtesy, Kansas City Royals.

Fred Bird and friend. The Cardinals' mascot is a favorite among fans. Courtesy, Missouri Division of Tourism

homeruns. The next year he hit 65. In 2001, he ended his career with a total of 500 home runs.

The Cardinals football team left St. Louis in 1988 for Phoenix, after a couple of years of spectacularly bad public relations. Most St. Louisans were not sad to see them or their contentious owner, Bill Bidwill, go. Shortly after they left, civic leaders agreed to build a domed stadium downtown to attract a new team. Originally christened the TWA Dome, it was renamed for the investment firm of Edward Jones when TWA disappeared in a merger with American Airlines in 2001. After lengthy negotiations, the Los Angeles Rams agreed to move from southern California to eastern Missouri in 1995. They were immediately embraced by enthusiastic fans. Since then, they have played in two Super Bowls, beating the Tennessee Titans in 2000 and losing to the New England Patriots in 2002. MVP Kurt Warner and Marshall Faulk provided team leadership and won the hearts of fans for their contributions to the city's children. (The Kansas City Chiefs, incidentally, played in the very first Super Bowl in 1967.)

The St. Louis Blues hockey team moved from the ancient (1929) Arena to the glitzy new downtown Savvis Center 1994. The center also hosts St. Louis University basketball games. The love-hate relationship between and among Blues fans, coaches, players, and management has made for an up-and-down history for the team.

Kansas City added a professional soccer team—the Wizards—in 1996. It brought home the MLS Cup championship in 2000. The team was one of 10 charter members of the newly formed Major League Soccer association. The new NASCAR Kansas Speedway is just across the state line from Kansas City and brings thousands of fans and dollars into the metro area.

Missouri's history has become a moneymaker for the state in the last few decades. The past holds a fascination for Americans.History buffs in search of nostalgia, antiques, and family roots crisscross the state. Other history lovers visit sites of importance to the state and the nation to ponder what life was like then.

Route 66, America's "mother road" and precursor of the Interstate system, crossed Missouri diagonally, from St. Louis to Joplin and into Oklahoma. All along the route today souvenir hunters find memorabilia to remind them of life 40 years ago. Another road commemorates the forced removal of Cherokees from Georgia to Oklahoma in 1838. Under military escort, Cherokees marched through southern Missouri before dipping into Arkansas on what became known as the Trail of Tears. The National Park Service has marked the trail for motorists to follow, and there is a state Trail of Tears Park with a museum near Sikeston. The Lewis and Clark route along the Missouri River from St. Charles can be retraced by canoe or automobile. The Santa Fe Trail, which began in Old Franklin and continued to Fort Osage where it left "the States" in 1821, is marked for those who want to experience the era of ox-drawn wagon trade. Archaeologists today are looking for signs of the

This statuary group in the Westport area of Kansas City commemorates Alexander Majors, the entrepreneur who helped make the Santa Fe Trail profitable for Missourians; John C. McCoy, who laid out the town of Westport in 1830; and Jim Bridger, the Mountain Man involved with the fur trade, who operated a store in Westport. Courtesy, Gregory M. Franzwa

The Pony Express still captures America's imagination. Courtesy, Missouri Division of Tourism

Underground Railway in Missouri, and reenactors gather annually at the sites of the various Civil War battles in the state.

Old buildings now get their share of admiration. For years architectural preservationists, such as the Landmarks Associations in Kansas City and St. Louis, lobbied to save historic buildings and worked to educate the public about their worth. The 1997 enactment of a tax credit for historic preservation projects gave a tremendous boost to renovation. Not only do refurbished historical structures draw visitors, they encourage recycling of old, elegant buildings that could not be duplicated today.

Renovation of Kansas City's venerable Union Station began in 1997. Two years later it reopened as a huge "hands-on" Science City. Smaller communities have converted their abandoned railroad depots into restaurants, theaters and art centers. One successful railroad recycling project has brought delight to bicyclists and hikers. The 200-plus-mile Katy Trail was once part of the Missouri-Kansas-Texas line, and ran alongside the Missouri River. The "rails-to-trails" project began in the 1980s, supported by Edward D. Jones and completed about 10 years later.

While some rails were torn up, others were reused. The Metrolink light rail system is one of St. Louis' favorite success stories of the 1990s. Operated by the Bi-State Development Agency, Metrolink uses existing rails to connect the East Side (Illinois) with St. Louis, meshing with the bus system. Its route takes passengers from downtown to Lambert International Airport and back via 27 stations. The system's design, engineering, and construction were financed through a one-cent gasoline tax. The quiet and clean-running vehicles are electrically powered from overhead wires and are bi-directional. Roughly twice as successful as anticipated, Metrolink registered 14.2 million fares in 2001.

In the late 1870s, Robert Brookings and Samuel Cupples had an idea for speeding up the transportation of goods by rail. They built a group of warehouses with a system to store merchandise before it was shipped elsewhere, making St. Louis a hub of commerce. Today, the Cupples Station warehouses have been transformed into hotels and office buildings.

Preserving old homes appeals to Missourians, too. Hundreds of historic homes have been saved and refurbished throughout the state. Many are open to the public, carefully tended by volunteers. Two communities that make their histories work for them are St. Charles

and Ste. Genevieve. Both have preserved their old buildings as mini-museums with costumed attendants; both have annual celebrations that draw thousands; and both have created a strong behind-the-scenes community.

One of the state's greatest contributions to science is the Missouri Botanical Garden. When Henry Shaw visited the Royal Botanic Gardens in London in the mid-nineteenth century, he was inspired to create a similar garden on his estate in south St. Louis. His country villa, now Tower Grove House, was built on a 1,800-

This elegant old home in Springfield was converted into a bed and breakfast. Courtesy, Missouri Division of Tourism

A Metrolink train runs alongside Lambert International Airport. Courtesy, Bi-State Development Agency

Main Street in St. Charles invites shoppers and history buffs. Courtesy, Missouri Division of Tourism

In 2000 Peter Raven was awarded the National Medal of Science, the nation's highest scientific honor. *Time* magazine called Dr. Raven "a hero for the planet" for his conservation work. Courtesy, Missouri Botanical Garden

acre tract at the outskirts of the city. The Shaw garden was first opened to the public in 1859.

The Garden remained "a nice place to visit" until Peter Raven became director in 1971. Deeply dedicated to plant ecology and conservation, Raven has built the Garden into a major research center with the primary mission of amassing botanical information collected worldwide. The herbarium has grown to 5.1 million mounted specimens and the library contains 9,000 rare books and 160,000 specialized monographs. Much of this material has been digitized and can be accessed by scientists anywhere on the globe. Its most ambitious project, a database called TROPICOS, includes information found nowhere else, plus more than 21,000 digitized images. A special project of the Garden is the study of tropical rain forests.

Washington University's new Donald Danforth Plant Science Center is also a center of botanical research, with a more practical aim, following in the tradition of the enterprising George Washington Carver, whose laboratories have been preserved by the National Park Service in Diamond, southeast of Joplin.

Monsanto is a partner in the Danforth Center, along with Purdue and the University of Missouri.

St. Louis-based Monsanto is almost synonymous with the development of agribusiness. It is known worldwide as a pioneer in genetically modified crops—"Franken-food," according to detractors. Whether biotechnology, including genetic engineering, is a boon or a bane will be discovered (and debated) in the years ahead. There is no doubt it is already affecting the way agriculture is practiced today.

Agribusiness today encompasses not only agriculture or the growing of food, but also processing, transporting, and selling it. One of every six Missourians is employed in agribusiness, an industry that generates $17.3 billion for the economy. The agri-chemical industry in the state showed a 24.2 percent increase in employment in the last decade.

North of the Missouri River is some of the richest farmland in the nation. Old-style, family-run truck farms are rare there today, but new-style family farms are still viable. As labor found a hundred years ago, cooperation is the key to survival. Farmland Industries of Kansas City, a Fortune 500 company, is a producer-owned cooperative made up of 600,000 family farmers throughout the nation.

Viticulture, or grape growing, is not one of Missouri's major agribusinesses, but it is one of its most pleasant. Today 33 small wineries produce 380,000 gallons of wine each year, and Missouri viticulturists hope to develop a "Missouri grape" that can withstand cold, damp winters.

Mining, the oldest industry in Missouri, continues to be important in the state's economy. Five hundred years ago, native peoples extracted minerals from the ground, and ore was a major reason the French came to the St. Francois Mountains 250 years ago. In Herculaneum today, a major producer of lead is the Doe Run Mine. The residue of lead smelting hangs over the town and has created serious problems in the com-

munity, reminiscent of the dioxin spill at Times Beach, just west of St. Louis on the Meramec River, 20 years earlier. The poisoned area couldn't be cleaned up, and the town disappeared as residents were forced to move elsewhere. Nearly half of Herculaneum's children show dangerous amounts of lead in their blood, and there is talk of a Superfund cleanup and mine buyouts.

Heavy industry began leaving the "rust belt" in the 1980s in search of cheaper labor. Missouri has consistently lost

The interior of the new Donald Danforth Center. Danforth is a familiar Missouri name. In 1893 William H. Danforth began an animal feed company that would become the giant Ralston-Purina. His son Donald headed the company next; one grandson was William, who became chancellor of Washington University; John C., another grandson, served as a U.S. senator from 1976 to 1995. The Danforth Foundation is known nationally for its support of educators. Courtesy, Danforth Plant Science Center

Augusta winery. Some of the most beautiful landscapes in the state are found in wine country. Courtesy, Missouri Division of Tourism

manufacturing plants since that time, but has made up for it with the growth of light industry. Today the state has the sixth most diversified economy in the U.S. Its exports are chemicals, agricultural products, machinery, electronics and transportation equipment, especially aircraft assembled at the Boeing (formerly McDonnell-Douglas) plant.

The Sprint Campus in metropolitan Kansas City is the prototype of the type of industry the state hopes to attract.

As commentators never tire of pointing out, the "new economy" of the 21st-century is knowledge-based. Within the last 10 years, the state Department of Information Technology was launched to help incubate and guide IT businesses in the state. Six of the 10 fastest growing occupations in Missouri are computer-related. All college and university campuses upgrade their technology courses to keep pace with the industry, and the Center for Advanced Technology at Mizzou concentrates on keeping ahead of the next wave.

The 1990s saw an increased commitment to improve Missouri's public educational system, which has always been weak. The Missouri Assessment Program (MAP) now measures student performance in both knowledge and skills. If a school is found "academically deficient," it has two years to get up to standard, or it is closed. Special school districts reach children with disabilities, and programs for the gifted have been strengthened. Still, the overall quality of education is uneven throughout the state, with affluent suburban schools at the top and inner city and rural schools lagging behind.

An incentive introduced in 1991 is the Gold Star Schools Program. Underwritten by the State Farm Insurance Companies in conjunction with the state Department of Elementary and Secondary Education, the purpose of the program is to recognize outstanding schools in Missouri. Once they have been identified and awarded a "gold star," they are studied for what they are doing right. The information is then shared with other schools.

Washington University in St. Louis devotes much of its energies to scientific research, both in its departments of science and in its medical school. Many of its faculty members have been recipients of various awards, and not just in science. In 1993 Douglass C. North was awarded a Nobel prize for "applying economic theory and quantitative methods to explain economic and institutional change." North had joined the faculty of Washington University in 1983, finding "an exciting group of young political scientists and economists who were attempting to develop new modes of political economy." In that heady atmosphere, North created the Center of Political Economy.

The dramatic changes in medical technology over the past 20 years have been mind-boggling, while the changes in healthcare delivery have not been as appreciated. Old-style hospitals, which treat only acute illness and trauma, have given way to regional medical centers, offering a wide variety of services. Along with traditional hospital care are rehabilitation facilities, outpatient surgery, trauma centers, sports medicine, workplace health, wellness clinics, home healthcare, mental health, dental care, long-term care, and hospice facilities. Regional medical centers are major employers in many Missouri counties.

The dispensing of medications has also changed. Express Script, a Fortune 500 company with headquarters in St. Louis County, offers "pharmacy management" to navigate the rocky shoals of managed care, third-party payments and complex group insurance plans. By buying in bulk, using Internet marketing, and offering overnight shipping services, Express Script has become one of the largest such services in the nation, with 47 million members.

A new facility in Kansas City promises more discoveries in medical science. The Stowers Institute for Medical Research opened in the spring of 2001, endowed by Virginia and James Stowers of American Century Companies, an investment firm. The $200 million center is drawing

The air ambulance from the Cox Medical Center in Springfield is outfitted with state-of-the-art, life-saving equipment and drugs. Courtesy, Cox Medical Center

Joyce C. Hall cared enough to produce the very best. "I'm hell-bent on quality," he used to say. From the first, Hallmark set the standard for greeting cards. This valentine appeared early in the twentieth century. Courtesy, Hallmark Archives, Hallmark Cards, Inc

top scientists to conduct research into genetic systems and their relation to the cause and prevention of disease, especially cancer.

The nationwide economic boom of the 1990s was especially beneficial to Missouri financial management firms. A.G. Edwards, American Century, and Edward D. Jones expanded exponentially, and A.G. Edwards added several new buildings to its headquarters in midtown St. Louis.

Despite mergers, buyouts and relocations, some of Missouri's old standbys continue to grow. The Anheuser-Busch brewery still anchors St. Louis' south side, and Hallmark Cards is vital to Kansas City. Its Crown Center is a family-friendly combination community, arts, and business center.

For most of the 1990s, Missouri's governor was Democrat Mel Carnahan, a popular moderate who was something of an administrative genius. Under his leadership, Missouri was ranked the third best-managed state by *Financial World* and was one of four states to receive top honors in *Governing* magazine's study of state governments.

A Valentine
to the
Nicest Married Man I Know

Like all Americans, Missourians responded with horror and outrage to the terrorists attack of September 2001—then got to work fighting back. Former Senator Jean Carnahan shares a meal with Mess Specialist 3rd Class Christopher Gray of Florissant on board the U.S.S. *Theodore Roosevelt*, part of Operation Enduring Freedom.

the November election, Carnahan's light plane crashed in Jefferson County, killing him, his son Ron, and his senior advisor. Within days, his widow, Jean Carnahan, agreed to serve in his stead and won the seat.

As the twenty-first century began, Missouri's fastest growing counties were located in the southwest corner, followed by a corridor in the central part of the state, benefiting from the expansion in Boone County. In numbers, St. Charles County led the growth sweepstakes, according to MERIC, the Missouri Economic Research and Information Center. The bootheel, where the poverty rate is 24 percent, twice the state average, continues to lose population, as do several farming counties in northern Missouri. Perry County in southeast Missouri has been judged as the county offering the most natural amenities to its residents. These amenities, which may attract retirees but not those climbing a career ladder, include mild temperatures, goodly amounts of sunlight, a river or lake, and "topographical variation." Whereas 150 years ago settlers wanted

Originally from the Ozarks, the Carnahans settled in Rolla, and Mel became involved in politics right away. He won 20 elections during his political career, as he moved from judge to state treasurer to lieutenant governor to governor. The state constitution didn't allow him to take on another term as governor, so in 2000 he decided to run for U.S. senator against conservative John Ashcroft, a race judged by most politicos as 50-50. Just three weeks before

open spaces, and chopped down trees to get them, today's resettlers seek out woodlands and hilly countryside.

The ethnic changes statewide reflect those in the nation. The one-time "either white or black" look has changed to a blending of ethnic identities. Immigrants from China, India, Thailand, and Vietnam have added an Asian cast to urban areas and universities. Middle Easterners, as well as Bosnians and Kosovars, have brought their ethnic riches to the area. The Latino population continues to grow, and Spanish is now the most common non-English language spoken in the home. Surprisingly, in the face of more exotic imports, German is the second most-common, reflecting the long history of Germans in the state.

Today a lifelong resident of the South would feel comfortable in Missouri's bootheel or mid-state Little Dixie; a city-loving Eastern sophisticate would feel at home in Kansas City or St. Louis;

a Smoky Mountain dweller would feel right in the Ozarks; and farmers from anywhere in rural America would recognize as their own the fields and small towns of the Missouri plains.

Diversity had always been Missouri's best hope, despite the strife it often engenders. When Freeman Bosley was elected as St. Louis's first black mayor in 1993, the election was hailed as ushering in a new era of racial harmony, but it did not. Muslims throughout the state received threats after the terrorist attacks of September 2001, and synagogues are still sometimes marked with hate signs. Will the growing Latino and Asian cultures be segregated or integrated? How will the economic pie be sliced up in the years ahead?

Coming to terms with a diverse population is the nation's biggest challenge as well. Missouri may be able to meet that challenge as it joins the global economy of the twenty-first century.

Fiesta Hispana in Kansas City draws all ethnic groups into its celebration. Courtesy, Missouri Division of Tourism

Facing page, bottom: Enthusiastic crowds greeted Pope John Paul II when he visited St. Louis in 1999. Courtesy, *St. Louis Review*

These people were hard at work at the Robertson Aircraft Factory on March 23, 1928, long before the war in Europe escalated the need for assembly-line production of aircraft. Courtesy, Missouri Historical Society

CHAPTER VIII

Chronicles of Leadership

Missouri's location in the center of the nation has been an important factor in its development as a center of manufacturing, agricultural production, and trade. Bounded on the east by the Mississippi River and bisected by the Missouri River, the state was heavily dependent upon river transportation in its early days. With the opening of the Eads Bridge across the Mississippi at St. Louis in 1874, the railroad came to dominate transportation. Today Missouri boasts several expanding airports, thousands of miles of railroads, primary highways, and waterways.

Two great cities dominate the state's economy—Kansas City on the western boundary and St. Louis on the eastern boundary. Both cities began as trading centers for the westward expansion movement of the nineteenth century, and both have retained a mercantile spirit. The capital of the state, Jefferson City, is the center for government offices, and nearby Columbia is the home of the main student campus of the University of Missouri. Springfield in southwest Missouri is a medical, financial, and manufacturing center for a three-state region.

Missouri's natural resources offer an abundance of riches. Fertile farmland produces soybrans, wheat, corn and other crops, making the state an agricultural leader. Mining is another significant part of the state's economy. Missouri is first in the nation in the production of lead. Barite ore, limestone, and several types of clay also come from the state.

Manufacturing is an important contributor to Missouri's economy and its base has become highly diversified. A large segment of Missouri's work force is employed in the service industries, including retail and wholesale trade, finance, insurance and real estate, community and social services, transportation, communications, and utilities.

The fastest-growing industry in the state is tourism. Billions of dollars are spent in Missouri each year at attractions such as: Mark Twain's home in Hannibal, Ste. Genevieve, the Gateway Arch and Six Flags Over Mid-America in St. Louis, Worlds of Fun and the Harry S. Truman Library in Kansas City, Lake of the Ozarks, and Silver Dollar City. The Branson area in southwest Missouri has become a vacation mecca, attracting visitors from all over the country.

The enterprises of Missouri have their own special histories, both short and long. New businesses are created every year; some prosper, others do not, and as time goes by, fledgling businesses become established firms, each with a history that touches thousands of lives both locally and worldwide.

The organizations whose histories are related on the following pages have chosen to support this important literary and civic project. They illustrate the variety of ways in which individuals and their businesses have contributed to the state's growth and development. The civic involvement of Missouri's businesses, institutions of learning, health organizations, and local government, in cooperation with its citizens, has made the state an excellent place to live and work.

AMERICAN BUSINESS WOMEN'S ASSOCIATION

Today, the American Business Women's Association spans the nation as one of the world's most diverse professional organizations for women. Tens of thousands of members gather throughout the country, united by a common goal—to support each other in professional development and career advancement.

ABWA has long been accepted as one of the leading businesswomen's associations in the United States, and its far-reaching influence has touched the lives and careers of so many. It's incredible to realize that it all began more than 50 years ago in Missouri, when the term "business woman" was an oddity, and an association dedicated to advancing women's careers was simply unheard of.

The year 1949 was part of the post-war era for Missouri. The American boys had come home from World War II, eager to exchange their soldiers' garb for the business attire and workman's clothing they had left behind.

But when the men initially had answered the call to arms, an immense gap was created in the American workforce, and the women remaining behind were expected to fill it. When that war whistle

Hilary A. Bufton Jr., 1919-1985, founder and executive director of the American Business Women's Association.

The founding members of the American Business Women's Association, Kansas City, Missouri, 1949.

blew, women left their homes in droves to serve their country, taking the places of the men who had gone to fight.

World War II was the first time that American women were recognized as a viable factor in the workforce. The end of the war meant that women were expected to leave their newfound careers and return to their homes; however, their desire to seek fulfillment as part of the working world was not easily suppressed.

Kansas City, Missouri, businessman Hilary A. Bufton Jr. recognized the positive impact women had been having upon the economy. He also realized what a widespread loss it would be to let women fade quietly out of the workforce. Yet given the times, he knew that they couldn't go it alone.

"It was my feeling all women were seeking and deserved equal business opportunities," he later wrote. "They had gained tremendous business knowledge during World War II, through necessity, and I felt that a new organization for all businesswomen was needed." Acting on his

feelings, Bufton registered the name "American Business Women's Association" in the summer of 1949, and the American workforce was changed forever.

On Sept. 22, 1949, Bufton and three Kansas City businesswomen incorporated the American Business Women's Association, and soon the first ABWA chapter, aptly named the Pioneer Chapter, was installed. By the end of its first year, ABWA boasted 21 chapters with more than 1200 members, yet despite this impressive start, the idea of a professional women's organization was not readily accepted.

"Many women were working in the early '50s," said Bufton. "But for most women, a job was a second career. The first responsibility was home and family."

Not only did many women of that time echo such career-discouraging beliefs, but even more husbands frowned upon the idea of their wives leaving the household to pursue a career. "Men believed that women belonged at home," explained Bufton. "In many ways, the first ABWA members were breaking tradition, and it wasn't always easy for them," he continued. "Without even knowing it, I guess they were paving the way for today's women."

As word about this exciting organization was spreading, new programs and ideas flooded the budding Association.

Carolyn Bufton Elman carries on the family tradition as executive director of the American Business Women's Association.

The idea that had taken root in Missouri flourished as women throughout the country discovered the values of networking and professional development that lay behind chapter doors.

Then in 1953, tragedy struck the Bufton family. After an extended illness, Hilary and Ruth Bufton's five-year-old son, Stephen, passed away. An ABWA memorial fund was created in his name, designed to further educational opportunities for members. The Stephen Bufton Memorial Educational Fund grew rapidly, soon becoming one of the Association's most prominent and far-reaching programs, and it is still thriving today.

Throughout the decades, the Association continued to grow and prosper. ABWA's place in American history was cemented when, in 1983, a joint Congressional resolution signed by President Ronald Reagan proclaimed Sept. 22, the date of the Association's founding, as American Business Women's Day. The proclamation set aside this date to annually recognize the achievements not only of ABWA members but also the mil-

lions of employed women in the United States.

Sadly, Association founder Hilary Bufton Jr. passed away at the age of 66 on May 24, 1985. Thousands of members mourned the death of the man who had helped so many women to achieve success in the workplace. In January 1986, the Association welcomed his daughter, Carolyn Bufton Elman, as executive director.

Today, under Elman's guidance, ABWA continues to serve as the ultimate source of professional development opportunities, networking support and well-deserved recognition for businesswomen. The organization remains firmly rooted in Missouri, with its national headquar-

ABWA's national magazine, *Women in Business,* is just one of the many benefits of membership in the association.

ters in Kansas City, yet many changes have occurred.

"ABWA is not the same association that it was 50 years ago," says Elman. "By continually reinventing itself, ABWA is able to give women what they want today in a professional organization. We follow business trends very closely, and with years of experience upon which to draw, ABWA is able to provide members with the professional tools they need to stay current and to succeed in today's market."

The keys to ABWA's success include developing different membership options and securing critical strategic alliances. Working with such preeminent groups as the prestigious Ewing Marion Kauffman Foundation, which focuses solely on entrepreneurial success, and Franklin Covey, the acclaimed time-management organization, allows ABWA to provide members with exceptional resources at below-market rates.

New ground was broken in 2003 with the ABWA-KU MBA Essentials program. This unprecedented learning opportunity provides master's degree-level basics in a variety of critical business subjects. The top-notch curriculum is designed and taught by faculty from the highly regarded University of Kansas School of Business and its KU Center for Management Education.

"The development of ABWA-KU MBA Essentials," says Elman, "is testament to the Association's continued commitment to bring the highest quality education and training opportunities to businesswomen nationwide."

For more than a half century, the American Business Women's Association has been a significant thread woven tightly in the fabric of Missouri history. Its unparalleled success in supporting the dreams and aspirations of working women across the nation shall continue well into the future, changing women's lives for many years to come.

Additional information about the American Business Women's Association is available at www.abwa.org.

BANK OF BELTON

"Countries without a community banking system don't have a viable small business community." So states James Blair, president of the Bank of Belton in Belton, Missouri. The statement characterizes his professional vision and also that of his great-uncle Alexander, who started the small community bank over 100 years ago.

In the 19th century, the availability of fertile, arable farmland brought Blair's great-uncle and great-grandfather to Cass County in western Missouri. Alexander Franklin Blair and James Harrison Blair "mustered out" of General Grant's Union army in Fort Scott, Kansas, and rode by train to Belton, Missouri, in 1866. James took to farming. His brother Alexander did not, and in 1884 Alexander, along with several neighbors and other citizens, obtained a charter. With a starting capital of $20,000 the Bank of Belton was created. Harry Truman would be born that same year in Lamar, Missouri. In 1885 bank officers bought a parcel of land at the corner of Main and Walnut Streets in Belton for $1,700—and constructed a brick building there that would serve as home to the bank for over 85 years.

Bank of Belton, 1950s.

On the Fourth of July in 1868, farmer James Blair had celebrated the birth of his son, James Franklin Blair. The date of his birth would not be "Young Frank's" only tie to United States history. He chose to follow his Uncle Alexander into banking and attended business school in

Bank of Belton, 1884. **Courtesy, Frankie Blair, Jr., collection**

Sedalia, Missouri. He then joined his uncle in the newly formed Bank of Belton in 1886. He was eventually appointed cashier, a high office for bank personnel, and remained with the bank in that capacity until his death in 1934. He had by that time managed to enlist his son, Frank Blair Jr., to join the bank as well, pulling Frank out of the local pool hall for assistance on the day that the bank's proof machine operator quit. Frank Jr. also took to banking and was elected president of the Bank of Belton in 1961.

In 1906 Harry Truman left his position as assistant teller in a Kansas City, Missouri, bank, called home by his family to the Blue Ridge family farm near Grandview, in neighboring Jackson County. Both of Truman's grandfathers had belonged to the fraternal order known as the Masons, an organization that counts Mozart, George Washington and Andrew Jackson among its former members. James Blair notes that his

Bank of Belton, today.

father, Frank Blair, served as "Masonry tutor" to the future 33rd president of the United States. He adds that the Truman family farm had an account with the Bank of Belton, and that the family retains a bank ledger written in his grandfather's hand, notating that account.

David McCullough states in his biography of Truman that "The man primarily responsible for Harry's involvement in the Masons was Frank Blair." When Truman in 1916 faced serious financial losses incurred through a business partnership with a local "promoter" involved in a zinc mining operation, McCullough notes that "Frank Blair at the Belton Bank had come to the rescue with a loan," after telling Truman what a mistake it had been to involve himself in the scheme in the first place. Truman would refer to the experience as "a liberal and expensive education."

In his history written for the bank's centennial in 1984, Frank Blair Jr. notes that the 20th century opened to "widespread financial disorganization and a substantial lack of central administration and policy" within the country's financial profession. When a currency panic in 1907 led people to hoard money for unknown reasons, the New York City bank that maintained an account with the Bank of Belton went out onto the streets of New York and "bought currency," shipping it

to the bank in Belton by parcel post. The bank's history continued to parallel the country's history with the selling of Liberty Bonds during World War I and defense bonds during World War II.

James Blair believes strongly in his bank's presence as a community bank. He speaks compellingly of the need for community banks that can provide small commercial loans of under $1.5 million to local businesses to support community economic growth. Blair, president as well of the Cass County Sister Cities Organization, a service organization linked to Manzanillo, Mexico, adds that in Mexico, many small businesses "remain family businesses forever," due to lack of capital for expansion. He notes that in the United States, small banking interests reflect community interests, in that depositor funds are used for community growth.

Blair encourages his staff to assume community leadership positions, and they willingly comply. Senior vice president John West, president of the local school board, also heads "Celebration Singers," a group of 80 youths who have traveled throughout the country to sing for various events. West also sponsors a Kansas City culinary competition for children from the United States Virgin Island of St. Croix, who stay with various bank employees during the competition. Compliance Officer Lanna Bernard serves on the Board of Directors for the Ozanam Home for Troubled Youth. James Blair

serves on the Board of Directors for the Foxwood Springs Living Center for the elderly, and within numerous other community organizations. Bank officers as well as employees serve in many community leadership positions, including that of PTA presidents. Blair's wife, Barbara, serves as the bank's executive vice president, following a tradition that dates from the 1930s, when two women served as board members for the Bank of Belton.

In accord with Blair's vision, the bank focuses its services on community needs. Its 35 employees provide to customers low cost deposit and transaction services as well as insurance, trust and retirement services. In 1999, as a result of a strategic planning process, the Bank of Belton purchased the First Trust of Mid-America. The trust company, with ten employees, now functions as a wholly owned subsidiary of the Bank of Belton, providing a "cafeteria plan" of services to customers with simpler financial needs.

Both federal and state regulators assign high ratings to the Bank of Belton, based on the bank's capital adequacy, liquidity, earnings, asset quality and management. In 1970 bank officers purchased from the town a tract of eight city lots located on Main Street between Cherry and Chestnut Streets. The bank built its current building on the site of the former First Baptist Church. It moves from there into the 21st century with its 19th century principles intact.

BRINKMANN CONSTRUCTORS

Pioneers in every field of endeavor have always demonstrated a gift for seeing the world a bit differently than others. That time-proven pattern repeats itself daily in the work of Brinkmann Constructors, the St. Louis region's foremost construction problem solver and one of the nation's leading fast-track, design/build construction firms.

Founder Robert G. Brinkmann, a civil engineering graduate of the University of Missouri-Rolla, is renowned for his way of "seeing" remarkable time- and money-saving solutions that yield quality construction for clients. His reliability as a practical innovator has placed the firm in the enviable position of negotiating 95 percent of its work in an industry where the low bidder is most often favored to win the project. This record has been sustained across his geographic markets—spreading throughout the midwestern, southern and eastern portions of the United States.

Brinkmann Constructors fulfills new construction and renovation needs in nearly every market sector, including retail, office, manufacturing, multifamily, data centers, entertainment, hospitality, schools, warehouse/distribution, develop-

Brinkmann Constructors' fast-track approach to the *St. Louis Post-Dispatch* printing facility expansion halved the time needed to build the $17 million project, without disrupting the daily's 24/7 operations. *St. Louis Construction News & Review* bestowed its Regional Excellence Award on Brinkmann's performance and passion for excellence. Photo by Peter Newcomb

The firm founded by Robert G. Brinkmann in 1984 is known as one of the region's foremost construction problem solvers. Photo by Suzy Gorman

ment services and other project types. Clients span developers, retailers, corporations, financial institutions, manufacturers, restaurants, country clubs, schools, not-for-profit organizations and others.

Practical Creativity. Brinkmann has accomplished what few innovators dare: he has cultivated his special talent for innovation and problem solving among Brinkmann Constructors' project managers, engineers and superintendents.

"We commit tremendous resources to training our full team in ways that speed the natural learning process in construction to deliver accelerated benefits to our clients," he said. "Most firms let their project team members learn through osmosis. It can take 20 to 30 years to develop the construction know-how that owners need for smart construction decisions. We accelerate that by conducting 26 three-hour sessions every year to teach, grill and drill our team members on building materials and processes, design concepts, value engineering, building codes, financial pro formas and related material."

"In our training, we also stress there are different ways of looking at a problem, and we develop the habit of seeking several good solutions," he said. "We break out of the traditional engineering mold of finding one correct answer to deliver creative and practical solutions that make the most of clients' investments."

By focusing constantly on devising better ways to deliver construction excellence through people, processes and systems, Brinkmann regularly shaves time and money from projects while meeting every challenge. Value engineering is integrated in all phases of development, pre-construction, design/build and construction. Consider these examples:

• At the *St. Louis Post-Dispatch* printing plant, Brinkmann Constructors completed a $17 million, fast-track 110,000-square-foot expansion and 97,000-square-foot remodeling of the *St. Louis Post-Dispatch* printing plant in half the time originally projected, without disturbing the newspaper's 24/7 printing operation. The client compared Brinkmann's work to "replacing a car engine while it's running." Brinkmann masterfully phased major components of the project to ensure printing presses kept pace with daily production demands. "The project was fraught with extraordinary challenges," described John Dennan, vice president of production, *St. Louis Post-Dispatch.* "Without drawings, Bob Brinkmann was able to value engineer the building in his mind and set a schedule that fostered optimal teamwork with our building partners. We originally thought it would take a year-and-a-half to complete the work. Brinkmann did it in nine months."

• American Multi-Cinema (AMC), Inc. had all but given up on developing a highly desirable site occupied by a two-acre lake for a new 16-screen theater in St. Louis County. That was before they met Brinkmann. The Brinkmann team offered a creative redesign solution that saved $900,000 and allowed the $10 million, 56,000-square-foot theater to

Brinkmann Constructors' leadership team includes (from left) Tim Breece, Tom Oberle, President Bob Brinkmann, Brian Satterthwaite and Gary Nelson. Brinkmann Constructors is one of the nation's top design/build construction firms. Photo by Arteaga

proceed. Brinkmann's plan eliminated the need for an expensive retaining wall and lowered the site grades by five feet. Water storage was moved from a wet retention basin to an underground concrete basin, and remaining water was used to create a small landscaped lake. "Brinkmann was able to bring critical issues to everyone's attention early in the development stage and come up with a creative solution to shore up site instability," said Brian Olsen, development manager for MBK Construction Ltd., who served as construction manager for AMC. "Brinkmann's knowledge of local building regulations gave us viable alternatives to solve storm water problems."

• Brinkmann Constructors built an upscale $20 million, 134,200-square-foot retail center in only 115 days, despite 39 days of rain. Retailers opened two-and-a-half months early due to Brinkmann's well-disciplined scheduling using three coordinated teams of subcontractors, overlapping design and construction efforts, and strategic construction procurement. The site was formerly home to a Bristol-Myers manufacturing and distribution complex, the shell of which was used as the structural frame for a

Schnucks Supercenter for the region's largest grocery chain. Craig D. Schnuck, chairman and chief executive officer of Schnuck Markets, Inc., noted, "Brinkmann's entire group did an outstanding job of constructing our new Schnucks Ladue Crossing shopping center in record time and in a first-class manner. This was done in spite of snow and rain that would have stopped most projects. Brinkmann's work really demonstrated to us and others the true ability of the organization."

Shaping Future Leaders. As a company that leads the work of many specialty subcontractors and vendors, Brinkmann places an emphasis on leadership development. Brinkmann's management team, which includes executive committee members Tim Breece, Tom Oberle, Brian Satterthwaite and Gary Nelson, has notched 10 to 18 years with Brinkmann. "People come to us, and they stay," Brinkmann said.

To nurture leadership skills, Brinkmann taps a retired Army major as coach. "To be a good leader, you must learn to be a good follower. Our staff finds themselves in both roles. They are trained to do all functions, to know the complete

Brinkmann Constructors used high-tech methods to keep pace with the changing requirements of this client's effort to consolidate staff in a new 180,000-square-foot headquarters in St. Louis County, Missouri, and accomodate a corporate merger as project completion neared. Photo by Sam Fentress

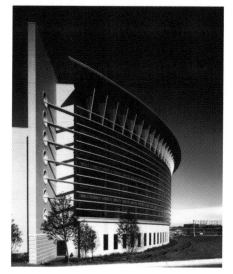

picture, to be well-rounded and to be specialists committed to excellence in everything," he notes.

"Our focus on courageous leadership yields relationships and results infused with candor and integrity," he adds. "Those qualities lead to the long-term relationships we enjoy with our clients."

Professionalism is critically important as well. "Our team leaders still wear white shirts and ties," Brinkmann said. "While many firms have adopted a less formal attire, we believe professionalism should be expressed in everything we do."

It's no surprise that Brinkmann is so deeply committed to training and mentoring those poised to follow him. His life was changed dramatically by the encouragement of one teacher who, when he was in sixth grade, informed him he would be going to college. She kept that vision alive in him, as he now does for others—both internally and externally.

He is passionate about inspiring dreams among area children. He is a board member and major supporter of the Junior Achievement (JA) program, which locally offers business education programs to students in grades kindergarten through 12 at more than 700 public, private and parochial schools. His eyes light up as he describes teaching fifth-graders in multi-week sessions at neighborhood schools each year. Each session ends with a visit to one of his construction job sites, where his students get a strong sense of how what they learn in school applies in real life.

Brinkmann is building the Dennis and Judy Jones Free Enterprise Learning Center for JA in Chesterfield, Missouri, where area fifth- and eighth-graders will experience two novel programs aimed at helping them experience the real world of personal finance and business.

His generosity is regularly felt throughout the St. Louis community, particularly among organizations catering to the health and well-being of children. Perhaps that speaks better than anything else to his passion for building—whether people, projects or community.

CENTENE CORPORATION

The concern, commitment and fortitude to see that low-income families with children and individuals receive access to quality health care resulted in the creation of Centene Corporation in 1984.

Centene's founder, Mrs. Betty Brinn, was devoted to helping poor people obtain good health care in Milwaukee, Wisconsin. As an orphan, who had lived in 17 foster homes when she was a child, and was particularly concerned about the health and welfare of children. As the Medicaid and commercial-managed care company that Mrs. Brinn headed grew more successful, she found ways to help poor and neglected children in the Milwaukee community. The company contributed money to a day care center for the poor. She also established a foundation to benefit community organizations that worked with low-income persons. In 1992 Mrs. Brinn died of cancer. A Board of Directors continued the success of the company and in 1994 took steps to open a second health plan in Indianapolis, Indiana.

In 1996, the Board of Directors undertook a national search to find a president and chief executive officer. Michael F.

Mr. Michael F. Neidorff, Centene's president and CEO.

Neidorff, who with the assistance of a group of prominent physicians, launched United HealthCare's Physicians Health Plan in St. Louis, Missouri, and grew the Plan to cover more than 400,000 people, was selected by the board of directors to head Centene. Mr. Neidorff was recognized in the St. Louis community as an individual concerned about families receiving quality healthcare. He was one of the first managed healthcare leaders in the country to speak out against drive-by overnight pregnancy stays at

hospitals. Mr. Neidorff changed the hours of health clinics he headed to include evening hours to make healthcare more accessible to St. Louis working families. After hiring Mr. Neidorff, the board directed him to build the organization's resources, expand the company and transform it into a publicly traded company.

To turn Centene from a base of 40,000 lives in three counties—two in Wisconsin and one in Indiana—into a national company, Mr. Neidorff moved Centene's headquarters from Milwaukee to St. Louis in early 1997. By locating the company in the Midwest, he knew he would save the company money in travel expenses when searching for national expansion opportunities, and the St. Louis community would help attract a high-level corporate executive staff. After carefully selecting a new management team, Mr. Neidorff went to work to build the Indiana expansion operating only in one-third of the state. Two years later, the Indiana health plan was operating statewide and is today Indiana's most successful Medicaid managed-care health plan.

In 1997 Centene bought a position in Superior HealthPlan, Inc., in Texas, which

Centene's headquarters.

resulted in a joint venture between Centene and Community Health Centers Network, L.P. (CHCN). CHCN is a Texas limited partnership created by the Texas Association of Community Health Centers, a group of Federally Qualified Health Centers located throughout the state, which has provided care to the Medicaid population for more than 25 years. After competing against other health plans, Superior HealthPlan was awarded a contract by the Texas Department of Health to provide Medicaid managed healthcare services for the El Paso, Texas, service area. In 1999 Superior HealthPlan opened its first office in El Paso and began serving members. In only one year, more than 26,000 persons had joined the health plan. Early in 2001, Centene acquired the Medicaid business from Humana, Inc., in Austin, San Antonio and Wisconsin, adding approximately 70,000 Medicaid persons to Centene's two health plans. Centene also ventured into the Illinois Medicaid market. The company later sold its Illinois health plan to focus its business in states where Medicaid enrollment was mandatory.

By September 2001, Mr. Neidorff and his staff had engineered a dramatic turnaround in the company. Under his leadership, Centene changed its focus to provide managed care services for only the Medicaid population, children of working parents who could not afford to purchase private insurance to cover their families, and the elderly, blind and handicapped. Centene's Mission Statement was changed to read, "Centene will be a recognized market leader in government-supported, physician-driven health care, creating enhanced value through positive outcomes for our members and clients." The company ended its commercial healthcare coverage. By the end of 2000, the company's strategy and hard work paid off, and it recorded a profit of $7.7 million. In the first six months of 2001, the company announced it had already earned a $5.4 million profit. When the IPO market had come to a standstill fol-

lowing the September 11 tragedy, the company forged ahead in October and filed with the Securities and Exchange Commission to go public. Two months later, Centene became a publicly traded company. The $14 per share offering was to raise $57.5 million for the company to repay subordinated notes and fund potential acquisitions.

In June 2002, Centene acquired the State Children's Health Insurance Pro-

Centene's claims processing facility opened in 2000. It allowed the company to maintain pace with recent technological advancements and process claims more efficiently for payment to customers.

gram business from Texas Universities Health Plan, Inc. The acquisition allowed its Superior HealthPlan to expand into Lubbock and Amarillo. Later in 2002, Centene acquired an equity position in University Health Plans, Inc., when it

Throughout the St. Louis community, Centene Corporation has supported many of the fine health organizations' projects, such as the American Lung Association of Eastern Missouri's Camp Superkids, a summer camp created for children who have asthma.

formed a joint venture with The University of Medicine and Dental of New Jersey, a statewide system for higher education, research, healthcare and community service. Centene's newest Medicaid health plan added 52,000 Medicaid-eligible persons.

At the beginning of 2003, the company announced it had recorded 14 consecutive quarters of increased profitability at the end of 2002 with revenues of $141.7 million, a 57% increase over the fourth quarter for 2001. Earnings were listed at $9.6 million, a 68% increase over the previous year. Centene's success led to Mr. Neidorff being honored with St. Louis' 2002 Ernst and Young's Entrepreneur of the Year award.

The St. Louis community has benefited economically and charitably by Centene's success. When first opened, Centene's corporate office employed 46 people in its St. Louis headquarters. Today, 124 persons are employed in St. Louis. The company also opened a claims processing facility in 2000 in Farmington, Missouri, with 34 employees. It currently employs 125, and the facility has expanded to accommodate 300 employees. Centene, its president and staff continues to be actively involved in the St. Louis community. For a number of years, Mr. Neidorff served on the board of the St. Louis Symphony. He also served a term as the symphony's chairman and helping secure funding during financially stressed times, transitioning a new conductor and negotiating a five-year contract with its musicians.

Centene and Mr. Neidorff have been supporters of the American Lung Association of Eastern Missouri based in St. Louis for years. The Lung Association

said, "The leadership and support Centene and Michael have shown to the American Lung Association has been a tremendous impetus and force behind the strategic direction of the ALA as it reaches its century mark." Centene and its staff have also helped support the Asthma and Allergy Foundation of America, St. Louis Chapter; Dance St. Louis; Greater St. Louis Area Boy Scouts of America; The St. Louis Opera Theatre; Steps Toward Empowering People, St. Louis County's Community Action Agency; St. Louis Crisis Nursery; The St. Louis American's Salute to Educational Excellence; and other community organizations and events.

Centene considers its greatest accomplishments as providing quality managed healthcare services for more than 400,000 men, women and children in need at the end of 2002 and saving a significant amount of money for the revenue-stressed states where it does business.

DALTON LUMBER

For the owners of Dalton Lumber, running a business truly is a family affair.

The Gatewood-based company specializes in producing stringers and deck boards for pallet stock and is located in the heart of southern Missouri's hardwood forests, where oak and sycamore abound. Like these native trees, Dalton family roots run deep and strong here.

Tom Dalton, now 53, started the company as a part-time sawmill operation in 1970. He purchased tracts of land and began harvesting the timber. After years of holding down two jobs, Dalton left his supervisory position with a vinyl advertising products company in 1984 and set up a family corporation with his wife and son. Today Tom is the president of Dalton Lumber, Marilyn is the secretary, and Tommy Wayne is the vice-president of operations. The company also employs eight additional workers. The main site includes a large mill building, maintenance and storage building, and office.

Dalton's interest in the lumber industry began with his father, who earned extra money cutting white oak blocks and selling them locally. The elder Daltons—Odes Dalton, now 94, and Ethel Dalton, now 92—used to help out at the mill. And now Tommy Wayne's 12-year-

Tom Dalton, president of Dalton Lumber, at the side one of the tractor trailers.

old son, Stetson, works on weekends, making the company a four-generation enterprise.

Sawed squares of lumber called cants are bought from sawmills in Missouri and Arkansas. The cants are loaded into an unscrambler and sent by conveyor to a cut-off saw where they are sized. The cants then go either to a junior gang saw or a bandsaw system to be sawn into deck boards.

Stringers are made in the big mill building. A bundle of cants is fed onto a roller bed. The bundle is broken loose and the cants fall over row by row. In the unscrambler the cants are separated out further, then they travel to the chop saw.

After being cut to a size of 40 or 48 inches on the cut-off saw, a gang saw splits the 6-x-8 cant into two 4-x-6 pieces. Then the wood goes through a notcher. Each notched 4-x-6 piece is fed to another gang saw, which saws it into four 1 3/8 inch-wide stringers. In the final stage, the pieces are fed into a stacker.

The finished product is transported via tractor-trailer to companies in Arkansas, Tennessee and Illinois, who use the stringers and deck boards as stock to manufacture pallets. Sawdust is sent to a Kentucky company, which uses it to heat boilers in its paper mill and to make carbon products.

The company generates millions in annual sales. Dalton attributes his success to "lots of hard work, and lots of hours." He typically works 11 hours a day, arriving at 6:30 a.m. to sharpen saws and ready the equipment for the day's production. He also goes in on Saturday mornings to do maintenance work.

"I started out with nothing. It's fascinating to see how things have fallen into place," says Dalton. "Looking back to when I started the business, it's amazing to watch it gradually keep growing and turning out more products. It makes you feel proud, like you've done something right."

Main mill building where both mills are fed with cants.

CENTERCO PROPERTIES, L.L.C.

When Centerco Properties first organized in 1961, IBM punch cards kept track of accounting practices. Much has changed procedurally in the profession over the years, but dedication to client service and appreciation of employee loyalty still serve as the foundation for the St. Louis real estate investment and management firm.

Four employees and two founders formed the basis for Centerco, established in Clayton, Missouri, in December 1961 as the Guild Management Company. Melvin Friedman, a practicing attorney, and Arthur Loomstein, a law student at nearby Washington University, established the firm to centralize bookkeeping and managerial functions for three family-owned properties. The new company founders, aware that Clayton was well situated to be a major location for corporate offices, chose the site to formalize the operations of Carondelet East, Carondelet West and the Guild Building, the three office buildings that formed the initial basis for Centerco's services. Investors, then as now, were primarily family, friends and private individuals, many of whom held interests in multiple properties.

Centerco moved into fee management in the mid-to-late 1960s. Managed properties during this time included the River Bluff Apartments, the Charter National

Woodchase Apartments, Chesterfield, Missouri, 186 units.

Life Building, the 200 South Hanley Building and the 7711 Building. The firm also ventured into development at this time with the construction of the Colony Hotel (now the Sheraton-Clayton Plaza) and, in 1971, of Chromalloy Plaza (now known as Clayton Center), a 275,000-square-foot office building located in downtown Clayton. Centerco Development, Inc., owned by Loomstein, Friedman and Donald K. Ross, an engineer and long-time family friend, served as developer and general contractor for the Chromalloy Plaza project. This property and its development company were both sold in 1979.

Developments during the 1970s included the organization of private syndications to conduct transactions. In 1977 the firm purchased Jaccard Apartments, a 94-unit complex located in University City, Missouri. The 1980s saw a period of increased activity for the Midwestern firm: in 1980, operations moved out-of-state for the first time with the purchase of Poco

Diablo Resort in Sedona, Arizona, which was subsequently sold in 1984. Delcrest Plaza, a 60,000-square-foot office building located in University City, Missouri, was purchased in 1986 and sold in 2000.

The 1980s and 1990s were characterized by similar acquisitions and sales, including those of the Hill Building in St. Louis, a retail/office complex; the Townehomes at Clarkson Court, a company apartment rehabilitation project of 78 units located in St. Louis County, Missouri; and Westline Office Plaza, a 36,000-square-foot property located in St. Louis County, Missouri. Several properties acquired during that period remain in Centerco's portfolio of investment properties, including Chez Paree Apartments, a 394-unit apartment complex in Hazelwood, Missouri, purchased in 1989; Woodchase Apartments, an apartment complex in Chesterfield, Missouri, purchased in 1998; and Greenbriar Apartments, located in Kirkwood, Missouri, purchased in 1999. Unfortunately, this period of time was also marked by personal tragedy for the company when one of its original founders, Friedman, died in January 1987 in an automobile acci-

Cross Lake Apartments, Evansville, Indiana, 208 units.

dent, leaving Loomstein as sole owner of Centerco. In 1998, Centerco's structure was changed to a limited liability company.

Company acquisitions after the year 2000 include 11628 Old Ballas Road, a St. Louis County, Missouri, office building; Riverpark Plaza Apartments, located in Wichita, Kansas, the company's largest apartment complex, with 584 units; and Cross Lake Apartments, located in Evansville, Indiana.

The three office buildings that formed the basis of Centerco's original services remain to this day under company management. Such longevity of service is key to Centerco's success in the real estate market and to its mission: the provision of property management services resulting in excellent working and living environments for tenants and equitable and competitive financial returns for investors. This service-oriented perspective of delivery of quality habitable apartment units is unique to the area. The company does not seek to position properties for resale, but to retain them for long-term appreciation and growth, while nurturing its tenant base.

In keeping with this philosophy, company plans for the future include decreased ownership in office buildings and increased ownership in apartment buildings. Company founder Loomstein believes that this is the better area of concentration, one where "hands-on management will have a great effect on results." Loomstein speaks from experience: as head of one of the oldest real estate companies in St. Louis, he has successfully navigated his company through a number of soft markets, enduring downturns in the economy that have defeated less solidly based enterprises. In 2002 the company almost doubled in size, acquiring close to $25,000,000 worth of investment property in Evansville, Indiana, and Wichita, Kansas, and completing two refinancings in excess of $35,000,000 on St. Louis properties. As a result of these transactions, company personnel increased by 25 percent.

Greenbriar Apartments, Kirkwood, Missouri, 208 units.

Not surprisingly, Loomstein credits much of Centerco's success to its history of collaborative relationships with company employees. Long-term employees serve as many of the company's officers: Jack Wolf, executive vice president (1970-present); Donna Maurer, vice president of administration (1978-present); Robert Downey, building services manager (1978-present); and Lin R. Meyer, vice president of residential properties (1989-present). Onesimus Boston, hired in 1958 before the company was officially formed, is still employed with Centerco on a part-time basis. Such loyalty is not surprising in a company that, in its official welcome to new employees, stresses quality management, competitive wages, equitable treatment and prompt and concerned conflict resolution. President Howard J. Smith describes the company's history of employee loyalty in more humanistic terms, noting that it reflects "the caring and nurtur-

ing culture that the founder and owner, Arthur Loomstein, has overlaid as a basic approach to business. He is a very caring person who takes care of his employees."

Such an approach to business is welcome in any climate, but may be especially welcome in an era of widespread misuse of corporate authority. On such a basis Centerco, now managing properties in three states with the help of 55 employees, can look forward to the future with optimism and confidence.

Pool and riverview at Riverpark Plaza Apartments, Wichita, Kansas, 584 units.

DELONG'S INC. OF JEFFERSON CITY

Home of the world's first steel bridge built at Glasgow in 1879, Missouri is also home of one of the nation's premier producers of structural steel for bridges. What began in a small blacksmith shop in Jefferson City nearly 60 years ago with a father and son grew into a multi-million dollar business that supplies steel for bridges and buildings all over the United States as well as overseas. DeLong's Inc., still based in Jefferson City, is a diversified structural steel fabricator serving the construction industry with bridge steel, structural and steel joists, ornamental steel and other products. Founder F. Joe DeLong Jr. was a man of great foresight and community commitment; his company has brought millions of dollars into the state of Missouri and employed hundreds of workers. As DeLong's enters its 59th year, it is still very much a family business with third-generation Joe DeLong III currently serving as president and chief executive officer.

In the highly competitive and volatile industry of steel fabrication, DeLong's has survived economic downturns, recessions, worker shortages and other challenges through a company philosophy of timely delivery, quality fabrication, complete product control from start to finish and employee involvement in all aspects of the company. "The intelligence,

In 1931 Fred DeLong invented and manufactured 3,000 of these corn fodder balers to be sent to drought-ridden states at a cost of $15 each.

Standing left to right: Phil DeLong; Greg Wankum; Greg DeLong; F. Joe DeLong, III; Jim DeLong; Darrell Chronister, CPA; Alan Becker and Bill Wise II. Seated left to right: F. Joe DeLong, John Hendren, Mozelle Delong and B.J. DeLong.

kindness, generosity and hard work of my parents in establishing our company's philosophy, and the good reputation that we've built as a result, are the keys to the success of our company," says Joe DeLong III. Joe DeLong worked for the company he founded with his wife B.J. every day until his death in 1996. B.J. is now in her 59th year with DeLong's and was recently re-elected to the board of directors, making her the longest serving member.

F. Joe DeLong Jr., founder of DeLong's Inc., learned about shaping steel and engineering enterprise in his father's blacksmith shop at 818 Jefferson Street in Jefferson City. Eleven-year-old Joe watched his father, Fred DeLong, invent and manufacture 3,000 corn fodder balers for drought-ridden states in 1931. By 1938 Joe's interest had turned to airplanes, and he went to work as a welding supervisor in the plant built by Clyde Cessna, founder of Cessna Aircraft Co., in Wichita, Kansas. As Cessna's business grew, Joe became plant supervisor at the age of 22. He also met and married Betty Jo Hargrove in Kansas.

The young couple was called back to Jefferson City to help Joe's ailing father. In November 1944 father and son started DeLong's with $1,300, B.J. as bookkeeper and one employee, who earned one dollar per hour. The company began with blacksmithing and general welding repair work. Next came custom-made truck bodies, tool trailers and wagons, along with ornamental iron for the Jefferson City area. DeLong's added five more employees and had total sales of $19,000 in its first year. After World War II ended, Joe's brother Phil DeLong joined the company, as machine work and structural steel manufacturing was added to the company's endeavors. Long-serving company attorney John Hendren also joined DeLong's in 1946. DeLong's was incorporated in

Bob Bachta on the left and Joe DeLong III.

1948, the same year that the company moved to 909 W. Dunklin Street. With 30 to 40 employees, more product lines were added, including commodity sales and extensive engineering work in the fabrication of steel.

By 1952 the company had outgrown its location and purchased seven acres at Dix Road and Industrial Avenue. DeLong's built its first plant in 1953 with facilities to manufacture long-span steel trusses and fabricate structural steel for bridges. Another important milestone for DeLong's happened in 1952 when Joe met Bill Wisch and Alan Becker, two young engineers from the Missouri State Highway Department. When Bill went to DeLong's for some welding repair work, he recognized design drawings for a bridge near Centertown; it was a bridge he had designed at the highway department. Since this was Joe's first attempt to bid, fabricate and erect a bridge, he had some questions for the engineer. The conversation that followed led to a successful bid, and the start of the engineering and drafting department at DeLong's after Bill and Alan joined DeLong's in 1954.

Alan Becker recalls the early project that successfully launched DeLong's as a fabricator of steel joist: "In the spring of 1955, a large project involving 1,100 tons of steel joists was advertised for bids in Chicago, Illinois. DeLong's was recommended to the contractor by a customer for whom several small projects had been

successfully furnished. After a thorough study of the plans, delivery and financial requirements, a bid was completed and the contract awarded to the company. This particular job was, in itself, many times larger than the combination of all that had been previously fabricated. It served the purpose of putting DeLong's "on the map," but it also led to an obstacle requiring a quick solution.

"The major joist fabricators at the time were all members of a technical organization—the Steel Joist Institute. This body wrote specifications for the design, testing and performance requirements of steel joists. DeLong's joists were designed in accordance with the same specifications, but had not been tested for required strength and performance. Since the company was not a member of the Institute, the project authorities insisted that design data be submitted and full-size testing of the product would be required.

"Undaunted by this decision, DeLong's complied by devising an innovative and unusual procedure for testing the 60-foot joists. A platform was fabricated consisting of two end frames upon which three joists were supported. A wooden deck was then applied to the top of the joists and layers of building brick placed uniformly over the entire area. Bricks were stacked layer upon layer until the calculated design load was attained. As a safety factor, specifications required the joists support 1.65 times the design load; additional layers were applied until this requirement was satisfied. No failure or distress occurred and the brick was then removed entirely to satisfy one additional requirement—after deflecting under the loading, a 90 percent recovery was specified. The joists performed admirably, averaging a 96 percent recovery. A huge sigh of relief was expressed by the entire DeLong's work force—officers, shop workers, secretaries—all of whom had assisted in loading the thousands of bricks."

As Alan notes, the project was completed successfully in 1956 with DeLong's steel joists, and the company went on to become a major steel joist supplier to hundreds of building contractors in many states, including Alaska and Hawaii. DeLong's was also accepted as an active member of the Steel Joist Institute

Employees gave Joe and B.J. a cruise after 40 years.

Standing left to right: Joseph DeLong IV; Bob Bachta; Steve Akre, attorney; Harry Otto, CPA; and Mike Smith, comptroller. Seated left to right: B.J. DeLong; Jim DeLong; Gary Wisch; F. Joe DeLong III; Ben Bielski, metal products; and Donna Coulter, secretary.

(SJI), which was pivotal in DeLong's development. DeLong's production of steel joists, which were now fabricated at the second DeLong's plant in Sedalia, increased to an annual average exceeding 10,000 tons during this period. A company snapshot from 1977 shows record sales of $12 million, 180 employees, customers over a 30-state area, a $3 million payroll, $6 million of steel purchased from domestic mills (DeLong's uses only domestic steel) and $1.5 million paid in tax revenue.

During the 1970s and 1980s, many new companies began fabricating steel joists and competition increased. Unlike DeLong's, some of the producers were associated or owned by basic steel-producing mills, giving them a competitive advantage. DeLong's decided to expand the successful arm of its business that fabricated steel highway bridges, ushering in a new era for a company that knows the value of diversification and versatility.

Bridge projects located in Missouri, Kansas and Iowa were bid successfully and DeLong's reputation for quality work and timely delivery spread, leading to bridge work across the United States. In the early days Bill Wisch headed the Bridge Division, which is now headed by his son Gary. More than 2,500 bridges have been built with steel supplied by DeLong's, and bridge work now makes up 90 percent of the company's total sales. Joe's younger brother Jim DeLong, who joined the company in 1963, is now executive vice president of purchasing and sales.

The year 1989 was another milestone for the company, as Joe and B.J. handed over the company leadership to the next generation and Joe III became the president and chief executive officer of DeLong's. Under Joe III's leadership, DeLong's continued its bridge work and expanded its facilities with a 50,000,00-square-foot addition to the main plant in 1990-1991. Joe continued to work at DeLong's without drawing a salary on a full-time basis until his death in 1996. B.J. continues her work with the next generation of DeLong leaders and employees through her expertise on the pension, profit-sharing and investment committees.

Looking after loyal employees has been part of the DeLong philosophy since the company was founded. In a 1983 interview, Joe praised his employees: "Whatever success we've had should be attributed to the many fine employees in our organization. They are the people who make it go." Many employees have retired after 35 years of service and several have worked at DeLong's for 50 years. Elmer Ott, who joined DeLong's in 1950, still handles commodities sales at the front desk, where customers and contractors can order a variety of ornamental gates, dividers, railings and other items including wood stoves, fireplace inserts, straight or spiral stairways and many other standard or custom steel products.

DeLong's established a profit-sharing trust for employees in 1954 and a pension plan shortly thereafter. To date, the company has contributed more than $2 million to the plan; the trust has earned more than $3.5 million and employees have withdrawn $3.8 million. Another aspect of DeLong's company philosophy

Curved bridge, layed out in yard at DeLong's Inc.

DeLong's Inc. work in St. Louis County, Missouri, located at I-44 and Highway 270.

is its "no layoff" policy. No matter what market conditions are, DeLong's finds a way to keep from implementing layoffs, a strategy started by the founder and continued by his son. "When market prices drop, as they do every 10 years or so, we continue to bid and book enough work to keep everyone busy even at a loss to maintain our quality, experienced work force," says Joe III.

The company also practices what Joe III calls "participative management." Employees are involved in management decisions and kept closely informed of company developments. After 35 years as a union organization, DeLong's became non-union in 1986. Joe and B.J.'s daughter, attorney Marian Mozelle Bielski, was instrumental in helping the company make the transition.

Participative management at DeLong's includes bi-monthly plant meetings in which issues regarding sales, plant improvements, safety, backlog and any other topic initiated by an employee are discussed. General Manager Robert Bachta credits DeLong's continued success in a competitive industry to employee participation and "treating our employees as highly valued individuals, encouraging their input and providing them with sound benefits and wages." The respect is mutual on the employee's part, as evidenced when they expressed their appreciation to Joe and B.J. with a pair of

tickets for an ocean-going cruise in 1984.

Along with his employees and family members, Joe DeLong cared deeply about his church, his community and the state of Missouri. He spearheaded the industrial development of Jefferson City and served on many civic organizations. He was a board member of Central Bank and Central Bancompany, past president of St. Mary's Health Center Advisory Board, past chairman of the Jefferson City Industrial Development Committee, former vice president of the Jefferson City Housing Authority and was instrumental in establishing the Capital Plaza Hotel in Jefferson City.

He also served as a board member of the Great River Council of the Boy Scouts of America, a former trustee of the YMCA, former chairman of the Selective Service Appeals Board of the Missouri Western District, and a trustee of Westminster College, Fulton. He received the Jaycees Award in 1955 and the State of Missouri Meritorious Service Award. He was also the first recipient of the

Jefferson City Tourism Award and Missouri's Community Development Award in 1976. The Sisters of St. Mary's awarded him the Mother Odelia Award in recognition of his work with their hospital in Jefferson City.

B.J. DeLong shares a distinguished history of community and civic service along with her husband and many DeLong employees, past and present. Her activities have included serving as chairwoman or president of the Jefferson City Commission on Environmental Quality, Hawthorn Garden Club, St. Mary's Hospital Auxiliary, Immaculate Conception School Association and the Jefferson City Country Club Women's Golf Association.

DeLong's remains very much a family company, with Joe IV joining the board of directors in 2002 and making it a fourth-generation business. Joe and B.J.'s daughter Mozelle is chairman of the board of Metal Culverts, a company founded by her father. Son Gregory DeLong, now an Edward Jones broker and partner in Springfield, joined DeLong's after completing a master's degree in finance and was instrumental in helping the company meet the requirements to qualify as an AISC Category III Shop.

From shaping horseshoes to shaping the industrial development of Jefferson City and the state of Missouri, F. Joe DeLong Jr. provided an inspiring legacy to his family, his company, his church, his community and state that will be felt for generations to come.

DeLong's Inc. drafting department.

DRURY UNIVERSITY

A Focus on Students, a Tradition of Excellence. Drury University, located in the historic Midtown area of Springfield, was the first institution of higher learning in southwest Missouri. In the early 1870s, Drury University's founders—James H. Harwood, Charles E. Harwood, Nathan J. Morrison and Samuel F. Drury—and the members of the Springfield Association of Congregational Churches banded together to form a private liberal arts institution. Little did they know that their work would result in the nationally recognized school that Drury is today.

Springfield College, the school's original name, quickly became Drury College, the name she held for more than 125 years. The transition to Drury University happened on January 1, 2000. Throughout its long and rich history, the Drury name has stood for excellence.

From its inception in 1873, Drury has adhered to its original goal of providing a high standard of instruction and scholarship. This commitment to quality has helped Drury become a strong university

Drury University's first class of 39 students included seven American Indians—five men and two women. The men are pictured below with other members of that first class.

Dr. Nathan J. Morrison, Drury University's first president.

today. Excellence is expressed in a variety of ways across the 80-acre campus. From academics to campus housing, Drury continually improves and updates its facilities. That dedication and commitment helped the university earn a place on *Yahoo! Internet Life's* "Most Wired Small Colleges" list.

With the support of some 600 trustees and friends of Drury, science students today study in a truly state-of-the-art facility, the Trustee Science Center. Spacious, well-equipped classrooms and teaching laboratories form the heart of a center designed around a ground-breaking, collaborative and interdisciplinary approach to science education. Research opportunities abound for undergraduate students, giving them a jumpstart on graduate studies or professional preparation. The university's commitment to undergraduate research helped it earn the Heuer Award for Excellence in Undergraduate Science Education from the Council for Independent Colleges.

For architecture students, excellence is the rigorous and well-respected Hammons School of Architecture, the first of its kind on a liberal-arts campus. Immersed in the tradition of liberal arts, the Hammons School of Architecture prepares students professionally for architecture with the well-rounded critical thinking skills of a comprehensive education.

Academic excellence is found wherever you look in the Drury community. The Breech School of Business Administration fosters the international award winning Students in Free Enterprise team. Drury music students can be found performing at concert halls and prestigious conferences around the world. While Drury students pursue excellence, they are not alone in their endeavors. Drury professors routinely receive recognition from state and national associations for their research and publications.

Recognizing that today's graduates will work and compete in a global environment, Drury created the Global Perspectives 21 core curriculum. In the GP21 program, students learn to place their lives, interests and beliefs in a global context so they can adapt and succeed in a rapidly changing society. Closely tied to a liberal arts education, the GP21 curriculum teaches the kind of problem solving, creativity, communication and critical thinking skills needed

for success. As a benefit of studying the Global Perspectives core curriculum at Drury, every student receives a minor in global studies, a unique opportunity in higher education today.

This concept of diversity and multicultural understanding has been a part of Drury from the very beginning. Of the first group of 39 students enrolled at Drury in 1873, seven were American Indians. In the ensuing 20 years, there were only two years without American Indian students as part of the college's roster. Looking forward 125 years, this foundational emphasis on diversity bore fruit when university administrators and trustees worked with neighboring historic Washington Avenue Baptist Church to help the city's oldest African-American congregation find a new place of worship. The university then relocated the historic church building and reconstructed it, returning it to the original design, using the original bricks, wood, furniture and stained-glass windows. The building now serves as the university's Diversity Center, committed to providing and hosting activities, forums, educational opportunities and other events for the Springfield community.

With 1,500 traditional undergraduate students and 2,900 students in the College of Graduate and Continuing Studies, Drury is small enough to meet the indi-

Drury University's Trustee Science Center, where interdisciplinary research, technology and academics come together in one place.

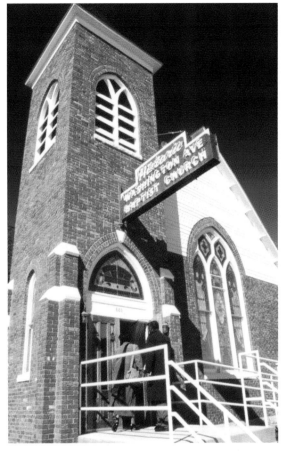

Springfield's Historic Washington Avenue Baptist Church, now fully restored, serves as Drury University's Diversity Center, a place for multicultural seminars, forums and community events.

vidual needs of its students, yet large enough to offer more than 45 majors. Efficiently using financial resources helps meet the needs of an ever-growing student population. Drury continues to be

recognized by *U.S. News & World Report* as the top institution on their "Great Schools at Great Prices" list, and is listed in *Barron's Best Buys in College Education*. The students at Drury recognize the quality of their university. When asked by the National Survey of Student Engagement, Drury students ranked the university near the top in areas such as academic challenge, active and collaborative learning, student-faculty interactions, supportive campus environment and enriching educational experiences.

The Drury experience spreads far beyond Springfield's boundaries. Students at the university find numerous international study opportunities, including Drury's own satellite campus in Volos, Greece. The experience includes more than traditional college-age students as well. In the early 20th century, Drury began offering courses specifically tailored to the schedules and needs of working professionals. What began as professional development for teachers at area schools grew quickly. Today, the College of Graduate and Continuing Studies serves non-traditional students with undergraduate and master's degrees in more than 35 areas. The courses are offered at the Springfield campus and at satellite campuses in several Missouri communities. Online courses have added another new dimension to the university's ability to take the excellence of Drury around the world.

Drury has a long tradition of excellence, built on the foundation of four men with a passion to provide high-level scholarship in Springfield. The foundation they provided stands true and firm today, and is a base for future innovation in teaching and leadership, always with a focus on serving students.

EFCO CORPORATION

Terry Fuldner's first job after college didn't last long. The young Washington University graduate with the degree in Industrial Engineering was selling windows for Republic Steel, when the company's president asked him what he thought of their training program. Terry replied, "What training program?" The next day, he was asked to clean out his desk.

This brief setback worked in Terry's favor, however, as he and his college buddy George Eberle decided to go into business for themselves, selling windows for a manufacturer based in Florida. Borrowing $2,500 dollars each, they formed EFCO Product Company in 1951, and began selling jalousie windows to lumber yards and home improvement contractors in the St. Louis area. That first year, as the only two employees, Terry and George each took home a salary of $200 a month. Soon, the company was manufacturing screens for the windows they sold, and by 1953, it was incorporated as EFCO Corporation.

From its original offices in the basement of a laundry on Brentwood Boulevard, the company began its expansion with light manufacturing capabilities including louver-type jalousie windows and single-panel storm sashes. New aluminum products required a bigger manufacturing facility, so EFCO Corporation moved to a 5,000-square-foot building on Grant Road in St. Louis County in 1954.

One area of growth followed another, and in 1955, the company decided to branch out into residential windows with the idea of expanding distribution to areas outside the St. Louis market. EFCO purchased the tooling and inventory of Melco Window Company of Magnolia, Arkansas, to facilitate this expansion.

By 1957, following an organizational picket imposed by the carpenter's union, the partners began to think about moving their headquarters to a more favorable climate. At the same time, the city of Monett, Missouri, was losing a major employer upon the departure of

Terry and Chris Fuldner.

Frisco Railroad—a situation that prompted them to try to attract EFCO to their community. The next year, EFCO Corporation signed an agreement with the Monett Industrial Corporation for the financing and construction of an 13,000-square-foot plant in Monett, which began operating with 25 employees on November 8, 1958.

As they tend to do in the face of diligence and hard work, opportunities continued to present themselves to the growing company. EFCO secured a contract in 1961 to construct aluminum cargo boxes for aircraft parts, and expanded its facilities again in 1962, this time to 25,600 square feet—almost double the size of the original Monett plant. The new plant provided space for two more production lines and etching tanks. A second plant was started in Aurora, Missouri, for making windows for metal building manufacturers. In 1968, with annual sales hovering at around $3 million, EFCO sold their residential window products and committed exclusively to commercial sales.

The 1970s brought more changes, challenges and innovations. In 1972 the

plant was expanded for a new, integrated horizontal paint line, which allowed architectural products to be offered in a variety of colors—and in turn drove increases in sales. The big news came in 1973, when the Arab oil embargo sent fuel prices spiraling and prompted the development of new, energy-efficient construction technologies. EFCO Corporation's insulating glass units were enhanced with the introduction of thermally broken aluminum frames, a process consisting of extruding a channel in the aluminum frame, filling it with high-density polyurethane, and then cutting out the bottom of the channel, thereby isolating the exterior metal from the interior metal. This greatly reduced heat loss as well as condensation and frost on the metal frames. Despite setbacks including a 1979 fire that destroyed the plant's paint line (a serious disruption that was to repeat itself in 1998), innovations like thermally broken frames contributed to the company's growth.

EFCO was known as the first company in its area to offer health insurance as an employee benefit in the early 1970s and, in turn, grew to 130 employees, occupying a group of facilities totaling 78,000

EFCO CORPORATION
MONETT, MO

ISO9001 REGISTERED
SEPTEMBER 14, 2001

square feet. Profit sharing and an employee stock ownership plan were also implemented. Employees now own about 25 percent of the company.

In the mid-1970s, the company underwent a fundamental change in sales philosophy that sparked its exponential growth. Under the original philosophy, sales were managed to be at a specific backlog level. When the backlog was up, prices were raised; when it was down, prices were lowered. The new thinking of Chris Fuldner in 1977 did just the reverse. EFCO held prices constant and managed its capacity to meet the demands of its backlog. Prices were set to provide good value to the market and a fair return to EFCO. The result was a steady increase in business that has driven EFCO ever since. By the end of the decade, the pace of growth was more intense than ever before.

With sales having risen from $3 million in 1974 to $17.5 million in 1981, the company built a new 125,000-square-foot plant in Monett, followed by yet another expansion, again of 125,000 square feet, in 1985—this time to include an upgrade of anodizing facilities. Curtain wall products were added to the line in 1986, along with the company's Express program (an arrangement by which customers can receive pre-engineered, custom products in three weeks). The Express program was instituted by Chris Fuldner, who that year became president of the company and assumed management of its operations. Expansion was necessary again in 1987, when a 2,500-ton, 7-inch extrusion press was added along with an additional 50,000 square feet. The growth coincided with sales increases that met the company's hard-won goal of "90 in '90"—$90 million in 1990.

The burgeoning manufacturing capabilities and expanded product lines (including storefront and entrance systems added in 1989) required new means of service and distribution, and EFCO an-

In 2001, EFCO achieved ISO 9001:1994 certification for the Monett facilities.

swered these needs with the Chicago facility in 1990 and the Oklahoma City facility in 1992. That same year, the company completed the world's largest window replacement project, Stuyvesant Town and Peter Cooper Village in New York City, consisting of 58,416 window units.

Unprecedented destruction caused by Hurricane Andrew in 1993 pointed out critical shortcomings in coastal construction standards, including the lack of impact-resistant windows designed to keep wind and water from compromising buildings' structural integrity. As a result, the south Florida counties of Dade and Broward revised their building codes to include compliance with strict impact-testing certifications. EFCO Corporation has fulfilled these and other stringent standards with a variety of products, including the recently introduced Impact Grade line of premium windows.

Throughout the 1990s, EFCO continued producing custom fenestration products based on a philosophy of quality, value and timeliness, achieving MRP II, Class A certification from the Oliver Wight Corporation in 1994 and breaking the $100-million sales barrier in 1995. Meanwhile, the company added another 50,000 square feet of space to the Monett plant to accommodate a new 2,500-ton, 8-inch

extrusion press, added silicon gasket curtain wall (now known as E-Wall) to the product line, and added three new plants: service and distribution facilities in Verona, Virginia; Dallas/Fort Worth, Texas; and the new 220,000-

Stuyvesant Town and Peter Cooper Village in New York City, the world's largest window replacement project in 1992, consisting of 58,416 window units.

square-foot manufacturing plant in Barnwell, South Carolina, which was awarded ISO 9002:1994 certification in 1999.

The new century continues to offer challenges and opportunities. In 2000 sales broke $200 million. In 2001 EFCO purchased two CNC-controlled machining centers for storefront and window production and achieved ISO 9001:1994 certification for the Monett facilities. The 2002 introduction of Impact Grade products demonstrated the company's continuing dedication to innovative design and execution.

Over the years, EFCO Corporation has worked to be not only a strong, successful company helping provide livelihood's for more than 1,800 families, but a helpful partner for its own communities and other worthwhile organizations that benefited from EFCO's assistance. EFCO has donated windows to the Monett Schools, Southwest Missouri State Uni-

EFCO Products Company started manufacturing of a louver type jalousie window to be used in the home-improvement market. Window products were sold under the brand name "Holiday."

versity, the University of Missouri, the local hospital, Monett City Hall and other public buildings. The company has also donated funds for scholarships to the local high school; the architectural schools at Drury University; the Universities of Arkansas, Kansas, Kentucky, and Clemson; and the engineering programs at Washington University. EFCO annually provides funds to numerous civic organizations in Monett and the surrounding towns. The city of Monett was instrumental in providing EFCO resources, people and a home. Four decades later the partnership between EFCO and Monett is as strong as ever.

Since George Eberle sold his stock and left the company in 1962, EFCO Corporation has been held by the Fuldner family—with three generations now involved in the company's operations. Founder Terry Fuldner, honored as "Small Businessman of the Year" by President Ronald Reagan in 1984 and inducted into the Glass Hall of Fame in 1997, retired from the company in 1999, handing over the functions of chairman of the board and CEO to Chris Fuldner. Chris has since been chosen as the chairman of the board of the American Architectural Manufacturers Association, the window and door industry's trade association.

In 2003 EFCO Corporation celebrates 50 years of providing solutions for a host of fenestration design and construction challenges. From its humble beginnings as the two-man shop in the laundry basement, the company has grown to 1,800 employees in two manufacturing plants and three service centers, with facilities totaling 901,000 square feet—an organization that pumps about $60 million annually back into the community's economy through payroll, purchasing, local taxes, local and national charitable donations, sponsorships and more. With its cornerstone beliefs in value and integrity, EFCO Corporation's outlook epitomizes the confidence that comes from decades of living up to a higher standard.

EFCO Corporation Project: Lincoln Triangle, New York City, New York.

FAULTLESS STARCH/BON AMI COMPANY

For more than a century, four generations of Kansas City's Beaham family have guided the Faultless Starch/Bon Ami Company in taking the wrinkles out of household activities.

In 1886 Major Thomas G. Beaham relocated from his native Zanesville, Ohio, to Kansas City, Missouri, in search of new business opportunities. Beaham soon became a partner in Smith & Moffit, producers of coffee, tea and spices, and the name was changed to Beaham & Moffit. Beaham, recognizing a potential success, purchased the formula for Faultless Starch from Bosworth Manufacturing Company also in 1886.

In the 1880s, laundry was still a sticky business for many housewives—the all-natural fiber clothes of the day required

Major Thomas Beaham.

starch, which in turn required a lengthy boiling process. Major Beaham introduced the first convenient commercial starch proclaiming, "No cooking, just add water!" in his advertisements.

The product quickly became a success and a household staple in the Midwest and Southwest. In 1891 Beaham bought out his partner, and Beaham & Moffit became the Faultless Starch Company. It was incorporated in 1902, one year after Gordon T. Beaham, Major Beaham's son, joined the business.

Gordon and Nancy Beaham.

The product increased in popularity, due in part to its diversity, discovered by creative housewives. Alternative uses for Faultless Starch included adding a crisp finish to decorative needlework, treating skin irritations and as both a baby powder and bath powder.

In a very progressive marketing effort in the 1880s, Faultless Starch began publishing small books, intended to serve as a substitute or supplement to school texts and primers. John Nesbitt, a salesman in the Texas and Indian Territory, attached a free book with a simple rubber band to each box of Faultless Starch sold. As there

were 36 books published, customer loyalty was established, and Major Beaham's company grew.

The Faultless Starch Library, which was published into the 1930s, included childhood staples like *Hansel and Gretel* and *the Owl and the Pussycat*. Many people in the area learned to read through these small paperback books, which today are collector's items.

The company found great success as a leading manufacturer of dry laundry starch for more than 70 years. As time progressed, the need for even more convenient products grew, and Faultless Starch had the vision to move ahead with its line.

In 1960 Gordon T. Beaham III joined the company as director of research and development. That same year, the family business purchased Reddi Starch and also partnered with Arthur D. Little, Inc. The partnership resulted in the development of high-quality aerosol starch.

The addition of the high-speed aerosol line was a great success, and led to more diversity for the company. Soon

David Beaham, center, with two business friends.

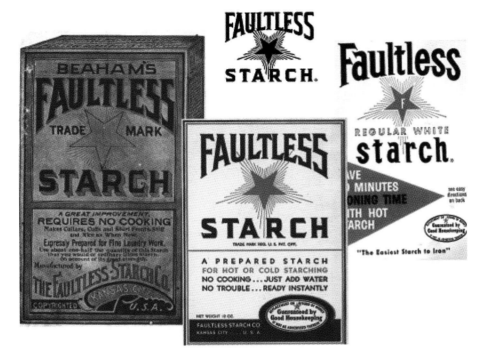

The Faultless Starch box has evolved through the decades of its history.

after, Faultless Spray-On Starch was added, followed by Faultless Fabric Finish in 1964, Faultless Hot Iron Cleaner in 1965 and Faultless Spray Pre-Wash in 1968.

The total aerosol starch category was among the top-ten fastest growing categories in the nation's supermarkets for three years in the 1960s, due in part to Faultless Starch's pioneering of the 22-ounce aerosol can.

The period of the 1960s was a decade of great change, and Faultless Starch was no exception to experiencing current trends. In 1962 the company embarked on selling its products internationally through U.S. commissaries and exchanges. In 1964 the company began distributing to commercial laundries.

International sales have been a strong part of the business. In 1962 Faultless began working with the Blattmann Company in Switzerland, and in 1964 it began producing Hoffman's Spray Starch, a market leader for Hoffman's Starkefabriken AG in Bad Salzuflen, Germany. The company also assisted in introducing the Remy brand spray starch and fabric finish to Belgium and France.

Spray starch was becoming a top laundry product choice; however, so were the new man-made fabrics that were becoming available in the 1970s. Promising easier care, synthetic fabrics brought with it a decline in the starch and fabric finish market. In 1976, the company began to see an increase in sales. The cost to produce petroleum-based fabrics rose, and consumers found natural fabrics to be softer and more comfortable, particularly in warmer climates.

In 1968 Faultless starch made its first major acquisition by purchasing the Kleen King Company and its line of metal cleaning products. The Kleen King line is one of the leaders in the consumer metal cleaning products category.

The next step was acquiring the Bon Ami Company in 1971. Bon Ami also shared a long and profitable history in the household goods market. Established in 1886, just one year before Faultless Starch opened its doors, the Manchester, Connecticut-based company's producer was manufactured by J.T. Robertson Soap Company.

Bon Ami polishing soap was known as a superior cleaning product because of its mild abrasive content. It was also known for its catchy packaging and advertising approach featuring bright red and yellow colors, a new-born fluffy chick and the slogan "Hasn't Scratched Yet!"

In 1974 Faultless Starch added the Bon Ami name to its own, becoming the Faultless Starch/Bon Ami Company. Gordon T. Beaham III, who was then serving as executive vide president, anticipated a movement towards nostalgia. He stated, "We live in a time, I believe, when many 'old fashioned' reliable products are about to become new products and products of the future."

The company, following Gordon Beaham III's vision, embarked on a new advertising campaign, promoting Bon Ami with a clever slogan: "Never underestimate the cleaning power of a 94-year old chick with a French name." The witty approach gained not just attention, but sales. Within six months, Bon Ami sales had increased 12 percent.

Acquisitions Bon Ami® and Kleen King®.

Having a proven history of providing better solutions to household tasks, the Faultless Starch/Bon Ami Company embarked on expanding its product line, but this time outside of laundry products and cleansers. In 1976 the company branched into the gardening business. Faultless Starch/Bon Ami purchased exclusive rights in the United States to the Garden-Weasel, through a partnership with the Gebr.vom Braucke Company, of Bielefeld, Germany.

Between 1979 and 1981, the Garden-Weasel was the top-selling spring TV item of all the products sold through chain drug stores. The company has sold millions of Garden-Weasels and continues to sell this popular German garden tool through various hardware distributors.

The company experienced great success with the Garden-Weasel and in the 1990s developed the opportunity to offer similar imported and domestically produced items. They soon introduced the Weed Popper, the Hoe-Down, ThatchMaster and the Garden Claw.

Faultless Starch/Bon Ami has continued a successful partnership with Gebr.vom Braucke Company for more

than 25 years. Together they have also successfully manufactured and distributed the Ruxxac folding material cart, which can transport up to 300 pounds, yet folds down to only a mere few inches wide. These two family-owned companies continue to operate together on nothing more than a handshake deal.

Overall growth continued for the company as it acquired one of its competitors, the Magic line of aerosol sizing and fabric finishes in 1997.

The same year, the company entered the home and gift market with its addition of the Trapp Private Garden line. Created by Robert Trapp, a Midwest botanical, floral, fragrance and interior-decorating expert, the line of premium aroma candles and room sprays have added a new dimension to the company's portfolio.

The company has an exciting future as well as a rich history. Faultless Starch/ Bon Ami has remained in Kansas City through the many decades and many

Trapp's Private Gardens Candles.

changes. The original facility was damaged beyond use during the flood of 1903. It was rebuilt in the West Bottoms area.

Through success and growth, the company required more space, so the plant was expanded on West Eighth Street. Another growth phase brought about the 1968 purchase of the New England Building, which coincidentally was built the same year Faultless was founded. The offices were then moved to Ninth and Wyandotte Streets in 1978.

Although Faultless had grown to be an international company at this point, exporting to Europe, Central and South America, the Caribbean and the Near and Far East, the Beaham family decided to keep the company's headquarters in its original hometown. In 1991 the offices relocated to its current location in the River Market district of Kansas City. The company maintains its manufacturing plants located in Kansas City on 8th Street.

Faultless Starch/Bon Ami is proud to be a privately held family business. And the employees are part of the family as well. Several employees have 20-plus years of tenure in a satisfying career at

The company's 1903 plant with 1967 additions.

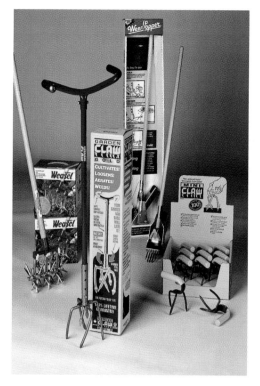

The Garden Weasel, left, and the Garden Claw.

The Weed Popper®.

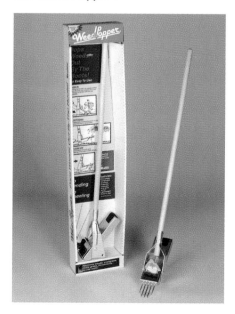

the company. Staff members earn competitive wages and benefits. And of the most remarkable perks, every employee is paid double-time for vacation. The company's philosophy is that the additional pay will allow employees to relax and enjoy time off, returning refreshed as well as productive.

Gordon Beaham III now holds the position of chairman of the board. Like his father and grandfather, he is a graduate of Princeton University, and he holds a master's degree in business administration from Harvard Business School. He served in the Navy from 1953 to 1956. Gordon Beaham III brought not just a lineage to the company, he had industry experience. Before joining Faultless, he worked for Proctor & Gamble Company in Kansas City as a production department manager for Lava, miniature Ivory and Zest bar soap-packing departments.

In 1954 Gordon Beaham III married Nancy Davidson. Nancy, who joined the company in 1971 to assist with the purchase of Bon Ami, currently serves as director of consumer relations.

The future of the company will undoubtedly continue to be a family affair. Two of Gordon and Nancy's four children are actively involved in the day-to-day operations of the Faultless Starch/Bon Ami Company. Son David joined the company in 1987 and is president; son Robert, who has been with the company since 1989, is vice chairman, treasurer and president of Trapp Private Gardens.

Bon Ami is currently a leader in the cleanser market, ranking as the third-best-selling powdered cleanser in the United States and retaining about five-percent share of the national cleanser business. The home and garden tool line continues to expand with

new ideas and new imports and domestically produced items.

The International Division continues to bring strength to the company through increased sales of imported hardware, gardening and specialty products. For more than 20 years, Faultless Starch/Bon Ami has sold its products worldwide and continues to work on licensing and joint-venture agreements. Faultless products can be found in 40 different countries.

The future holds great promise, with another generation of Beahams readying themselves to run the company, honoring the vision, hard work and philosophy of their great-great grandfather. This fifth generation is preparing to continue growing a private company. They are looking toward market expansion within the U.S. and globally.

Today, the company continues to thrive in an overly competitive market for consumers' loyalty. The Beaham family has established and grown a company that can not only change with the times, but make the best of them through innovative products.

The heritage of Faultless started with the invention of one product and the pursuit to make it better. From no-boil starch to carts, garden supplies and candles, the future seems to be wide open.

The Ruxxac cart fully loaded.

FIRST STATE BANK OF JOPLIN

The First State Bank of Joplin was chartered in 1925. Almost 50 years later, in 1974, Paul Buerge acquired it as part of his growing chain of local banks. Today, it is the flagship of the four banks owned by the Buerge family in Missouri and a comfortable place for thousands of area families to do business.

The story begins with a Mennonite farm family in southwest Missouri, in Jasper County. Farming is always challenging, but the depression years of the 1930s, plus the drought that gave rise to legendary stories of rich farmlands turning to a dust bowl, were especially difficult.

Frank and Annie Buerge's four sons—Robert, Marvin Eugene, Paul and Orville—were born between 1914 and 1927. They worked in the fields beside their parents. Marvin Eugene, Paul and Robert completed only eighth grade, while Orville finished high school. The two elder sons married and worked their own land.

In the late 1930s Frank was injured in a farming accident and Paul took on the care of his parents and youngest brother. World War II came, and the sons, working in an occupation essential to the war effort, held deferments that kept them in the fields.

The return for this hard work, however, was meager, and after several years of frustration, Paul and his wife, Margaret,

Left to right: Orville, Paul, Marvin Eugene and Robert Buerge.

Paul Buerge.

decided to move 90 miles north, to Cass County, which had been blessed with more rain and rich land on which crops grew aplenty. In 1946 they settled near the Sycamore Grove Mennonite Church. Paul's parents and brothers followed to the area north of Garden City.

Paul's discipline and intelligence offset his lack of formal education as he found avenues and skills to lead his family to success and community leadership.

Settled onto their new farm, Paul decided to pursue a new venture: Selling anhydrous ammonia, a fertilizer. He and Orville sold this new product to local farmers and applied it to their cornfields. Their first location, in East Lynn, was little more than some signs and storage. Two years later, in 1948, they moved operations to Harrisonville, the Cass County seat. Their quarters were still unimpressive but effective—a phone in a wooden box nailed to the trunk of a tree with sacks of fertilizer under a tarp near a railroad siding.

This humble entry into the retail agri-service

business soon expanded to other locations. In 1950 Buerge Bros. bought the Belton Missouri Grain Company. Paul managed this new facility, which included a grain elevator, while Orville ran things in Harrisonville.

Next, Paul and Orville bought grain elevators in Adrian and Archie. In 1958 they sold Belton to Robert, their eldest brother, and his son, Frank, and in 1960 Paul, Orville and brother Gene built a new elevator in Garden City. They ran it together until 1964 when Paul and Orville sold their shares to Gene.

That same year, Paul and Orville decided to divide their business. Paul bought the grain elevator in Butler, the Bates County seat, and became a part owner in the Butler International Tractor dealership.

Throughout this time, while the agri-service operations followed U.S. Highway 71 south, the family farms also prospered. The four brothers shared the belief that hard work, determination and honesty would make them successful and they were proven correct. Father Frank and the brothers added cattle even as Paul's entrepreneurial spirit and drive led the family into a new arena.

Paul went into banking in 1965, when the Federal Deposit Insurance Corp.

Alden Buerge.

(FDIC) took control of the First National Bank of Butler (chartered 1919). Because of his extensive knowledge of agriculture and his relationships with area farmers, Paul believed he could become an effective banker.

Paul joined, for technical support, with his CPA friend John Coke, in buying the bank. It recovered from its difficulties and, in 1967, Paul bought John's share. In 1968 he began buying and establishing additional banks, a process that continued for more than 20 years.

Paul's three sons, Steven, Alden and Robin, all became part of the expansion. In 1965, Steve went away to college. Paul, hampered by his truncated formal education, began bringing home letters that needed to be written for the bank. He asked Alden for advice and Alden began helping his dad improve the quality of business correspondence.

Paul's second bank purchase, in 1968, was a small but venerable operation in Metz (chartered 1906). Two years later, he sold it to his brother, Gene, and Gene's son, Scott.

Scott became a full-time banker while Gene continued to run the Garden City elevator and manage the family farms. He went on to serve as president of the Missouri Independent Bankers Association, which represents more than 200 community banks, and as a director of the Independent Community Bankers Association of America, which represents more than 5,000 banks nationwide. Scott, an accomplished pilot with commercial and multi-engine ratings, expanded his bank

Scott Buerge.

by locating a branch in Nevada, the seat of Vernon County.

Paul, in 1970, bought the First National Bank of Clinton (1945), in the seat of Henry County. He continued to expand, moving outside of Missouri for the first time in 1972 to purchase the Security State Bank of Fort Scott, Kansas. He added the First State Bank of Joplin in 1974; the First National Bank of Jenks, Oklahoma, in 1976; and the First National Bank of Sarcoxie (1881), Missouri, in 1978.

By this time, Paul's sons had completed college and were actively into banking. Steve moved to Fort Scott in 1972 and bought the bank there from his father in 1977. He became a successful businessman and cattle rancher in Kansas. Alden moved to Clinton in 1974 and bought Paul's bank there in 1979. He also built a restaurant called "The Sirloin Steak House" and became involved in numerous commercial real estate ventures. Robin moved to Jenks in 1976 and bought the bank there. He also added cattle ranching to his activities, as he became a successful Oklahoma businessman.

In 1982 Steve and Alden joined Paul as equal partners in buying the Grand Lake Bank (1975) of Grove, Oklahoma.

Above: First State Bank in Joplin, Missouri.

Below: First National Bank, Butler, Missouri.

Justin, Trisha, Alden, Jaxon, Kathy, Aaron and Brandon.

The late 1970s and early 1980s were a difficult time to be in business. Interest rates skyrocketed to 21.5 percent, oil prices shot up, and the national economy in general and farm economy in particular suffered. Along with these general problems, the Buerges faced a more personal tragedy: In 1983, Paul was diagnosed with cancer. He died January 11, 1984.

Alden and his wife, Kathy, moved to Joplin. He, like Scott, was an active pilot and felt his skills would help him cover the territory served by the banks. His interest in and understanding of flying—he holds an Airline Transport rating, the highest certification awarded by the Federal Aviation Administration—led him to establish a national airplane financing division at the First National Bank in 1987. This niche operation, which makes general aviation loans, has benefited both the bank and many aircraft owners around the country.

Alden, like Scott, served as president of the Missouri Independent Banker's Association. He is chairman of the Marketing Committee of the Independent Community Bankers Association of America and of the Joplin Regional Airport Board of Directors. As chairman of the boards of the three banks, Alden still oversees them from his office in Joplin.

As the 1980s wound on, bankers faced continuing economic challenges. The economy improved, and the Buerge banks grew, meeting the increasing demands of their customers. Alden, his brothers and cousin believe community bankers have a vested interest in the success of their communities and must work hard to improve quality of life. They finance their customers' dreams and provide security for their savings. The dream may be to own a home, a car, a tractor, a business. In helping customers secure these goals, the banks fuel the economic engine of their communities.

In 1990 the family sold the bank in Butler. Today, a third generation of Buerges is moving into the banking world, each member instilled with the work ethic of his grandfathers. Alden and Kathy have three sons: Aaron, Justin and Brandon.

Aaron graduated from the University of Missouri with a degree in engineering and from Clemson University with an M.B.A. At Clemson, he found an interest in finance. With a pause during 2002 to be ABC television's second "bachelor" in the reality-based show, *The Bachelor*, he serves as senior vice president at a new branch, the First National Bank of Clinton, which opened in Springfield in 2002.

Justin had always been interested in the banks. An outstanding collegiate soccer player, he earned degrees from Missouri Southern State College and an M.B.A. from the University of Phoenix and is senior vice president in commercial lending, the manager of a division

at First State Bank of Joplin and part of First National Bank of Sarcoxie's management team.

Brandon has a fellowship at Washington University in St. Louis, where he is working toward a graduate degree in Mechanical Engineering.

With the exception of a restaurant, Trolley's, that Aaron started, and some real estate interests in Joplin and Clinton, the family today concentrates on banking, with an emphasis on providing outstanding customer service. It acknowledges the important role the banks' many employees have played in their success. Outstanding senior managers through the years include Elaine Paxton and Nancy Carter, who have both been at the First National Bank of Clinton for more than 30 years; Richard Beydler and Judi Cox in Sarcoxie; Allen Davis and Betty Robey in Butler; and Carl McConnell, Sharon Benford and Pat Jones in Joplin.

Currently, the Buerge banks in Missouri, including Scott's in Nevada and Metz, have total customer assets exceeding $250,000,000, 12 locations in six cities, eighteen ATMs and more than 30,000 valued customers. In an era of massive banking consolidation, the Buerge family continues to offer competitive products with local management and a personal touch. As befits an operation based in family, the Buerge banks are in the people business first.

First National Bank staff of Clinton, Missouri, in December 2002.

THE LEARNING EXCHANGE

Making education meaningful and relevant is what The Learning Exchange is all about. For the past thirty years, the groundbreaking work of this Kansas City not-for-profit agency has had an impact on students and educators across the nation. Through interactive learning programs, reform initiatives and educational consulting, The Learning Exchange continues to pave the way for "new visions of teaching and learning."

Two teachers, Mary Watkins and Gail Taylor, launched the organization in 1972 in a church basement. The first year's budget of $20,000 was contributed by area foundations. Today, The Learning Exchange is housed in a building on the Penn Valley Community College campus with a staff of 50 and an annual budget of more than $4 million.

From the beginning, The Learning Exchange has emphasized the importance of hands-on learning that takes students out of a traditional classroom setting and into a real-world environment. Two of the agency's most successful experiential programs, Exchange City and EarthWorks, are now being replicated throughout the nation.

Exchange City was developed in 1980. This eight-week curriculum teaches the

Earthworks, a 35,000-square-foot facility located in an underground limestone cave, transforms young learners into scientists at they investigate five midwestern habitats to learn key environmental science concepts. The soil habitat is pictured below.

principles of economics and entrepreneurism to fourth, fifth and sixth graders. The highlight of the course is a one-day trip to Exchange City, a simulated city where students put their knowledge into practice. Here the students govern the city, interview for jobs and manage the bank, factory, newspaper, radio station, snack shop and several other businesses. Since its inception, over 800,000 students in Kansas City have participated in the program—a successful venture that has replicated in 25 cities across the nation, serving 200,000 students annually.

Building upon the huge success of Exchange City, in 1996 the organization created EarthWorks. This award-winning environmental science program teaches third and fourth graders about midwestern habitats, animals and native plants. Students take part in a six-week course capped off with a visit to an underground laboratory in a limestone cave. Each year some 15,000 students from Kansas City area schools take part in Earthworks. Like Exchange City, the program is now being replicated in other communities.

Since the 1980s, The Learning Exchange has broadened its focus to include education reform. Through regional initiatives such as Urban Part-

Since 1980, Exchange City has given over 1 million students across the nation the opportunity to learn economics through immersive, hands-on experiences in a simulated city environment.

ners, Metropolitan Instructional Leaders Program and Great Expectations, educators have shared ideas, devised solutions to needs and transformed learning environments. The organization is also a strong advocate of the charter school movement and was instrumental in the formation of 24 charter public schools through its Charter School Partnership since 1998.

The corporation created a for-profit subsidiary called Experiencia in 2001 to establish Exchange City and EarthWorks facilities in markets outside the Kansas City area.

Most recently, The Learning Exchange created the Experience Design Group to developed customized curricula and learning experiences for schools, businesses, museums and visitor centers. The Smithsonian, American Century Investments and Ford Motor Company are among its clients.

President and CEO Tammy Blossom says the organization will continue to work on the front lines to transform education in the 21st century.

"That's the core of our mission," says Blossom. "When a majority of young people are finding their classroom activities are not applicable to the real world, we are here to make learning more meaningful and relevant."

FRANCISCAN SISTERS OF MARY

On April 30, 1823, Anna Katharina and Maria Anna, twins, were born in Bavaria to Alois and Katharina Berger. Years later, Anna Katharina would be known as Mother Odilia, founder of the Sisters of St. Mary, now known as the Franciscan Sisters of Mary. As the inspiration and pacesetter for the first congregation of Catholic sisters to be founded in St. Louis, her life's journey planted the seeds that continue to flower in her followers.

Long before devoting herself exclusively to religious life, Katharina, as she was then called, lived a simple-but-busy life with her parents and siblings. When she was four years old, her father sold his brewery in Regen and moved the family to the town of Plattling, where he took over another brewery. There the family lived in a three-story house, with a distillery on the first floor and living accommodations on the second floor. To bring in more income, Katharina's mother rented rooms to travelers on the third floor.

Life in Plattling would soon be full of trials for the Berger family. Katharina's father, who had contracted tuberculosis, began to grow weak. Katharina's mother gradually took over his work responsibilities to keep the family going. Because

As years passed, the sisters increased their knowledge and skills, developed technology and established institutions.

The heritage of faith, love and compassion of the Franciscan Sisters of Mary grew from their founder, Mary Odilia Berger, who with four companions, arrived in St. Louis from Germany in 1872.

of his illness, it was decided that 15-year-old Johanna would not return to school but would, instead, help care for her father and be in charge of renting rooms. As for the twins, they would continue their studies with the Ursuline sisters in Straubing, along with their youngest sibling, Maria. On November 13, 1832, Katharina's father died at the age of 43. Katharina was nine years old.

When she was 14 years old, Katharina took Johanna's place helping her mother rent rooms. Independent, business-minded and social, Katharina enjoyed on-the-job learning that gave her experience beyond most girls of her age.

From her early years, Katharina was attracted to religious life. Anna, her twin, had become a nun with the Institute of the Blessed Virgin Mary. Happy that her sister achieved her dream of the religious life, Katharina continued to hope that her own wish would one day come true.

As a young adult, Katharina declined two marriage proposals. In her late 20s, she thought she had finally found true love, but when she told her suitor she was carrying his child, he gave her money, suggested she move out of town, have the baby and put it up for adoption. Then he abandoned her. Disillusioned and angry, Katharina refused his money and chose to go on living right where she was. Her sister and a trusted friend helped her throughout the pregnancy. Once her condition became obvious, however, she was the subject of gossip around town, lost her job and had difficulty finding another.

Katharina gave birth to a beautiful baby girl on February 21, 1853, and named her Maria Walburga. While Katharina looked for work, the child was placed in the care of her mother. Soon, she secured a bookkeeping position. As time permitted, she would travel to see her daughter and mother. Walburga, as she was called, thought of her grandmother as her mother, and both women felt it best to let her think that way—especially since Katharina had finally made the decision to pursue her life's dream of joining a religious congregation.

On June 13, 1857, Katharina, who was now 34 years old, was officially accepted as a sister in the congregation of the Poor Franciscans of Pirmasens and given the name Sister Odilia. Dr. Paul Joseph Nardini, founder of the congregation, was understanding of Katharina, as he himself was a child born out of wedlock. He allowed Walburga to live at the Poor

In the spirit of St. Francis, the Franciscan Sisters of Mary are committed to promoting justice, peace and nonviolence.

Franciscan's orphanage when Katharina's mother was no longer able to take care of her. At the age of 10, however, Walburga died of an unknown illness.

Gifted with a sound business background, Sister Odilia was given the responsibility to collect monies for this new fledgling community to which she belonged. This ministry required frequent visits to surrounding regions and gave her the opportunity to identify the needs of women in different areas. Eventually, she and another sister traveled to Paris to help Father Victor Braun with German girls trying to make a living for their families back home. These girls were often forced into prostitution. Sister Odilia saw this situation as an opportunity, and she set about to help them. She received a dispensation from the Poor Franciscans and joined Father Braun in founding the Soeurs Servantes de Sacre Coeur de Jesus. He appointed her superior of the community and, from then on, she was known as "Mother Odilia."

Mother Odilia and the other sisters were passionate in their zeal to help persons who were poor. They often comforted the dying, attended to the sick and cared for orphans. When the Franco-Prussian war broke out in 1870, the sisters helped German girls leave Paris. At one point in this endeavor, the sisters were mistaken for German spies. On the day Paris was seized, Mother Odilia and a companion escaped to Rhineland.

During the war, the sisters nursed injured soldiers at a medical hospital. It wasn't long though, because of religious

We respect, appreciate and live in harmony with creation and direct our actions to preserve the earth. (FSM Declaration of Nonviolence)

persecution by Bismarck, before the sisters turned their eyes to America. Fearing for their safety and desiring to establish their own permanent religious community, they gladly accepted an invitation from the Wegmann family to settle in St. Louis, Missouri. In 1872 Mother Odilia and four companions came to this country, arriving in St. Louis on November 16 with $5 to their name.

Life in America, though, was far from ideal. The whole country was suffering from various epidemics—yellow fever, smallpox and cholera—plus devastating heat waves that killed people and livestock. Within that milieu, St. Louis was experiencing a raging smallpox epidemic. The sisters' arrival quickly became a blessing, as they immediately began nursing those afflicted by the disease. Through their devotion to these dangerously ill patients, they became known as the "Smallpox Sisters."

Soon, instead of living in rented rooms, they were able to build their own convent, utilizing one wall of the adjacent St. Mary of Victories Church. Seeing their close proximity to the church, the people of St. Louis began to call them Sisters of St. Mary. The name stayed.

During those early years, the sisters established themselves in the care of orphans, working girls and persons who were sick. As the need for health care increased, the sisters opened their first hospital in 1877. St. Mary's Infirmary provided care regardless of a patient's ability to pay. Account books from the 1800s identify almost 60 percent of the patients as "ODL," which stood for "Our Dear Lord's." These patients could not pay for their care. The Infirmary had a long and rich history. In 1933 it reopened as St. Mary's Infirmary for the Colored with an organized medical staff of black physicians and a school of nursing.

With characteristic generosity, the sisters responded to calls for help from the southern states during the yellow fever epidemic of 1878. Five of their 31 members died in this epidemic, a heavy toll indeed for the young congregation.

Kathleen Mary Maloney, FSM, plays with children who live with their mothers at Almost Home, an FSM-sponsored transitional living experience for teen mothers and their children who are homeless.

In 1880 Mother Odilia received the news that the congregation was acknowledged as an official religious congregation in the Roman Catholic Church, thereby allowing the sisters to profess public religious vows. Shortly after their first vow ceremonies, Mother Odilia became ill, apparently with a ruptured appendix. On October 17, 1880, at the age of 57, and 14 years to the day that she had founded her beloved Parisian Soeurs Servantes du Sacre Coeur de Jesus, Mother Odilia died.

During those early years, the sisters responded to epidemic outbreaks of smallpox, diphtheria and scarlet fever in St. Charles, Missouri. Always a significant number of sisters from their small group were sent to nurse those who were ill. By 1884 the citizens of St. Charles recognized a need for a hospital in their town. A local resident offered his home for this purpose in gratitude to the sisters who nursed his infant son through diphtheria. St. Joseph's Hospital opened in 1885 and continues today as a thriving medical center.

In 1894 Sister Mary Augustine Giesen, imbued from her novice days with the spirit of Mother Odilia and St. Francis, along with six other Sisters of St. Mary, formed a new religious congregation in northwest Missouri. They came to be known as the Sisters of St. Francis of Maryville.

Ninety-three years later, in 1987, the Sisters of St. Mary and the Sisters of St. Francis of Maryville reunited. To reflect the newness of this reunified congregation in the church, they named themselves "Franciscan Sisters of Mary" (FSM). They now proclaim their Identity and Mission in this way: "As Franciscan Sisters of Mary, we live the Gospel as sister to all. We give our life by being present, hospitable and compassionate, choosing to stand with our sisters and brothers who are poor and on the margins of society."

Today, the Franciscan Sisters of Mary, headquartered in St. Louis, sponsor SSM Health Care with health facilities in Missouri, Illinois, Wisconsin and Oklahoma. In 2002 SSM Health Care became the first health care organization to receive the Malcolm Baldrige National Quality Award—the nation's premier award for performance excellence and quality achievement. SSM Health Care, a non-profit Catholic organization, comprises 21 hospitals, three nursing homes, 5,000 physicians, 23,000 employees and 5,000 volunteers.

Besides SSM Health Care, the Franciscan Sisters of Mary also sponsor Almost Home, providing transitional housing for teenage mothers and their children who are homeless and Woman's Place, a drop-in center of hospitality for adult women who have experienced domestic violence, both located in St. Louis, Missouri; co-sponsor Holy Family Services, the country's only Catholic free-standing birthing center, in Weslaco, Texas; and The Sarah Community, a collaboration of five Catholic religious

Franciscan Sisters of Mary have had a presence in Brazil, South America, for over 30 years. Central to their choice of gospel living is extending hospitality to their sisters and brothers on the margins of society.

Jane L. Rombach, FSM, a social worker at SSM Cardinal Glennon Children's Hospital for 20 years, gives evidence in her work to the concern all Franciscan Sisters of Mary have for the plight of women and children.

congregations of women providing a continuum of care for their members and the general public, in Bridgeton, Missouri. Individual sisters, who are health professionals, pastoral care providers, social workers, massage therapists, authors and artists, continue to be active in Wisconsin, South Carolina, Missouri, Oklahoma, Illinois, Arizona, Ohio, Texas and Brazil.

As pioneers in a new country, Mother Odilia and the members of her sisterhood had no idea how vast their influence would be. Over the years, their health care services included the following Missouri locations: Hannibal, Marceline, Maryville, Kansas City, Jefferson City, Blue Springs, St. Louis, Pilot Knob, Ironton, Chillicothe and Moberly. SSM Cardinal Glennon Children's Hospital in St. Louis, Missouri, is the only Catholic children's hospital in the nation.

Following in the footsteps of their courageous and compassionate leader, many sisters, through the ensuing years, have made significant contributions to health care and humanity in general. To name a few: Sister Mary Francis McRory, the first sister registered in the Midwest as a medical technologist, and who, in

1910 worked with Dr. Louis Rassieur to establish one of the first organized laboratories in the United States; Sister Mary Beatrice Merrigan, the first certified x-ray technician in the United States and Canada; Sister Mary Philomena Peters, a 1920s licensed engineer, who was in charge of the engineering and maintenance department at St. Anthony Hospital in Oklahoma City for 47 years; Mother Mary Concordia Puppendahl, a founder of the Catholic Health Association, who became a national influence in health care and established schools of nursing and allied health professions; Sister Mary Servatia Risse, awarded the first degree in medical records science in

1938 by Saint Louis University; Sister Mary Celeste Nix, a noted laundry manager who wrote a book about scientific laundry service for hospitals; Sister Mary Geraldine Kulleck, a consultant to the Bureau of Medicine for the Army and Navy; Sister Antona Ebo, an African American participating in the March to Selma with Martin Luther King, Jr.; Sister Betty Brucker, initiator of services for the HIV/AIDS population; Sister Leo Rita Volk, genetic researcher whose research contributed to the discovery of chromosome abnormalities that predispose a person for developing cancer; Sister Agnita Claire Day, whose work in neurophysical research affecting postural reflexes contributed to the Gemini Space Program's understanding of weightlessness; she also was a consultant to the St. Louis Cardinals baseball team in 1966, helping the players develop corrective exercises to improve their swing. The following year, they won the World Series.

Today, the Franciscan Sisters of Mary continue to work towards the betterment of humanity through leadership in health care and social ministries—and in promoting nonviolence, healing and hope.

Like all Franciscan Sisters of Mary, the ministry of Eleanor Krieg, FSM, at Mercy Hospice of Horry County, Myrtle Beach, South Carolina, expresses compassion and healing.

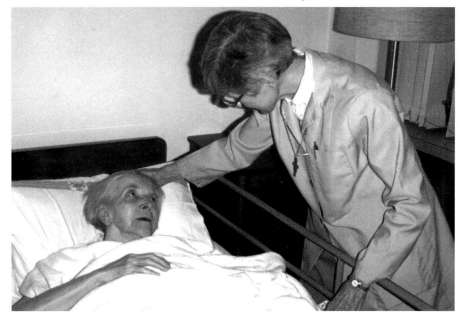

JOPLIN BUILDING MATERIAL COMPANY

Two young energetic brothers-in-law, working for the same building material company since 1954, decided to venture out on their own when the company sold. Dale Lundstrom and John R. Goostree gave their two-weeks notice, but the new owner handed them checks for a two-week vacation instead. They cleaned out their desks and started to leave, then realized they had driven company cars to work and needed rides home.

Although both had immediate job offers elsewhere, they were determined to go into business for themselves—in the business they knew, building materials, in the town they knew, Joplin. With nine years of experience under their belts, they struck out on their own with a company name, an old desk and a coffeepot. On April 15, 1963, Joplin Building Material Company opened its doors in a small Quonset hut beside the Kansas City Southern Railroad tracks with nothing to sell but their philosophy—"Business should be based on quality, service, fairness and friendliness." They also had one employee, Onie Wisdom. He'd promised to be their first employee, whether he got

Dale Lundstrom on the left and John R. Goostree in 1963.

paid or not, as long as they had a coffeepot. That's when business began; Onie was a volunteer, and the coffee was perking.

The firm's first sales line was aluminum windows, storm sashes and garage doors. They hustled to add suppliers to

their list: Ash Grove Cement, Dickie Clay, USG Plaster and Owens Corning Fiberglass, among others. When the opportunity arose to represent a brick company, Lundstrom recalls that the partners believed it was not a good business to become involved in. Money wasn't readily available, and they'd have to borrow funds to buy a forklift, a truck with a boom unloader and put in a railroad spur. The partners argued the pros and cons for two weeks. At one time one would be in favor, with the other against, and vice versa. Onie Wisdom listened to these confrontations and one morning presented Lundstrom and Goostree with an article from *Reader's Digest* that said if two partners always agreed, then one wasn't needed.

"You two must be the most needed partners there ever was," Onie said.

To settle the matter, the partners decided to take their proposal to the bank. (Small business loans were not prevalent in those days.) If they got the loan, they'd go into the brick business. Goostree met with a banker. When he came back to the office, Lundstrom asked if the banker had said "yes" or "no." Goostree replied that he'd never said either one, just, "When do you want the money?"

So Joplin Building Material (JBM) went into the brick business, but not without mishap. The area where the bricks were stocked was over an old mine drift, and on one occasion the owners and employees watched helplessly as 18,000 bricks disappeared into a hole in the ground. Seventy-five truckloads of fill were required to close the hole.

The partners incorporated in 1965 and dealt primarily in hard building materials: brick, cement, sand, lime, flue lining, fireplace units and accessories. The next expansion involved Redi-Mix Concrete, which required land and more financing. After inspecting a plant in Springfield that was closing, the pair purchased the

Aerial photo of Joplin Building Materials at 15th and Illinois, Joplin, Missouri.

plant equipment and relocated it in Joplin. Lundstrom reflected that in 15 minutes they had spent $100,000. "Not bad for a couple of old country boys," Lundstrom recalled, "but a bit frightening."

The company grew, fueled by many hours the partners dedicated to their work. Along the way, they vowed to contribute to the community that had helped their business prosper. Goostree joined Rotary, and Lundstrom joined Kiwanis. They volunteered time for club projects, and JBM provided a home for Kiwanis Apple Sales, with JBM employees spending countless hours unloading and handling apples. JBM became a stalwart supporter of the United Way Fund.

Business ventures included purchasing the old IGA Warehouse and incorporating the Joplin Warehouse Company, a 120,000-square-foot, five-story storage facility. In 1972 they purchased the Con-

crete Masonry Products Company in Joplin and in 1978 bought the Alexander Block and Building Material Company in Baxter Springs, Kansas. JBM began to concentrate on making and selling concrete blocks, establishing and maintaining a reputation for excellence.

With the death of John Goostree in 1983, Dale Lundstrom became the sole owner, purchasing Goostree's interest in JBM. The company acquired its present location at 15th and Illinois Avenue, and all operations were consolidated at one location. The Redi-Mix plant was sold, and the company focused with great success on masonry components.

Contrary to Lundstrom's first impression years earlier, the brick business was a good business, and in 1998, the company opened Springfield Brick Company in Springfield. In 2000 a million-dollar modernization project at JBM upgraded machinery and automated methods of producing concrete masonry products.

Community involvement continued through the years. JBM donated material for every new Habitat for Humanity project in the Joplin area. Materials were also donated to Boy Scouts, Girl Scouts, Little Leagues, college and high school athletic programs, technical schools for student instruction and others. The business has made financial contributions to many worthy causes in the community—

from a safe house for battered women to the free community clinic.

Looking to the future, JBM employs second-generation family members. Lundstrom's sons-in-law, Troy Richards and Larry Shumaker, are instrumental in the business. One of the few family-owned and family-operated concrete masonry producers in existence, JBM serves Joplin and the surrounding area with a full line of masonry products. JBM manufactures and distributes over 2 million concrete masonry units each year and sells and distributes over 6 million bricks annually.

What has made Joplin Building Material Company such a success story? Was it the dream of two young men who set out with a philosophy of quality, service, fairness and friendliness? Was it the principle that every customer is treated the same, no matter the size of the sale— or was it the coffeepot? The reason for the success of this small business may never be known, but one thing is for sure: Joplin Building Material Company remembers that it is the customer who signs the paycheck.

Stop by anytime; the coffeepot is always on.

Block plant operations in 2003.

KING COMMERCIAL, INC.

Citizens of St. Louis, Missouri, looking to lease a Hummer limousine or a 1957 Rolls Royce need look no further than King Commercial, Inc. This equipment leasing company has handled such exotica in its day, along with the more mundane items that constitute company transactions: high-tech equipment, manufacturing and medical equipment, office furniture, computer software and hardware and, in some cases, ambulances, aircraft and street-cleaning equipment for municipalities.

Dave Heyl, president, chief executive officer and 50 percent owner of King Commercial, teamed up with John King in 1987 to create the leasing concern. King, a native of St. Louis, served in both the military and private industry before creating his own leasing company. The founder and chairman of the board of King Commercial, he brought to the firm an extensive sales experience in insurance and real estate, as well as stints with Chevrolet and with Pillsbury. King's curriculum vitae also included stock-broking experience. Heyl, a 1982 graduate of Central Missouri State University in Warrensburg, also brought impressive credentials to the firm. These included a background in banking and experience, like King, running his own leasing company.

The two originators of King Commercial first met professionally, when Heyl,

King Commercial co-founders, John King and Dave Heyl (standing), with Assistant V.P. Jane Kohler and Executive V.P. Scott Hawkins (seated). Courtesy, Mark Buckner

employed by Landmark Bank in St. Louis, counted J.W. King Associates as one of his banking customers. Heyl left banking in 1984 to work for a competitor of King's before forming his own leasing company. The two men joined up in June 1987 and have worked together closely since that time. "He's like a father to us," Heyl said, noting also that King's integrity and strong sense of ethics provided the basis on which the new company was built.

A small space on Hampton Avenue in south St. Louis housed the firm's first

offices. Two phone lines and a part-time secretary provided administrative backup. The fledgling company generated revenues in 1987 of $240,000 with this slim support network. By the year 2000, company revenues were approaching the $20 million mark. Scott Hawkins, who serves as the firm's executive vice president, director of marketing and sales manager, signed on in 1988 as the company's first sales representative. Ten years later he bought into the firm as 50 percent owner, matching Heyl's ownership interest. Hawkins brought over ten years of valuable sales experience to the firm. Jane Kohler, a graduate of Benedictine College, serves as the company's assistant vice president.

King Commercial's role over the years has evolved into that of financier for its vendors. Although it sometimes contracts directly with clients, it primarily represents the third link in the lending chain, providing financing to clients who contract directly with equipment sales companies for their purchases. Toward that end, the company has devoted much of the past decade to the acquisition of funds to meet customers' financing needs. Its relationships with the St. Louis banking community have proved invaluable in this regard, helping the firm to meet its goal of supplying clients with the best possible financing alternatives.

King Commercial, centrally located within the United States, efficiently serves all 50 states, but emphasis in recent years is more toward regional development. Heyl notes that the company has "pulled in its horns" to focus primarily on the Midwestern states, noting that it's easier to "kick the tires" within a smaller geographical area where salespeople are familiar with the areas they are covering. The company finances every imaginable type of new and used equipment, from $5,000 items to $1 million plus trans-

Despite a gleaming modern skyline, St. Louis remains a city firmly connected to its roots in the mighty Mississippi, home to the renovated *Robert E. Lee* paddlewheeler. Courtesy, Mark Buckner

actions. Its leasing contracts can also include such expenses as insurance, freight, installation, maintenance and taxes, items that may be excluded from other firm's leasing arrangements. Additional benefits of leasing vs. buying include preservation of capital, tax advantages and the provision of hedges against inflation and obsolescence.

King Commercial's staff provides excellent service to its clients, who range from individuals to small businesses, vendors, municipalities and Fortune 1000 companies. Municipal and government agencies enjoy the benefit of low municipal interest rates on their transactions. With the advent of current e-business transactions, eligible clients can now be approved for service within a matter of minutes, allowing them to receive equipment and services as quickly as possible.

The completely renovated *Robert E. Lee Riverboat* is once again a jewel of the St. Louis riverfront and represents a new venture for Heyl and Hawkins of King Commercial. Courtesy, Mark Buckner

A number of King Commercial's vendors take advantage of e-commerce by offering sales service over the Internet. These websites are designed for use online at the point of sale and provide for preparation of proposals, input of credit information, retrieval of credit decisions and printing of contracts. This "online, real time leasing and financing program" represents cutting-edge technology in sales methods.

In August 1999 the company moved to its present location at 10024 Office Center Avenue in South St. Louis County. Although its focus during the nineties was on the St. Louis market, plans for the future include a greater emphasis on doing business in Illinois. Heyl and Hawkins also see growth at a steady pace as a desirable aim. Local banks have made bids for the successful St. Louis concern, but the

King Commercial's offices are centrally located in suburban St. Louis. Courtesy, Mark Buckner

company officers have not found them sufficiently attractive.

Business may be branching out to other states, but Heyl's and Hawkins' interests remain firmly entrenched in St. Louis. "It's home," Heyl said of the area. He discussed the entrepreneurs' latest project, which represents a radical departure from the world of finance. In 1999 Heyl and Hawkins, in conjunction with the Downtown St. Louis Development Corporation, took on the renovation of the *Lt. Robert E. Lee,* a replica of a steamboat dating from earlier days. The four St. Louis businessmen involved in the project spent more than $1 million for renovations to this bit of St. Louis history, which was originally built in the late 1960s from an old U.S. Army Corps of Engineers boat. Built as a riverfront restaurant, the steamboat was named for the Confederate General who served as a young man in St. Louis with the Army Corps of Engineers. Success appears to be following this venture as well: the *Robert E. Lee* opened as a restaurant in May 2003, and business is doing well.

LEWIS AND CLARK IN MISSOURI

In 1804, when Meriwether Lewis and William Clark journeyed through what is today Missouri, they frequently recorded their impressions of the land and its features. The landscape and the Missouri River left an indelible mark on Lewis and Clark and their Corps of Discovery. Today's explorers can still see the many features mentioned in the expedition's journal and visit facilities that commemorate this momentous event in the state's and nation's history.

The Lewis and Clark Expedition spent a total of 103 days in what is now Missouri. The expedition began to ascend the Mississippi River on November 20, 1803, and arrived at Wood River, opposite the mouth of the Missouri River, on December 12, 1803. On May 14, 1804, the crew entered the Missouri River at St. Charles to begin the journey westward.

The time they spent in Missouri would prove to be a training ground in many ways. The 45-member crew included men from many cultures and backgrounds. While most were young soldiers, the group also included interpreters of French-Shawnee parentage, French

This sculpture of figures from the Lewis and Clark Expedition can be seen at Lewis and Clark Point in Case Park in Kansas City.

boatmen, several of whom had French fathers and mothers from the tribes of the upper Missouri, and Clark's black slave, York. The young crew had to battle the swift and dangerous currents of the Missouri River. By the time they left Missouri on July 18, 1804, the men of the expedition were an efficient and motivated team united behind the common goal of reaching the Pacific Ocean.

The Corps of Discovery's journey within Missouri was well documented. There are numerous journal references about everything from the "beautiful and pleasing landscape" to "a respectable Indian" wanting to buy Lewis' dog, Seaman, and tales of almost losing the keelboat in the swift currents.

Once the expedition returned to St. Charles on September 23, 1806, Lewis and Clark went on to help create the future state of Missouri. Lewis served as territorial governor until his death in 1809. Clark spent a long life in St. Louis, always playing a key role in Missouri's growth and development. He served as general of militia, territorial governor and finally as U.S. Indian agent for the Missouri River. He died in 1838 and is buried in Bellefontaine Cemetery in St. Louis.

For today's explorers, there are numer-

The Discovery Expedition of St. Charles uses replicas and reenactments to tell the story of Lewis and Clark.

ous ways to follow in the footsteps of Lewis and Clark. The Lewis and Clark National Historic Trail has been designated by the National Park Service. In Missouri, the trail follows state highways on both north and south sides of the Missouri River. The North Trail begins in West Alton, Missouri, on Missouri Route 94, and the South Trail begins on U.S. Route 40 near the Jefferson National Expansion Memorial (the Arch) in downtown St. Louis.

For those who want to get closer to the trail than a highway, Katy Trail State Park offers another way to follow the river. Operated by the Missouri Department of Natural Resources, the walking and bicycling trail is the longest non-motorized segment of the Lewis and Clark National Historic Trail. For more than 150 miles, the Katy Trail etches its way along the Missouri River, tracing the route of the explorers.

To showcase the many areas and facilities in Missouri related to the Lewis and Clark Expedition, 90 interpretive markers have been developed at publicly accessible locations along the Missouri and Mississippi rivers. Developed in cooperation with the Missouri Lewis and Clark Bicentennial Commission, the Missouri Department of Natural Resources, the Missouri Department of Conservation and the Missouri Department of Transportation, the signs are placed on state and local properties to provide information about relevant Lewis and Clark sites such as campsites or features mentioned in the journal. These range from Tower Rock in southeast Missouri, where they described a whirlpool as "immense and dangerous," to the oxbow lake where they spent July 4, 1804, and is today preserved in Lewis and Clark State Park in northwest Missouri.

For any person wanting the Lewis and Clark experience, there are several key sites that should not be missed. A good place to begin is the Jefferson National Expansion Memorial in St. Louis for exhibits that give perspective on the westward expansion. Also in St. Louis is the Missouri Historical Society, where visitors can see hundreds of rare and priceless artifacts and documents and view an exhibit that tells the story of the expedition.

In nearby St. Charles, visitors can see full-size replicas of the keelboat and pirogues used in the expedition at a

The new state park at the confluence of the Missouri and Mississippi Rivers near St. Louis will interpret the Lewis and Clark Expedition.

boathouse/interpretive center. Here, the Discovery Expedition of St. Charles relives this historic time.

Nearby is the confluence of the Mississippi and Missouri rivers. This area is preserved in the Edward "Ted" and Pat Jones-Confluence Point State Park, which provides interpretation on Lewis and Clark. On the other side of the Missouri River is Columbia Bottoms Conservation Area, where an overlook provides a view of these two mighty rivers joining.

At Clark's Hill/Norton State Historic Site in Cole County, visitors today can stand atop the same hill that Clark did in 1804 when he viewed the confluence of the Missouri and Osage Rivers.

Bluffs along the Missouri River overlook Katy Trail State Park, which is the longest non-motorized segment of the Lewis and Clark National Historic Trail.

Farther upriver, the expedition members spotted a hill they thought would offer a commanding location for a fort. In 1808, Clark returned to the site to build Fort Osage. Today, tours of this reconstructed fort in Jackson County are offered to visitors.

When the expedition came to the mouth of the Kansas River, they camped above the future site of Kansas City. A hill that Clark climbed is now known as Lewis and Clark Point in Case Park. A sculpture in this park stands as a tribute to the Corps of Discovery.

In addition to journal notations about St. Michael's Prairie where St. Joseph was later founded, the St. Joseph area today contains many links to the opening of the West, including the Pony Express.

The impact of the Lewis and Clark Expedition on Missouri and the nation is undeniable. For today's explorers, there are many ways to follow in their footsteps and experience this part of history.

For more information on Lewis and Clark in Missouri, visit the website at www.lewisandclarkmo.com or call the Missouri Department of Natural Resources.

MIDWEST HAULING

There are many father-and-son stories in the trucking industry, but stories of mothers who have tried this difficult field—let alone been successful—are rare. Midwest Hauling is that rarity: The tale of a woman who has built a strong business in a tough industry and has the good fortune to be passing it on to her daughter.

Rebecca Johnson was born in St. Louis. Just after World War II, her parents moved outside the city, to Overland, where she and her older sister, Pat, grew up. Her father worked for Sears automotive, one of the few union salesmen working for the company in St. Louis. Her mother was a housewife. Rebecca was a tomboy, active in sports.

When Rebecca graduated from high school in 1960, she went to work at the L.J. Ross lumber company in Overland. She was a "Girl Friday," handling all the odds and ends that needed to be done. Ross, a commercial lumberyard, sold to contractors, and Rebecca answered phones, did the books and took orders. She also married that year.

It was as order taker that Rebecca's inquisitive mind and eagerness to learn stood her best. A hard worker who never missed a day in nine years with Ross, she learned the yard's inventory, every knot and grain. She spoke with the contractors, asking about their businesses and absorbing a wealth of details that would serve her well in the years ahead.

In 1969 Rebecca became pregnant and had to leave her job. Her daughter, Mary

Rebecca's very first brand new rock truck purchased in 1985, pictured with her daughter, Christine, and her nephew, Don, in the driver's seat.

Rebecca and Christine Johnson in 2002, at the time of Rebecca's 60th birthday.

Christine, was born in October and a few months later Rebecca was back at work. Her new boss was a salesman she had worked with at Ross who had gone out on his own as a contractor. He built apartments and homes, and Rebecca handled general office responsibilities, including hiring managers for the apartment buildings.

In 1972, newly divorced, she and Chris moved into one of his buildings, where she forged a long-term friendship with Barbara Burton, the woman she had hired to manage it. Chris and Barbara's oldest daughter, nine-year-old Dawn, became close friends. This lasted over the years and, in 2000, Dawn went to work as a valued secretary for Midwest Hauling.

In 1974 Rebecca went looking for a parcel in south St. Louis county on which to build her dream home, complete with a white picket fence and a barn. The property she found was too expensive for her, so she showed it to her boss, who bought it to develop. She watched him work and, realizing the value of the land

as an investment, when she found an adjacent 19-acre plot, she bought it herself and used the opportunity to go out on her own.

Rebecca had the parcel surveyed, divided it into lots, contracted for infrastructure—sewers, streets, water—and sold it to a builder who put up houses. During the mid-1970s, Rebecca also built and sold three homes—one at a profit, one at break even and the third at a loss.

These activities gave her practical experience to go with the knowledge she'd garnered with her questions, and the profit from her 19 acres gave her funds to start her own business.

Another opportunity came in a casual conversation with a close friend, an expert in concrete flatwork—foundations, sidewalks, streets, etc. They agreed to join his expertise with her connections, money and business sense and formed a partnership that would last into the early 1980s. At the end of that time, her partner offered to buy her out. This left Rebecca free to build her trucking company, Midwest Hauling.

Rebecca in 2003 standing next to a few trucks in the fleet.

She had started Midwest in 1980 with the purchase of her first dump truck. By 1984 she had 28 trucks and more than 30 employees: 28 drivers, a mechanic, tireman, secretary and herself. Her number one driver was the older of her nephews, Donald Frey, and the tireman was his brother, David. David also became a driver. Both stayed with her for many years. Today, Donald drives for J. H. Berra Construction Company, one of Midwest's major clients, and David works for Central Stone Company, a quarry that was once part of Berra and is still one of Midwest's sources for materials.

In 1985 Midwest bought its first new dump trucks, four Fords, but then the industry ran into trouble. Insurance costs climbed and conditions tightened, so when one of Rebecca's customers offered to buy her out, she agreed. He, however, ran into the same kinds of problems, and, after 2-1/2 years, she bought back her business, by then down to only four trucks. She hired Randy Hackworth as a driver and, shortly, promoted him to superintendent, the post he still holds. Chris, then in high school, had worked a couple of part-time jobs after school and began helping out at Midwest, doing the payroll and other bookkeeping.

With Chris involved, Rebecca had another reason to make her business the best it could be. Driven by her innate curiosity, her willingness to work hard and her abiding insistence on quality service, Midwest Hauling prospered. The fine details she learned at Ross enabled her to understand the needs of her clients and give them the best possible service. While Rebecca dipped into a variety of other ventures, including developing a few parcels of land when they presented themselves, she never lost focus on her primary goal.

Rebecca focused early on delivering exemplary service, even if that meant taking on fewer projects. She was, and remains, a stern taskmaster, insisting on "keeping a hammer on the men" and never tolerating carelessness or incompetence. Yet, even while she was making her mark in a tough, male-dominated business, Rebecca's heart did not toughen. She believes in giving a break to people who are willing to work. "If someone works hard and does a good job, I pay well," she notes. "I can't do this by myself, and I value the good people around me."

Chris, meanwhile, having grown up in the business, tried a few college classes after she graduated from high school. She found they didn't satisfy her interests. Rebecca suggested that—if Chris wanted to learn trucking and was willing to be tough enough—she would make a lot more money at Midwest than she would after completing a degree. Chris agreed. She went to work full time in 1989.

"You don't need college to be a success," says Rebecca. "Common sense, street smarts, good math skills and the ability to work with people can take you far in business."

Rebecca barrel-racing in Tulsa in 2001. In 2000, she broke three vertebrae in her neck after falling from a horse.

Midwest trucks in the quarry.

In the years that followed, mother and daughter rebuilt their fleet, reaching a high of more than 30 trucks in 1996. It wasn't easy, with the industry highly competitive and confronted with ongoing and escalating demands of regulators and unions.

"We're in the paper-pushing business now, not in trucking," Rebecca observes. "Things used to be easy. Now there's far more to do with insurance, laws changing and increased exposure to liability.

"If there's an accident and someone's hurt, they take you to court—even if they were at fault. Dump trucks are a target. They see one, and they sue. We had a case where the other insurer conceded responsibility but five years later we're still in the courts.

"We also have more responsibility for the people we hire, with tighter safety procedures and periodic drug screenings."

In 1997 Rebecca and Christine shifted their emphasis to brokering; they enter exclusive contracts with independent drivers and other trucking companies and line up the work. They started trimming Midwest Hauling's own fleet. By 2003 it was down to 18 trucks, and the company's payroll consisted of Rebecca, president; Chris, vice president; Dawn, office manager; Randy, superintendent; an assistant superintendent; a mechanic; and 18 drivers. Midwest operates in St. Louis and St. Charles counties, basically within an area 100 miles across. It works with several of the area's largest contractors.

Rebecca said she'd like to see it still smaller and more manageable, and Chris says she'll keep Midwest Hauling much as it is. She's happy with the mix of owned and brokered trucks and, while she might consider branching out should a possibility present itself, she's happy with the status quo.

While Rebecca says she's almost ready to retire and concentrate on her home, her animals and her hobbies, 2003 is turning out to be a landmark year for Midwest Hauling. The company is building a new headquarters on five and a half acres in Pacific, a St. Louis suburb. The building, expected to be completed in mid-autumn, will be 8,500 square feet with offices and a three-bay shop for maintaining Midwest's trucks. It will be the first time Midwest's offices have been outside Rebecca's home, and the first time its entire operation will be in a single location. In the past, the trucks were kept at quarries with which Midwest worked.

Running Midwest Hauling is not the only love Rebecca and Chris share. Rebecca, for many years, has had a passion for horses. In 1975 she bought her first horse and started competing as a novice in barrel racing. After about two years, she decided she didn't have time to compete seriously, and for the next several years she limited equestrian activities to trail riding. Her passion for horses was only banked, however, and

Midwest Hauling's construction of new shop and office, 2003.

Midwest's management crew, from left to right: Garry Thomas, mechanic; Dawn Huelsmann, office manager, Randy Hackworth, super-intendent; Rebecca Johnson, owner; Greg Crocker, fore-man; and Christine Johnson, owner.

when Chris was about 21, Rebecca found she had inherited that love, too.

They bought a horse and began barrel-racing. They quickly discovered one horse wasn't enough, and today they have three, and many of their weekends belong to rodeo. After a long week running Midwest Hauling, mother and daughter pack up two of their quarter horses and head out to whatever rodeo is running that weekend. It's not uncommon for them to drive hundreds of miles to an event, compete, drive home and be back at work bright and early Monday.

The horses live on the 30-acre spread Rebecca bought in 1993, which includes indoor and outdoor arenas for riding, a barn, a utility shed, a place for her boat, two dogs and the requisite barn cats. While the white picket fence she once thought she wanted has been replaced by a long, attractive white plastic fence, she has no regrets and looks forward to spending time in her garden and perhaps traveling in an RV with sister Pat, while cheering Chris on as she takes over full management of Midwest Hauling.

Looking back, Rebecca concludes that the secret of her success in a com-petitive, male-dominated field has been her ability to make the tough choices every successful man has made. At the same time, she had to work harder to break through so many barriers.

"Trucks are a masculine thing," Rebecca says, "and, frankly, I can't take an engine apart. But I do know how to run a business, and I have the street smarts and common sense you need to make decisions. I've got drivers, mechanics to take the trucks apart, and superintendents to do dispatching. Having good people around is the way to succeed."

Rebecca has a reputation for being tough and fair. She was a pioneer in her industry and has fought major battles with the unions. "They want us to be union, but I pay more than union wage," she notes. Still, she acknowledges it's still a man's world, even to the size of paychecks.

"Men are accepted easier. Women have to work harder to be taken seriously. Even with the best ideas, we sometimes have to be louder to be heard."

Rebecca has overcome much of that, establishing a track record that bodes well for projects she might want to take on, and for Chris and Midwest. For example, she has had the same banker for 27 years, so she can make a call, describe a project and know there will be no problem with financial support. The days of having to convince everyone that she knew what she was doing are long past. The track record that accompanies her name makes her a great bet.

Looking back, Rebecca says, "It was difficult, at times. I had to give up part of my relationship with my daughter. And now I'm almost ready to retire."

Remembering a freak horse accident three years ago that broke her neck, Rebecca adds, "Most of all, I'm glad I'm still alive.

"I'm proud of my life. There's been a price to pay, but it's been very rewarding. If I had to do it over, I would. I've done it all, but now it's time to smell the roses."

Midwest's current fleet showing 10 of 18 Kenworths, Fords (Sterling) and Macks.

MORRIS OIL COMPANY

Raised in Campbell, a small town in the bootheel, known as the Peach Capital of Missouri, Jim D. Morris became one of the foremost industrialists and philanthropists in the state.

His is a true Horatio Alger story; his characteristic ambition, drive and strong work ethic carried him from poor beginnings to great success. Throughout, he has remained true to his ideals and given back to the communities that supported him.

"My early years were poor in material things, but rich in family," Jim recalls. "I wanted to rise above poverty. That has been a driving force in my life. It's worked out, and I feel deeply blessed."

Jim was born in 1934, in the heart of the Great Depression. Jim and his brother, two sisters and his parents, Homer and Daisy, farmed in Southeast Missouri. He learned the value of hard work picking cotton and peaches on the family's farm and shining shoes on the Venice and Ocean Park Pier after school in California, where his parents worked during the winter months.

"I've had a life of faith and family," says Jim, who married his high school sweetheart, Catherine Farmer, in 1953. His family includes three daughters—Debbie, Pam and Stephanie—and a grandson, Brandon. "The best moments of my life were when my children and grandson were born," says Jim. "Life is so amazing!" He especially enjoys being with his family and going to his grandson's sporting events. Jim also tries

Jim D. Morris.

to find time to enjoy his antique car collection. His love for automobiles led him to own Jim Morris Chevrolet and Geo, which included a fishing and leisure boat dealership, located at Morris Plaza in Branson West.

At 18, when Jim graduated from high school, he started driving a gasoline bulk truck for Phillips 66. The next year, he became sales agent for the Standard Oil of Indiana Agency in Campbell. His salary was $120 a month. Five years later, with the help of a 100-percent loan from Standard, he bought that agency, founding Morris Oil Company on March 1, 1958. He was the youngest person ever to own a Standard Agency.

Jim worked hard, his agency grew and he began expanding his interests beyond oil. He invested extensively in real es-

tate, starting in 1959 with agricultural land around Campbell. He eventually accumulated some 2,500 acres, farms that produce row crops ranging from cotton to rice in river-bottom land and peaches on Crowley Ridge. "This area is the garden spot of the world," he says.

In 1961 Jim's success led Standard, through district manager G.E. Ogden, to invite him to sell the Campbell agency and buy the larger Branson agency. There, in 1964, he added propane to his product mix. On January 1, 1966, Ogden and Standard (later Amoco) promoted him to head the Springfield location. Already Standard's largest agency, Jim's aggressive marketing tripled its size in the years that followed. In 1969 Jim added a retail LP business and, in 1975, Morris Oil became fully independent when Standard sold Jim all of its assets in the Springfield market and encouraged him to buy back Branson, which he did.

Indeed, in the 1980s, Morris Oil was the largest independent marketer for petroleum fuels in Missouri. It wholesaled Amoco, Phillips 66, Total and Texaco products in 15 counties and lubricants in 45 counties. It supplied retail products through 50 outlets in the Springfield and Branson areas. All told, Morris Oil sold 40 million gallons of gasoline and diesel fuel, 4 million gallons of propane and more than 650,000 gallons of motor oil annually. This lasted into the mid-1990s,

One of Morris Oil & Gas Company's convenience stores and one of its tank trucks in Branson, Missouri.

Jim D. Morris, March 1, 1958, the founding of Morris Oil Company.

when Jim decided to sell parts of the business.

In 2001, after British Petroleum bought Amoco, Jim affiliated 17 of his 25 owned convenience stores with Conoco and the rest with Phillips 66. All are in Springfield, Branson and their surrounding area.

Jim has been an active advocate within his industry. He sat on the Board of Directors of the Missouri LP-Gas Association from 1975 to 1977. He served as president of the Missouri Petroleum Marketers Association (MPMA) in 1992–1993 and remained a key person in MPMA and the Missouri Association of Convenience Stores, which affiliated in 1993. John Pelzer, executive director of MPMA, states, "As president of the Missouri Petroleum Marketers Association, Jim transformed what had been a relatively stagnant organization into one of the most pro-active and powerful lobbying forces in the state. He is a man of

Top: Morris Plaza, Branson West, Missouri.
Bottom: Jim's love for automobiles led him to own Jim Morris Chevrolet in Branson West, Missouri.

vision, willing to do whatever it takes to preserve our industry." Jim wrote a popular series of columns under the heading "Jim Sez" in the MPMA's publication, *Missouri Pipeline*.

Jim was on the Petroleum Marketers Association of America's board in 1994 and 1995. He was a member of the Amoco Jobber Forum for 20 years, including chairing it from 1984 through 1987, and sat on Amoco's National Jobber Council for four terms, longest of anyone in Amoco's history. He helped found and served as chairman of the Board of Trustees of Fuel Marketers Insurance Trust. His fellow Amoco marketers in the 10-state Western Region elected him to be their spokesman on the Amoco National Advisory Board in 1995 and 1996.

Gordon Hankey, regional manager for Amoco Oil Company comments, "Jim

Above: Jim D. Morris, founder of Signature Bank at a ribbon-cutting ceremony.

Morris and Amoco have a long history together which I know we both treat with special respect. Our association began in 1953. One of the best loans Standard ever made was to that 23-year-old entrepreneur named Jim Morris, who became a Standard Oil agent and built his business

Morris Oil Company, Inc, Springfield, Missouri. One of Morris Oil Company's convenience stores and one of its tankers.

one satisfied customer at a time. Today, Morris Oil is a key strategic Amoco jobber in Missouri and a valued customer."

On Morris Oil's 40th anniversary in 1993, William D. Ford, then president of Amoco Oil Company, wrote: "I personally appreciate our relationship that goes back to the St. Louis district and the candor with which you shared your thoughts both then and now as a leader on the Marketing Advisory Board."

Jim has been an active advocate for his customers, becoming the driving force in 1995 in eliminating the Discount for Cash program, which cost consumers, who used their credit cards, an extra four cents a gallon. Amoco gave him the honor of announcing the elimination of that charge to his fellow jobbers.

He has also taken a keen interest in the well-being and future of the cities where he has operated.

In 1961 Branson was a small town known worldwide for its fine fishing. He worked to develop the area and was one of the pioneers of the Ozark Marketing Council, which has helped promote Branson into an international entertainment attraction. He served on the council's board from 1988 to 1994. Says Pete Herschend, executive vice president and co-owner of Silver Dollar City, "There has hardly been a time in the economic history of Branson and its remarkable growth that Jim Morris hasn't been a factor. I am convinced that much of what has happened in Branson today would

Springfield, Clarion Hotel owned by Morris Group Hotels.

not be taking place had it not been for the early work he did in helping us get a sense of community working for the area."

In Springfield, Jim worked in organizations such as Citizens for a Better Springfield. He was treasurer of that group in 1987 when it began its successful effort to pass a sales tax increase to finance needed capital improvements.

Development is one of Jim's passions that has not diminished over time. In the mid-1990s, he bought a 55-acre tract on the Shepherd of the Hills Expressway in the heart of Branson. The site holds the only amphitheater ever built in the city, a 10-acre, 8,000-seat facility made obsolete by indoor theaters. He plans to raze the amphitheater and redevelop the site within the next three to five years.

Morris Oil frequently joined forces with other companies, and was a pioneer in developing gas/convenience store/restaurant complexes. When Morris Oil and McDonald's broke ground in 1996 at James River

Freeway and National Avenue for a building to house the three entities, it was the first alliance between Amoco and McDonald's west of the Mississippi and their second alliance nationally. It was not, however, Jim's first joint venture with a restaurant. Morris Oil also shares buildings with Hardees, Blimpies, Papa Johns and A&W. His locations hold some of the most attractive and highest traffic convenience stores in Springfield and Branson.

Jim is founder and owner of Morris Group Hotels, which consists of five hotels in Branson and one in Springfield. The six have 1,000 guest rooms, a convention center and a reunion facility.

The Ramada Hotel, sets on 24 beautiful acres, is the largest hotel property on the Branson strip. They are presently in the planning and development stage for a 73,000-square-foot facility to include a 1,000-seat live music theater, an automobile museum featuring a private collection of each and every auto manufactured in 1957, along with other memorabilia of the '50s, and a well-known, music-themed restaurant featuring memorabilia of rock and roll stars of the '50s, '60s and '70s. This facility will occupy the eastern 3 1/2 acres of the 24-acre Ramada Resort and Conference Center. Additionally, negotiations are underway to construct a 30,000-square-foot interactive Nascar Sport Museum and Hall of Fame.

The Springfield Clarion Hotel has 200 guest rooms and more than 17,000 square feet of convention space. It has hosted former president George Bush, an array of local and national political figures, and the St. Louis and Kansas City baseball teams.

Jim has also been active in the financial arena, sitting on the boards of the Bank of Green County (1966–76), Bank of Springfield Centerre Bank (1976–82), Boatmen's Bank (1982–94) and First City National Bank (1994–96). He watched local banks succumb to mergers and buyouts, shifting their focus away from the individual customer, and in 1997 he started the Signature Bank to combat this

The Ramada Hotel in Branson, Missouri, owned by Morris Group Hotels.

trend. David A. Kunze, president and chief executive officer of Signature, states, "The founder of Signature Bank, Jim D. Morris, created one of the fastest growing banks in the United States. In six short years, Signature Bank has become the largest independently owned Springfield-based bank, with assets in excess of $400 million." Signature has three locations.

An active member of the Downtown Springfield Association, Jim Morris was one of the prime movers behind renovation of the city's center. He dreamed of its rebirth years before it became a reality. "A big part of [downtown's] progress has been due to Jim's personal commitment to the heart of our city," said Mayor Tom Carlson. "He did it at a time when it was not fashionable, but his contribution helped carry us over the hump. Jim has always been a primary investor in the downtown area."

Jim Anderson, president of the Chamber of Commerce, added, "With Jim's guts, financial resources and sheer determination, he has been the lightning rod for the tremendous redevelopment we are seeing occur in our Center City. Jim put his money where his mouth is and acted when most people were satisfied to moan, groan and complain. Jim has many lasting legacies in our region, but one that will always be close to me is what he has done and what he continues to do in our Center City. He continuously amazes me with his almost unlimited energy and enthusiasm and the way he gives of himself without want of any recognition."

"The City of Springfield is indeed a better place to live," said former mayor Leland Gannaway, "because of Jim's philanthropic efforts and his endless hours of working to improve the quality of life in our community." To Jim, he said, "I would also be remiss not to take this opportunity to express my appreciation to you for the tremendous amount of public service which you have so unselfishly given over the years."

Signature Bank locations in Springfield, Missouri. Bottom photo shows Jim standing in front of the building he purchased that became Signature Bank's first location in 1997.

Evidence of Jim's presence is everywhere.

There is the Gillioz Theater and the Jim D. Morris Arts Center being developed in adjacent downtown landmarks. Jim saved the Gillioz, a magnificent building built in 1926.

Initially, preservation of the theater was impossible because the lobby and the auditorium had different owners. In 1988 Jim bought the lobby. He talked to the owners of the auditorium about selling it to them but, when he heard they were considering turning the theater into a night club or a parking lot, he turned buyer and purchased the auditorium. In 1991 he turned both over to the Springfield Landmarks Preservation Trust. Without Jim's efforts, says Nancy Brown, president of the Trust's board, "downtown would be absent this architectural and acoustic masterpiece. Along with donating property, he has been the largest single cash contributor toward its restoration and reopening as a community performing arts center."

The Arts Center is in the former Netter's Department Store Building, renamed for Morris in recognition of his role.

Jim gifted a substantial portion of the old Trailways bus depot along with the land on St. Louis Street, which is now the new Discovery Center Children's Museum. He was one of the original planners of the Discovery Center and a prime donor of capital towards the project.

With Jim's support, and, with the efforts of him and others, the downtown now boosts new attractions such as the Jordan Valley Park, which includes an indoor ice rink, a minor league baseball stadium and an expo center.

His gift to Southwest Missouri State University resulted in the Jim D. Morris Center for Continuing Education. Each year, the Center accommodates some 10,000 young adults who want to further their educations.

With the help of land donations from Jim Morris to the City of Springfield, the major intersection of Walnut Lawn and Campbell was renewed in 1999.

Jim was appointed to the Springfield Regional Airport board in 1984. He served through 1989, including three terms as chairman (1984–1986). He believed the airport needed to expand to accommodate additional airlines. During his time as chair, it undertook $25 million in building projects, including a $12 million terminal building. In the words of Rob Hancik, director of aviation, his tenure "caused the staff to rethink some of the issues and evaluate solutions from another point of view."

Maintaining a sense of his beginnings, Jim is an active supporter of children, seniors and others in Campbell, Branson, Springfield and their environs.

Among other projects in Campbell, he built a new senior nutrition center, dedicated in March 2003, as the Daisy Morris Nutrition and Activity Center. The Center provides meals and a meeting place for senior citizens and is

Morris State Park, Campbell, Missouri.

named for Jim's mother, who is still going strong at age 89. His father died in 1980. The City of Campbell honored Jim by naming its 20-acre city park and a street for him.

In 2000 Jim donated 161 acres of virgin forest on Crowley Ridge to Missouri. He had bought the land, his playground when he was young, in the 1980s. A geologic and historic treasure trove, the forest was home to the Qupaw Indians until they migrated after the 8.0 magnitude New Madrid earthquakes of 1811 and 1812. In what is now Morris State Park, there are snake carvings on trees more than 200 years old, Indian artifacts taken from the woods make up the best collection in the state, and you can still find white sand and sea shells deposited thousands of years ago. The park, called "a treasure uncovered" by the Department of Natural Resources, also contains plants found nowhere else in Missouri.

In 2001 Jim donated land, which includes his grade school, to the Southeast Missouri Scenic Byways. With the help of a state grant, the school, an historic site, is being renovated and will be opened to the public.

Operating under the philosophy that all individuals owe a debt of service to their community and to say you are too busy is unacceptable, Jim sat on the Board of Directors of Springfield's Community Foundation from 1984 to 1990.

He provided substantial funding to Boys and Girls Town of Missouri (completely renovating its Social Services, Education and Administrative Center, now the Jim D. Morris Facility) and to the Good Samaritan Boys Ranch, which gives troubled children the opportunity for better lives.

He donated property and improvements to the Southern Stone County Fire Protection District. The District's headquarters and major fire station occupy the improvements named for him. He is also

Morris Farms, Campbell, Missouri.

a contributor to the Developmental Center of the Ozarks.

Jim provided start-up funds for Lost and Found, an organization that helps children who have experienced deaths of loved ones. He supports the American Cancer Society, Ronald McDonald House Charities, the American Heart Association, the Boy Scouts and Girl Scouts, Families for Children and the Children's Miracle Network.

He helped the Springfield Park Board, and particularly in its efforts to build bridges via softball with sister city Isesaki, Japan.

Jim Morris, along with country music legend Roy Clark, in 1991 co-founded the Branson Country Pro-Celebrity Fish Off to raise money for Habitat for Humanity and was a financial supporter of Skaggs Hospital expansion in Branson, where one of the family waiting rooms is named in his honor.

Jim's efforts and influence have been recognized by his neighbors and his peers. In 1984 he was chosen by the people of Springfield as one of the five best-known Springfieldians. In 2000 he was named Outstanding Philanthropist by the Ozark chapter of the National Society of Fund Raising Executives, cited for contributing not only time, effort and resources to the non-profit community, but also heart and soul.

Good common sense, Jim Morris says, is his best asset. "This means having to say no, at times, when you want to say yes. It means trying always to present the truth to people." Add into the mix, graciousness and humility, a soft-spoken demeanor and a basic kindness, and you have a man who, despite great success, values family and has no more forgotten the communities that were good to him than they will forget him.

NEW LIFE EVANGELISTIC CENTER, INC.

Over thirty years ago, a 22-year-old preacher and his wife sensed God calling them to launch a ministry to the poor in the inner-city community of Wellston, Missouri. With only meager resources, Larry and Penny Rice rented a 50-foot trailer in a mobile home park and invited people into their tiny living room for Bible studies. They offered overnight shelter and food to the homeless, despite the uncertainty of when their own next meal might come. Yet miracles kept happening, and in January 1972, the New Life Evangelistic Center was born.

The couple's first outreach program was a 24-hour-a-day devotional telephone line called "Dial-A-Message." Seeing first-hand the overwhelming needs of the homeless, the Rices decided to expand their operations. Several months later they were blessed with the opportunity to acquire a three-story former mansion built in 1869. And because the house was located in St. Louis, the Rices were able to extend their outreach to the homeless, the elderly, the mentally ill and to prisoners.

"We saw a great need to reach out to people in the community. There seemed to be a wide gap between the man and woman on the street and the man and woman in the pews. We wanted to bridge that gap," says Larry, the center's director.

Remaining true to their mission, Larry and Penny have seen their work blessed beyond measure and have in turn helped to transform many lives. What started out as a dedicated staff of six now consists of about 100 full-time workers in the United States, a network of hundreds of volunteers, and over 200 employees serving in southern India.

Today New Life Evangelistic Center, Inc., continues to reach people through hands-on assistance. Through a network of "free stores" in Missouri, Arkansas and Illinois, the needy can pick up food, clothing and household items without charge. The organization offers direct aid in times of natural and man-made disasters. NLEC also offers a two-year

Penny and Larry Rice with trainees of KNLJ-TV, Channel 25, in New Bloomfield, Missouri.

rehabilitation and job training program that has enabled countless numbers of people struggling with alcohol and drug-related problems to get their lives back on track.

"Some of these people have been cast out by society. When they discover their God-given talents, it gives them a sense of dignity and self-worth," says Rice.

NLEC also ministers to the community via the "Here's Help Network" of television and radio stations. The network consists of nine television stations including KNLC, Channel 24, which serves the St. Louis metropolitan area; KNLJ, Channel 25, which airs in the Jefferson City/Columbia areas; and 17 radio stations broadcast throughout the Midwest. The stations offer locally and nationally produced shows covering public affairs, entertainment, education, inspiration and children's programming.

The organization publishes a newspaper called the *ZOA Free Paper*, which has worldwide circulation. (*Zoa* means "life" in the Greek language.) NLEC also prints a bi-monthly newspaper entitled *Cry Justice Now*, which is dis-

tributed to inmates and their families.

The New Life Evangelistic Center training program is giving the previously homeless the opportunity to demonstrate that America does not have to use oil in order to function. In the heart of America, wind generators and solar panels are going up, electric vehicles are being built, used vegetable oil is being converted into diesel, solar hot water, radiant floor heating and solar cookers are being put to work. The Missouri Renewable Energy division is showing that people do not have to rely on polluting coal generator power plants, but can be free to enjoy the clean energy from sun, wind and other renewables.

"It has been exciting to see the growth of individuals and to see their ongoing legacies in the community," said Rice. "The ripples of our work now stretch far beyond our institutional walls. We want to continue to let the love of Jesus Christ shine through us to be a source of light and inspiration."

MURPHY COMPANY

It's time to forget Murphy's Law and pay attention to Murphy's Principles.

As espoused by Murphy Company, the largest mechanical contractor in the St. Louis area and 12th largest in the nation, it's simple: *"Provide valuable solutions to our customers."*

The corollary is "Anything that can go right will," an outcome rooted in the company's core values of employee well-being, enduring relationships, integrity and professionalism.

"The culture in which we operate creates win-win relationships with our customers, the people who work with us, and the vendors and subcontractors who work for us," said James "Jim" Murphy, Jr., the company's third-generation chief executive officer and its president since 1979.

"The relationship must be mutually beneficial," he added, "not one that takes advantage of others. That's a key factor in those we choose to work for and those we select to work with us."

The company traces its roots to a small plumbing shop founded in 1907 by an Irish immigrant, John C. Murphy, who

Murphy Company's nimble Quick Response team members bring the firm's vast resources to bear on small mechanical and plumbing installations in need of smart, cost-effective and responsive solutions.

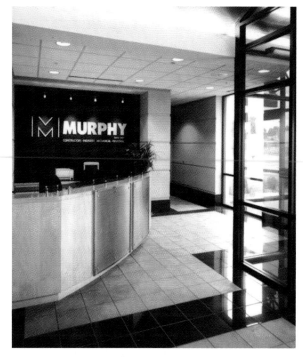

Murphy Company was founded in 1907. Today it is the St. Louis area's largest mechanical contractor.

had traveled from County Cork at age 14 to his adopted country. Murphy worked as a plumber when the historic Union Station was built in St. Louis. Eight decades later, the firm he began served on the renovation team that brought Union Station back to life.

Grandfather Murphy, who died in 1952, raised a family of eight children. His sons, the late James, Sr., and Jerry, joined the enterprise and widened its scope to include today's mechanical contracting functions of heating, ventilation and air conditioning (HVAC). Jerry's son, Patrick Murphy, Sr., joined the company in the early 1960s, just as his father and uncle were expanding capabilities to meet the needs of industry. The company changed its name to Murphy Company Mechanical Contractors and Engineers as a reflection of its heightened sophistication.

When Jim joined the firm in the 1970s, he cultivated an even greater range of diversity in projects and geographic reach. Moving beyond the St. Louis market, Murphy Company won contracts in Southern Illinois and throughout Missouri. By 1975 it began

investing heavily in fabrication facilities and equipment to improve the quality and efficiency of its installations.

As the third generation began leading the firm in 1979, the company formed a management group to formulate executive level decisions. That move set the stage for organizational depth and growth.

The company became an early innovator in the realm of design/build mechanical construction, with its many advantages over traditional bid-and-build. Its project management excellence quickly made Murphy Company the favorite of industry. In 2002 Murphy's work included more than 100 industrial retrofits, renovations and installations at major facilities operated by such firms as Anheuser-Busch, Daimler Chrysler and General Motors. By 2003 its exceptional performance in providing valuable solutions for commercial, industrial, healthcare, municipal and institutional markets took Murphy Company to a new high-water mark for revenues—$183.5 million.

Delivering Valuable Solutions. In the mid-1990s, Murphy Company noticed an unfulfilled need among customers for sophisticated and cost-effective skills on relatively small projects. It organized a new method for meeting the need with its Quick Response Group. It also retooled its service department to better deliver the customer savings associated with preventive maintenance and sound emergency service.

Murphy's Quick Response team brings the talent, technology and efficiency of a big company to relatively small mechanical and plumbing projects. Just as "minor surgery" is always significant, businesses in need of speedy projects to move their operations forward consider them critical endeavors.

A Quick Response project can range from $1,500 to $500,000 in value, and can require anywhere from two days to several weeks to complete. A single team led by a versatile project manager handles design, estimating and installation. The manager oversees all tasks and stays in touch with the customer. The work is completed efficiently and within budget.

Murphy's Quick Response Group delivers HVAC, plumbing, refrigeration and process piping services with the help of 20 well-equipped vans. Its members primarily serve healthcare, commercial, office, industrial and retail clients.

"Customers enjoy continuity in the skilled craftsmen who are assigned to their work and dispatched quickly," Jim said. "Murphy Company engineers provide fast and effective design services and solutions. This is what customers want, and this is what we deliver."

Sharing the credit for Murphy Company's strong growth is a service department that responds to emergency situations and service needs. With a fleet of 70 service trucks, it ranks as the largest in the St. Louis area. Its emphasis on preventive maintenance helps clients avoid disruptive emergencies in the first place. The service group completed 12,000 calls in 2003.

"Just as our Quick Response Group has tripled in size in the past seven years, our Service Group business has doubled in the last five years," said Patrick Murphy, Jr., a great-grandson of the company's founder and senior vice president. "Our service team performs at a level that attracts projects of every size to the firm. Clients can make one call to tap the full range of our services as they need them."

Market Diversification. In 1983 Murphy took a giant step beyond Murphy's original sphere of influence to open a regional office in Denver, Colorado. "Denver was about halfway between St. Louis and the West Coast," he said. "We could grow the company while also giving our people the chance to expand their horizons and run something on their

Commercial, industrial, municipal and institutional property owners rely on Murphy Company's design, engineering and construction solutions. In the commercial market, projects range from massive HVAC equipment replacement (as shown) to preventive maintenance programs for existing equipment.

own. Our expansion also helped us pursue work nationally on a selective basis for our customers."

"We are very competitive in the Denver marketplace," he added. "While we started from nothing, we were confident that our continued investment in resources would ensure the operation's success, and it has."

Murphy Company's commitment to deliver valuable solutions to customers led to its 1986 acquisition of Grossmann Sheet Metal in St. Louis to deliver greater value and responsiveness to customers on

sheet metal and HVAC projects. Extensive fabrication facilities now surround the corporate office at 1233 North Price Road in Olivette.

A key hire in 1987 brought the firm extensive experience in smokestack-industry work, including refineries, steel mills and power plants. Murphy Company became a contractor relied upon by industry to complete high-speed turnaround work safely and within stringent schedules.

The firm attracts some of the most complex and demanding work in North America, from a grassroots $250 million combined cycle power plant for Reliant Energy near Las Vegas to the hometown projects where St. Louisans cheer their favorite teams to victory —most recently, Savvis Center and the Edward Jones Dome.

Murphy Company also delivers its plumbing and mechanical contracting expertise to St. Louis' most significant facility owners, spanning every major healthcare institution, university, commercial property owner and manufacturer.

The firm is a major contributor to regional vitality, with Jim Murphy serving as president of the thriving Regional Business Council (RBC). Its 100 members are the largest mid-cap companies in the region. They bring their collective talents to bear on regional governance, education, business diversity, arts and culture, and philanthropy, while deepening the involvement and investment of members in the region.

People Count Most. Murphy Company employs more than 230 people, including 18 officers and 40 engineering staff. It also employs about 800 union craft workers, primarily from the AFL-CIO pipefitter, boilermaker, plumber and sheet metal unions. It is licensed to do business in 32 states.

Jim believes the company's deepest strength is its employees. "I'm a great believer in a balanced lifestyle," he said. "We don't want any workaholics. We want our people to take their vacations. We want them to spend quality time with their families, and to take advantage of cultural and leisure opportunities. That's good for a person's physical and mental health. It's good for our corporate health, too."

Construction safety is a passionate commitment. "The safety of our people truly is our highest priority," said Jim, past president of the Mechanical Contractors Association of America. "We want our people to go home to their families the same way they came in. It requires constant effort by every member of our team."

Murphy Company also strives to build unity among employees. "The larger a company becomes, the more difficult it

is to maintain a family-friendly, team-oriented operation," he said. "But we strive very hard to do that."

That approach includes letting employees know how the company is doing. "We want them to know the company's big picture, not only their particular area," Jim said. "We regularly share what we know, the good and the bad."

Murphy employees extend this family spirit to the greater community by generously giving to the United Way, which funds more than 200 social service agencies. Employees gave more than $100,000 to United Way in 2002 and again in 2003.

"Certainly, we all want to be successful financially," he added, "but that can't be accomplished over the long haul without motivating, challenging and making our employees happy. If they want to move ahead in their careers, the company will be moving ahead with them. That's

Murphy Company operates its own state-of-the-art fabrication and warehouse facilities for piping, sheet metal and plumbing.

one of the reasons we expanded in Denver."

A major factor in hiring is assessing whether the prospect meshes with the company's culture. "People must enjoy what they do or else there will be all kinds of family and health stresses," he described. "They won't be satisfied, and neither will we. Once we know where each person stands, then we talk economics."

One of the firm's major strategic goals is to attract the best people by providing opportunities for them to reach their career potential. The concept has driven the firm's growth and led to a culture in which Murphy retains people during cyclical slow times while other companies choose layoffs.

With this employment philosophy, Murphy Company flies in the face of national patterns. "When we hire, we want that person to retire from our company," Jim said. "We are looking for long-term relationships."

Murphy Company's commitment to streamlining the delivery of small and large projects alike is seen in the installation and relocation of heating, ventilation and air conditioning (HVAC) systems for temperature and humidity control.

RHODEY & SON CONSTRUCTION

Rhodey & Son Construction of St. Louis, Missouri, had its humble beginnings in the basement of John and Kathleen Rhodey's home. Having the support of his family and core values that exemplified honesty and quality, Rhodey was able to build a business that has reached its second generation and is being headed by his daughter, Pam Duffy.

For 22 years John worked for a large, national construction company. He was frequently transferred from one project to another. With every transfer, John moved his family with him. His two daughters and son were all born in different states. Moving was a way of life for the Rhodeys. Pam even refers to herself as a "construction brat," having moved nine times before she was in the fourth grade. But in 1972, Rhodey took a chance and turned down a very lucrative job with another construction company to work for himself.

While operating the company out of the basement and garage of their home, Kathleen Rhodey set one rule. The bathrooms were off limits to the construction workers they hired until a certain

John Rhodey (wearing hardhat) in his days with Frazier-Davis.

John and Kate Rhodey at annual company picnic.

hour in the morning. In 1990 this problem was alleviated when Rhodey & Son moved into their own offices. They now employ approximately 50 people, and handle general contracting, building design and construction management in the areas of healthcare, industrial and civil construction.

The construction business is a volatile industry because of the fluctuating economy, high risk and high cost factors involved. In addition to the challenges

of building his business, Rhodey had an even greater challenge when it came to breaking into the tight St. Louis business community. Being a native of St. Louis can play a very important part in the success of one's business. Pam admires her father's tenacity and work ethic. "The fact that he succeeded in such a tight community says a great deal about his work," she says. "His priority has always been customers and not the jobs." With this attitude, his reputation has allowed Rhodey & Son to continue growing at a slow but steady pace. And when they moved from their home to office space, they found that their business had tripled.

John Rhodey and Pam Duffy at the annual company Christmas party.

Even though his daughter now runs Rhodey & Son Construction, John Rhodey is still very much involved in the company. His expertise in construction is invaluable, and he is the number one resource for the company's marketing and consulting needs. Duffy declares that her father could not have been a better mentor. He taught her how to be self sufficient, strong and knowledgeable of every detail of the business. She is amazed at the trust her parents have given her by allowing her to run the business that they put so much effort into— but then she, too, doesn't waiver from the same core values established by her father. Perhaps that's the reason for the success of Rhodey & Son Construction.

NATIONAL ENZYME COMPANY

Proper nutrition, active lifestyles and exercise are very much in vogue in today's health-conscious society. At National Enzyme Company, however, the importance of a nutrient-rich diet has always been in fashion.

Headquartered in Forsyth, Missouri, NEC stands out as a leader in the dietary supplement industry. For more than seven decades, the company has used meticulous research and innovative technology to create enzyme-based products that are improving the general health of people worldwide.

The organization owes its very existence to a dedicated physician who embarked on a quest to improve the diets of his chronically ill patients. Dr. Edward Howell's fascination with enzymes and human nutrition began in the 1920s while working at Lindlahr Sanitarium in Chicago. Howell believed nutrient assimilation could be enhanced by replacing enzymes lost in the cooking and processing of food. What was needed was the creation of an enzyme-based product. In the course of his investigations, Howell found that microbial and plant enzymes performed the same types of functions as did digestive enzymes present in the human body. After extensive clinical and laboratory research, Howell devised a way

Anthony W. Collier, president and CEO.

Dr. Howell and Mr. Collier in the banana grove in Dr. Howell's backyard.

to cultivate and extract specific plant enzymes. He added these enzyme-based digestive supplements to the diets of his patients. Soon other doctors recognized improved health in these same patients.

In 1932 Howell established National Enzyme Company and featured his general digestive enzyme-based formula. He called it "Genuine N-Zime #1." The company was later incorporated in 1942. Today NEC is the oldest enzyme company in North America. Its dominance in the field is a legacy to the pioneering efforts and compassion of Dr. Howell.

Anthony Collier, a recent DePaul University business school graduate, began working for the corporation in 1977 as the office manager. He purchased the company in 1979. In that year, sales of the Genuine N-Zime products totaled $78,000. NEC was moved to Missouri the following year. Located just east of Forsyth, company operations are currently housed in nine buildings on Highways 160 and 76. More than 100 employees offer their expertise in the areas of product development, manufacturing, quality assurance, technical services, marketing and customer service.

Following in the footsteps of his predecessor, Collier believes strongly in the quality and effectiveness of the product he sells. "Dr. Edward Howell founded our company on the belief that supplemental enzymes greatly enhance a person's health," says the NEC president. "I believe this and would like to see enzyme-based dietary supplements on every table, every medicine cabinet, every doctor's office and in every hospital around the world."

Enzymes play a crucial role in the digestive process. Each step of the way, these substances break down different types of food. Digestion begins in the mouth, moves down into the stomach, and

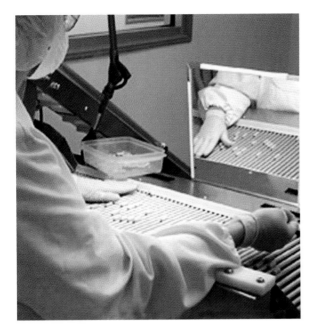

Quality is very important to NEC. Above, capsules are checked for powder consistency.

then travels into the small intestine. When food reaches the upper section of the small intestine, pancreatic enzymes are released to break down the food further. The remaining molecules of food pass into the lower small intestine for final break down.

These organic catalysts occur naturally in food and are responsible for all of the human body's metabolic functions. Enzymes jumpstart all normal biochemical reactions in the body and are highly specialized as to what they do and under what conditions. The foods we eat are composed of proteins, fiber, fats, and carbohydrates. During the digestive process, enzymes break down these materials into their basic building blocks. These freed components can then be absorbed into circulation and used for energy, for maintenance and to help fight disease.

Most significantly, as part of the initial phases of digestion, the action of chewing along with the enzymes in saliva and those contributed by unprocessed food, begin predigesting the food. This process continues in the upper stomach, until gastric acid is released. When food is cooked or processed, however, the enzymes present in the raw food are de-

stroyed. In addition, stress, overeating or eating too fast, and the overuse of antacids, can all negatively impact the body's digestive enzyme supply. The loss of enzymes can make the digestive process become overstressed and incomplete. Essential nutrients may not be released from the food to be assimilated by the body, resulting in gastrointestinal problems. Supplemental enzymes can function as a replacement for those enzymes lost in the cooking process.

Benefits of enzyme supplements include an increase in the absorption and usage of nutrients, a decrease in stomach discomfort and a stronger immune system. Even people who are in excellent health can experience some benefits from these products. Increased energy, less fullness after meals, a faster emptying of the stomach's contents and regular bowel habits are just a few of the noticeable

improvements. Among the more popular supplements are those which assist in the digestion of milk sugars and proteins found in dairy products, and those enzymes which improve the absorption of phytonutrients.

Enzyme supplements typically consist of lipase, protease and amylase. Lipase breaks down fats found in butter, meat and cheese. Protease assists in the digestion of proteins found in meats and nuts. And amylase breaks down the carbohydrates, sugars and starches present in potatoes and other vegetables, fruits and snack foods. Some of the digestive products may also include lactase, cellulase, malt diastase, gluco-amylase, sucrase, papain and bromelain. By increasing the level of digestive activity in the stomach, more food can be broken down. This allows less partially digested food to pass into the colon, and makes more nutrients available for absorption.

National Enzyme Company takes great pride in its products. Through a

NEC's scientists are always looking for new and better ways to use enzymes as dietary supplements.

combination of science and art, research-ers have developed complex formulas blending just the right elements to create a complete dietary supplement package. Custom formulas are created by combin-ing microbial and plant-based enzymes, pro-biotics, herbs and other ingredients which meet specific requirements. The company also ensures that its source en-zymes are not derived from genetically modified organisms.

Expertise and knowledge in such di-verse fields as enzymology, phytochem-istry, biochemistry, and physiology are required to develop these complex for-mulas. Custom enzymatic blends are designed by product development staff using newly discovered applications and cutting-edge technology. The supple-ments begin with a product concept that is developed into a formula. The formula specifies the raw materials to be used, the quantity of each ingredient, and the end product, whether it be powdered, encap-sulated or bottled.

Among NEC's trademark products are special enzymatic blends called "n·zimes™" (pronounced *n-dot-zimes*). One such blend, "n·zimes™ fp," is a spe-cial combination of proteolytic enzymes which works by hydrolizing protein mol-ecules at the end of the peptide chain, thus liberating an amino acid to assist digestion; "n·zimes™ PA" and "n·zimes™ PA-L" were created as alternatives to ani-mal-based pancreatin. Both supplements contain lipase, protease and amylase iso-lated from fungal sources. Lipolytic en-zymes "n·zimes™AN" and "n·zimes™ RO" help break down fat found in cheese, but-ter and meat.

Other proprietary blends offered by the company include "CereCalase™" and "e·d·s™." CereCalase™ uses phytase, beta-glucanase and hemicellulase to synergis-tically break down fibrous plant cell walls and increase the bioavailability of cal-cium, iron, zinc and other minerals. e·d·s™ contains enzymes which assist in the absorption of vitamins and minerals from botanicals and other whole food sources.

Individuals who suffer from dairy in-tolerance and its associated symptoms of bloating, gas and diarrhea may find wel-come relief in a new product developed by NEC called Dairyzimes™. This special blend of protease and lactase enzymes enhances the digestion of proteins and sugar found in dairy products. Lactose intolerance and other forms of dairy intolerance are caused by a shortage of enzymes required to break down these elements. Over 70 percent of the world's population, including those of Asian, Af-rican, Mediterranean, Jewish and Native-American descent, experience difficulty digesting lactose. Those suffering from dairy intolerance often limit their intake of milk, cheese and other products or avoid these foods altogether. Dairy-zimes™ supplies these much-needed enzymes, however, and is said to be three times more effective than naturally oc-curring enzymes found in the stomach and small intestine.

NEC has filed for a patent on yet an-other new product, Isolase™, which is de-signed to increase the absorption of

Bottles are randomly checked for fill weight.

chemicals called isoflavones. Found to possess many health benefits, isoflavones are credited with the reduc-tion of incidences of breast cancer, with inhibiting the growth of tumors, lowering cholesterol, preventing cardio-vascular disease and osteoporosis, and can be used as a natural estrogen re-placement therapy.

Soy is the most common source of isoflavones and is present in numerous food and drink products. The bioavail-ability of soy isoflavones varies from 13 to 35 percent in individuals. In naturally occurring isoflavones, an attached sugar molecule renders them less bioavailable to the body's metabolic processes. Isolase™ works by cleaving the glucose molecule from the isoflavone, thus en-suring that the maximum amount of bioavailable nutrients can be absorbed.

Another new product is IsolasePro™, a proprietary enzyme composition de-signed to increase the absorption of isoflavones, plus increase the bio-

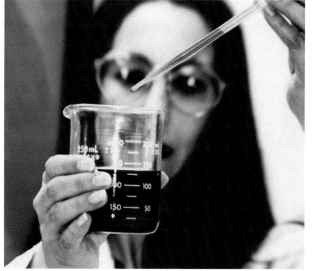

availability of soy proteins. IsolasePRO™ can increase the absorption of isoflavones and assist the body in breaking down soy protein, thereby increasing the positive benefits of protein consumption in those who consume soy protein products.

National Enzyme Company is committed to the quality and safety of its products. The manufacturing process begins with sourcing the highest quality raw materials available and double-checking the ingredients with specifications provided by the customer. The ingredients are then blended into a bulk powder of uniform consistency or encapsulated. The process must satisfy all U.S. Good Manufacturing Practices mandated by the Food and Drug Administration.

Every ingredient is required to pass a stringent testing process before it can be released for production. Tests include proof of identity for incoming materials and enzyme assays to verify activity levels. In-house laboratories analyze all materials for E. coli, Salmonella and other harmful substances. Additional testing involves taking samples, verifying weight and cross-checking batch formulation records. The finished product is tested again and held until cleared for release. A Certificate of Analysis is then issued to identify the ingredients of the blend.

The company has received a Good Manufacturing Practices registration by the NSF Dietary Supplements Certification program. NSF conducted an audit of the Forsyth facility and will conduct periodic audits to ensure these high standards are maintained. Included in the standards are guidelines for the manufacturing of the product and specific documentation regarding the composition, purity and strength of the ingredients.

In July 2001 the Occupational Safety and Health Administration (OSHA) awarded NEC its highest safety honor, the "Star Voluntary Protection Program." The award is given to companies who have outstanding health and safety programs in their workplaces and are recognized as models among their peer industries. This is a significant honor, since less than 0.1 percent of the six million companies OSHA oversees receive the distinction.

One of the objectives of the company's aggressive marketing strategy is to build demand at the consumer level. By using a comprehensive training, advertising and public relations program, National Enzyme Company seeks to reach the general public as well as retailers, health-care providers and clinical dieticians. Article-like advertisements, or advertorials, are placed in consumer magazines to better inform the public about the role of enzymes in digestion.

A consumer education website, www.enzymeuniversity.com, has also been developed. The website includes information about enzymes as they relate to dietary supplements. The articles and technical information are prepared by NEC staff and other medical and nutritional experts. In addition, NEC has raised public awareness of supplemental enzymes by sponsoring the nationally syndicated talk radio show *A Word on Health*.

National Enzyme Company's customer base encompasses both large and small businesses around the world. The sales and marketing staff are able to conduct business in English, Spanish, French, German, Portuguese, Mandarin Chinese and Taiwanese.

What began as one doctor's unheralded crusade to improve the nutritional health of his patients is today a thriving company that holds its position as a leader in the industry. Dr. Howell's legacy of quality, commitment and service are the same values that guided National Enzyme Company through its first 70 years of operation. And as the company embarks on its next 70 years, that's one formula for success that won't change.

Bottles moving down manufacturing line, waiting to be filled.

O.M.S. - OUELLETTE MACHINERY SYSTEMS

Joseph F. Ouellette, founder and president of Ouellette Machinery Systems, Inc. (OMS) has his own formula for success: "Success starts with a moment of desperation," he says. This creative inventor and his design team have resulted in O.M.S. holding patents on over 40 mechanical devices for the packaging industry, with 11 more patents in the works. Ouellette, a native of Canada, came to the U.S. in 1956 and soon after that he served three years in the U.S. Army. Before starting his own company, Ouellette had a number of good jobs. "I mastered each job well, but the appetite was there to move on."

With each position, Ouellette found that something was missing. Even though he put in extra time learning every aspect of the job—including other people's jobs—he still felt unfulfilled. "I wanted to get my hands into everything," he said. "I put extra time in learning all the jobs; it made people feel uncomfortable, but I wasn't trying to challenge anybody; I was just trying to learn."

Ouellette credits his father for his strong work ethic. "I have an appetite for work; it comes from my dad," he says. "My dad worked long hours for a pulp and paper manufacturing company; he had to master a lot, and ended up retiring from that same company as a manager."

At one point, Ouellette worked for Honeywell, Boeing and Xerox, but once again felt unfulfilled. Unhappy with himself and motivated by the prospect of achieving more than his current job offered, he thought about what he really wanted to do with his life. "You have to be in a situation where you can go as far as you can," he said.

After leaving Xerox, however, he found himself spending eight months watching television, cutting the grass, shopping, swimming and shooting pool. Finally he understood that anything was possible, and that he hadn't yet gone as far as he could. It was then that he knew he had to go into business for himself.

After that self-revelation, Ouellette took a job just to pay the bills, while he

Mr. Ouellette in 1977, standing on a version of the O.M.S. Earthquake Simulator.

tried to determine how to go about his new dream. At the time, his wife was expecting a baby, and he needed economic stability. After a year, he faced another dilemma: the company he was now working for, Crown Cork & Seal Company, was experiencing its own crisis and let him and other workers go at the end of February 1971.

Not to be deterred, Ouellette saw this event as divine intervention and kept remembering his dream of being his own boss. "I'm going to go to work for myself," he told his wife, who was not immediately thrilled with the idea. Determined to make a good living for his family, and in spite of many obstacles, Ouellette began advertising his skills, saying that he was available 24 hours a day, 7 days a week— as a consultant and automated machinery service engineer at an established rate. Interim to consultant and service contracts, Ouellette would work for mimimum wages to fill the voids.

On March 1, 1971, Ouellette Machinery Service, Inc., was officially born in Glendale, Missouri.

Ouellette worked 12 to 18 hour days contacting various bottling companies around the country. He knew that most of the bottling companies were experiencing economic slow down and had little choice but to cut back their workforce. Some were not financially able to buy new machines nor build new plants, so Ouellette wanted to offer them a way to incorporate their existing machines and plants with improved productivity. Through intensive telephone campaigns and mass mailings with the help of his wife Catherine, Ouellette informed the bottling companies of his services—and they let him know that they were, indeed, interested.

"It was feast, famine, feast, famine," Ouellette said. "It was a long, hard road."

Automatic Case Palletizer Model 530 equipped with heavy-duty, 3,500-pound pallet handling conveyors.

The O.M.S. "Smartly" Automated Production Line Level Bulk Bottle Palletizer Model Series 875-6.

When he averaged out his earnings in conjunction with the amount of time he was putting in, he figured he was making about 50 cents an hour. Still, he was poised to "follow their needs," sensing that all his hard work would eventually pay off.

In the middle of servicing his customers, Ouellette realized that many of them had great needs for certain special design devices. His attention became focused on this aspect, realizing that this was a way to both expand his business and provide the challenge he needed for his own personal goals.

In April 1973 Ouellette Machinery Service, Inc., was established as Ouellette Machinery Systems, Inc., by Ouellette and two partners. O.M.S. became a three-family-owned business, with Ouellette being the major stock holder. Both of Ouellette's partners eventually bowed out of the small-business venture. One left in the 1980s, and the other left in 1994. Ouellette then bought their shares in the company.

Just prior to the establishment of the three-family partnership, a client asked Ouellette to manufacture a special machine—something that would be able to remove the twist-off bottle caps from glass returnable bottles. The client, however, wanted this machine to remove the caps while the bottles were still in their cases. This was the break that Ouellette had longed for.

Although he had never seen a machine of this sort before, Ouellette and his partners gathered in the basement of his residence and created what is now known as "the world's first successful Incase Decapper." Someone later said to him, "It's unorthodox, but it works!"

"I suppose you've heard stories about guys building things in their basements and then they discover that they made something that's too big to get out the door," said Ouellette. "Well, that didn't happen in this case," he said, winking and tapping his head. "I planned it all out very carefully before I built it," he added, laughing. Careful planning has always been one of Ouellette's trademarks.

Very soon after its invention, the Incase Decapper was built, bought and delivered to a customer—and was soon given a U.S. patent. When the pleased customer began placing more orders for additional machines by the following September, though, Ouellette had to move his operations out of his basement and into a rented industrial manufacturing space. Labor Day marked the start of Ouellette's second Incase Decapper.

By 1974 O.M.S. was, in addition to manufacturing new equipment, rebuilding palletizers and depalletizers that its clients sent to them for improvement.

Also in the 1970s, O.M.S. ventured out into new territory by creating an earthquake simulator, which is now housed at the Seismology Department of the St. Louis Museum of Science. From taped command signals, the simulator is able to produce the shaking effect felt in an earthquake by transmitting frequencies and amplitudes ranging in intensity from 4 to 6 on the Modified Mercali Scale.

When Ouellette designed the simulator, he was asked specifically to make sure that the floor beneath the machine did not shake—that the vibrations should be contained within the machine itself. Ouellette, to the amazement of some scientists, achieved this goal. When demonstrating the simulator at the Science Center, though, the wooden floor did shake. No one could figure out what the problem was—until they realized that the shaking was coming from a person bounding up the stairs, and not from the machine!

A person wishing to try the machine, enters a booth and stands in the center of an 18-inch round platform, then holds on to a bar for support. As a video of an earth-

quake plays, the person(s) can actually feel the platform shaking beneath them.

Several museums around the country now have Ouellette's patented earth-quake simulators. Ouellette's design and manufacturing of specialty products have generally ceased since repeat machinery products must take priority over special projects. Still, the invention of the earthquake simulator has been much appreciated by its many visitors, who get a chance to experience what a real earthquake might feel like.

In July 1977 OMS introduced its first Automatic Case Palletizer and Semi-Au-

Design versatility provides for a variety of types of containers and shapes for palletizing as part of O.M.S. achievements.

tomatic Case Depalletizer, which had speed enhancement features. Another patented system, this invention allowed for increased production line speed and positive pallet destacking (palletizing) and stacking (depalletizing), which includes ease in handling defective pallets.

December 1981 introduced O.M.S.'s first Bag Palletizer, followed by a Drum and Pail Palletizer. By the summer of 1983, the company began designing and manufacturing a variety of Bulk Palletizers and Depalletizers to suit the needs of its clients. Offering small to large systems that range from low to high speed, O.M.S. continues to help clients pick out the right machine for their budgets and production line speed requirements.

As a pioneer of floor-level, row-forming, bulk palletizing systems, O.M.S. has the most operationally correct, fully automatic bulk palletization. By July 2002 the company's first "Fully Automatic Bottle Layer Bagging Palletizer" premiered.

A sales office display shows the amazing number and variety of containers that can be moved and manipulated on O.M.S. production line systems. They specialize in handling odd-shaped and odd-sized bottles, boxes, tins, cylinders, cans, pails, totes, crates and other containers. It also manufactures stackers, unstackers,

Intelligently Automatic Void Free Model 875-6 Bulk Bottle Palletizer.

palletizers, depalletizers, elevators, dispensers, inverters, rinsers and pneumatic conveyor systems, which are all tested for particular product handling application, speed capability and functionality prior to shipment.

To this day, Ouellette still works seven days a week, although he sometimes "cheats and works only 6 1/2 days," he laughs. "I take some time off now," he says, but admits that even when he's away he's always working mentally. "This is my hobby," he says. "In hard times and good times, I love it."

Ouellette thinks the world of his employees and credits part of the success of his company to them—to the teamwork they bring, saying that without teamwork, nothing would get accomplished. "It's kind of like an orchestra, and everyone knows their notes," he says. "I don't like the word 'I' or 'me'—if it were all about me, I'd never get it all done. We have to have great products to have great customers, and to have great products we have to have a great team of technical employees and dependable suppliers. Which comes first? It's a cluster that can't be disengaged."

Fully Automatic Bottle Layer Bagging Palletizers Model #LBGP-875-3.

With this kind of business philosophy, Ouellette has garnered great respect from his employees who refer to him as "JFO." "I love working with our employees; they're a great crew, and I also wear the green O.M.S. uniform as they do." says Ouellette. "I wouldn't ask anyone to do something I would not do myself. I also from time to time sweep the floor. A bell rings 10 minutes before the end of the working day. That's when we put away tools and sweep. It sets an atmosphere. Good for the mind and promotes safety and productivity." In fact, on various visits, the fire marshal was so impressed, that he wanted to use O.M.S. as a good example for other similar manufacturing plants to follow!

Ouellette's son, Richard, who is the vice president of design, describes his father as "ambitious, determined, intelligent and modest." James Hritz, vice president of sales and marketing, says that Ouellette is "the most innovative person I've ever met. He takes things out of the blue and turns them into reality."

O.M.S. is a company that sets no limits, just as Ouellette had once envisioned. During its humble beginnings, it employed one part-time worker and one full-time worker at a cost of $300 per week. Today this company, has 75 to 80 employees at a weekly cost of $55,000—and occupies 85,000 square feet of manufacturing facilities, now in Fenton, Missouri, part of St. Louis County, with state-of-the-art CNC manufacturing equipment.

Its client base has also increased, with both small and large companies in North America, South America and overseas. To date, O.M.S. holds 39 U.S. patents, 2 Canadian patents, 1 Mexican patent and has 11 patents pending. Some of the most recent patents granted to O.M.S. include; "Belt Conveyor Transition with Vacuum Stabilization," Conveyor Row Former, Array Rake and Sweep Mechanism for Conveying Objects Having Triangular Cross Sections" and "Early Detection Photo Controls." For more information, visit the company's website: www.omsinc.net.

When asked if he would recommend going into business for yourself to anyone today, Ouellette responded, "Absolutely, but one has to be prepared; it's a tough thing. You have to say, 'I'm going to do this, come hell or high water.' And, by Ouellette's experience, a moment of desperation wouldn't hurt, either.

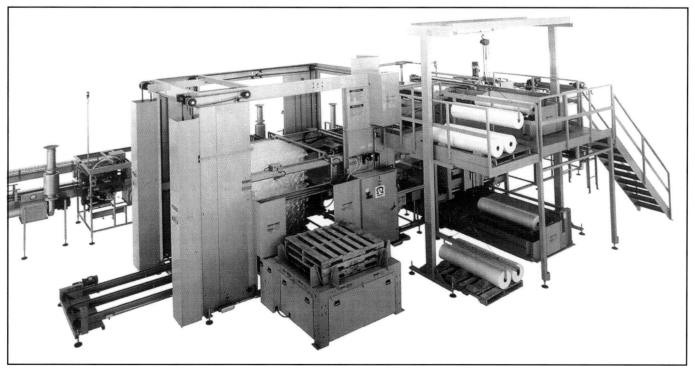

THE OUTSOURCE GROUP

Headquartered in Columbia, Missouri, The OutSource Group and its affiliated companies have served as a collection agency for healthcare, commercial and retail clients across the nation for the past quarter of a century.

The enterprise began as a partnership between two college friends working out of a one-room office. Today the company employs about 70 workers and operates out of one of the five buildings located in the Jay Ousley Plaza on I-70 Drive S.E.

For company owner and CEO George Ousley, Jr., the path to success involved a series of twists and turns, a life-changing tragedy and gutsy determination. The future looked anything but bright for the Jefferson City native when he quit high school during his senior year.

"My father told me I needed a high school diploma in order to get a good job, but I just didn't like school," explains Ousley. "If I wasn't going to go to high school, I figured the best thing to do was join the service."

The Vietnam War was raging, and Ousley's father feared for his son's safety. The young man opted to join the Navy and was assigned to the *U.S.S. Princeton* (LPH-5). He soon found himself on the other side of the world in Southeast Asia, toiling as a machinist mate in the engine room of the ship. It was hot, exhausting work. Many times Ousley questioned the decisions he had made.

His four-year stint in the Navy proved to be a training ground for future endeavors, however. It was here that he developed the qualities of discipline, organization and a strong work ethic. And he earned his G.E.D.

Ousley landed a job with Crown Finance, a small loan company, when he returned home to Jefferson City. "The ad in the paper said you must be at least 21, have a car, be married and be honorably discharged from the military. I thought, gosh, that's me!" recalls Ousley, who had no prior experience in the field. His starting monthly salary was $250.

Jay Ousley Plaza in June 2003.

After two years with Crown Finance, Ousley went to work for Berlin-Wheeler, a collection agency in Jefferson City. Soon thereafter the company hired a man named Wayne Sells to serve as a skiptracer for delinquent accounts. Ousley and Sells hit it off immediately. Sells was taking evening classes at Columbia College and urged Ousley to enroll. To his surprise, Ousley found the classes to be interesting and rewarding, especially those in the psychology and business departments. For the next four years, he took evening classes three nights a week while continuing to work at the collection agency. His perseverance paid off when he graduated with a bachelor's degree in 1978.

In the meantime, Sells had left Berlin-Wheeler, worked briefly at Boone Clinic, and joined forces with four partners to start up a collection agency called MediCredit Corporation in Columbia. Sells offered Ousley a full partnership in the new company.

"They needed someone to collect the money," says Ousley. "The other partners were more like investors. Wayne knew I could collect the money, and I knew Wayne could sell."

Ousley was not sold on the idea initially, however, and felt reluctant to leave the security of a job he had held for eight years. He waited another year before finally deciding to resign as collection manager and join MediCredit. He and Sells bought the other partners out and became a two-person operation. Ousley managed the office while Sells handled marketing and sales.

The inexperienced entrepreneurs learned through their mistakes, and the business began to prosper. "When we started out, the business grew at a rate of 30 percent a year, and we didn't know very much about what we were doing," says Ousley. "Our philosophy was to go out and work hard and do a good job. Word of mouth went out about us and we developed a lot of business that way."

And grow they have. Today the company has five divisions which fall under

George H. Ousley, Sr., receiving key to the City of Jefferson City, Misssouri, in 1981, upon retirement.

the umbrella of "The OutSource Group." MediCredit Corporation is a full service collection agency for retail and medical clients. MC Financial Services (MCFS), established in 1992, assists the client in the setting up and monitoring of payment arrangements. IntelliTrace (ITI) is an in-house skip service created in 1995. Through computer and software technology, consumers who have skipped with unpaid accounts are located. In 1996 TechPort was initiated to provide technical support services to The OutSource Group and its clientele. The National Healthcare Management & Billing Services (NHMBS) was also established that same year, specializing in insurance claims and reimbursement management. Its founding completed the wide range of accounts receivable management ser-

vices offered by The OutSource Group.

While in the midst of enjoying many professional triumphs, Ousley suffered a terrible tragedy that is every parent's worst nightmare. His eldest son, George H. Ousley III, was killed in an automobile accident in 1988 while serving in the Navy in Rota, Spain. He was just 19 years old.

"When you first hear news like this, time stands still. You don't even know how you're going to go on," says Ousley. "At some point you just start thinking about the good things."

The grieving father wanted to do something special to honor his son, who was known as "Jay" thanks to the nickname his grandfather gave him years ago. Ousley and Sells owned a parcel of land along I-70 and already had one building on the site. They received approval from city council to rename the property the "Jay Ousley Memorial Subdivision." They also began building a plaza and would later name it the "Jay Ousley Plaza" as a lasting tribute.

Ousley thinks his son, who was always giving generously to others, would be touched by the honor. "Jay was one of the most caring and easygoing kids you'd ever know. He would do anything for anybody."

Jay's grandfather, George H. Ousley, Sr., received a great honor of his own when he was handed the key to Jefferson City upon his retirement as foreman with the Division of Public Works in 1981. Ousley, Sr., was a dedicated employee of the city for 29 years.

These values of hard work and integrity were instilled in Ousley,

Jr., early on by the example of both of his parents. Sometimes his father would be called into work at the plant in the middle of the night, but he never refused to go, says Ousley. His mother, Hazel, also worked long hours as an LPN at Memorial Community Hospital.

Ousley and his business partner have applied a similar level of commitment in order to make their company a success. The OutSource Group serves some 200 clients all over the country. Most are located in Missouri, Arkansas, Nebraska, Kansas and Florida. Three years ago Ousley bought The OutSource Group from Sells, who wanted to retire and focus his attention on independent investments.

And the two remain close friends. "We worked together for 25 years. He's been like a brother to me," says Ousley.

Ousley is astonished at the success he and Sells enjoyed over the years. "I thought it would do okay. It's hard for me to imagine where it is today, and it's still growing. And it's got a long way to go. Our foundation is strong. We've got the right people there."

Bonnie Baker serves as president and has been with the company since 1982,

Sells and Ousley, front page, _Columbia Business Times_, 1995.

Ousley And Sells Create Winning Partnership

Gregory S. Ousley, 1988 Jefferson City High School graduation.

vice offerings, and have worked hard in the past few years to build up the infrastructure of the business," says Baker. Future plans include the addition of more retail business and possible expansion of the company's skiptracing services.

The OutSource Group is also involved in a number of community charitable events, including fundraisers for the Columbia Youth Football League and the American Cancer Society. Last year the company started a golf tournament to benefit NBA Woodhaven and contributed funds toward the purchase of a transportation van for its residents.

After years of hard work, Ousley is finally able to slow down and enjoy the simple pleasures of life. He and his wife own vacation homes in the Ozarks and in Florida. Whether he is playing golf, traveling or fixing up his red 1963 Corvette, Ousley has learned the importance of savoring every moment of life, especially time spent with family and friends.

George H. "Jay" Ousley III, 1986 Jefferson City High School graduation.

where she started out as a computer programmer in the Medi-Credit office. The general manager, Don Wright, has worked with The OutSource Group for 11 years.

Ousley's family has also played important roles in the business. His younger son, Greg, worked in the company for five years and served as vice president of sales before launching out on his own. For the past eight years, Ousley's sister, Marilyn, has been involved in the skiptracing division. And now his wife, Gayleen, works in computer programming.

Ousley firmly believes that quality service has been the key to the company's success. "We give the clients what they want. We're not one of the big agencies that are out there. But we've had some of the same clients since the beginning. I don't know many in this business that can say that."

Baker credits the vision of the company's founders and their management staff for making The OutSource Group what it is today. The business world continues to change, and entrepreneurs must be prepared to meet these challenges.

"We are very proactive on technology utilization and ser-

This statuary group in the Westport area of Kansas City commemorates Alexander Majors, the entrepreneur who helped make the Santa Fe Trail profitable for Missourians; John C. McCoy, who laid out the town of Westport in 1830; and Jim Bridger, the Mountain Man involved with the fur trade, who operated a store in Westport. Courtesy, Gregory M. Franzwa

PETERSON MANUFACTURING AND PETERSON CORPORATION

To millions of people around the world, the name Peterson Manufacturing is virtually unknown. Yet these same millions see and use the products and services of this Grandview, Missouri-based corporation every day of their lives.

From the lighting assemblies on countless cars, trucks, trailers, motorcycles and other vehicles to air charter services; from ground transportation fleets for railroad and airline crews to cutting-edge technology in tool and die engineering and plastics; from global import sourcing to the exciting world of motorsports collectibles and more, the Peterson Corporate Group is truly a multi-faceted company.

Even the company admits that most people don't know the real Peterson Manufacturing (PM). "Since 1945 we've been a vibrant, growing part of the automotive original equipment and aftermarkets," says PM President and CEO Don Armacost, Jr. "Today our family of some

Don R. Armacost purchased Peterson Manufacturing in 1956.

11 companies is serving transportation-related industries around the world."

As a multi-industry corporation, Peterson's humble origins trace to 1945 when the company officially began supplying the automotive aftermarket with an eclectic assortment of products that

included safety lighting, reflectors and tire pumps.

In October 1956, Don R. Armacost, a young Kansas City businessman, acquired the company by paying all the cash he could muster and borrowing the remaining 86 percent of the purchase price. Prior to purchasing Peterson Manufacturing, Mr. Armacost served as a Navy lieutenant during World War II and worked for his father, a Kansas City Studebaker dealer, both before and after the war.

In his first year, Mr. Armacost boosted the company's total sales more than 25 percent over the previous year and began looking for ways to expand his customer base beyond the automotive aftermarket. In the early 1960s, Armacost and his chief engineer invented and patented the Vibar® socket, a breakthrough in safety lighting technology. This exclusive, resilient socket, destined to become an industry standard, was designed to absorb road shock and vibration for longer bulb life. It opened the door for Peterson to begin doing business with the much larger market of original equipment manufacturers.

The Vibar® innovation was the first of many for Peterson. Over the years, the company has been among the first to develop rustproof, stainless steel housings; Lexan® lenses that are virtually indestructible; a unique way to seal lights against moisture and road salt; leading LED optic and circuitry technology; plus other product and packaging innovations too numerous to list.

Today, the ever-expanding Peterson product line covers more than 2,200 different types of vehicle safety lights, reflectors and other automotive accessories. An integral component to each and every product is quality—something that Don Armacost, Jr., says starts with the people who make the product.

"We don't inspect quality into a product, we build it in. Our big competitive advantage is our people and their total commitment to quality. Many of them are second- and third-generation associates

The lobby of Peterson Manufacturing's Grandview, Missouri facility serves as a welcoming location for guests and a showcase for the company's vehicle safety lighting products.

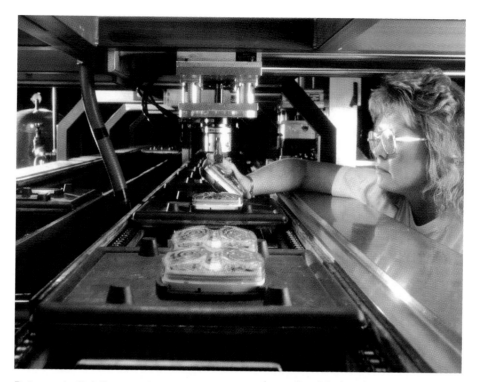

Peterson's lighting products not only meet federal requirements but exceed them by 25 percent.

and they truly care about our customers and take pride in what they do. It's their dedication and skills which are the heart of our growth."

Quality is very much a core value to Peterson, driving the company to become the first in its industry to obtain ISO 9001 and QS 9000 certification. Quality is why Peterson builds products that not only meet federal specifications, but also exceed them by 25 percent. And quality is why the company boasts the industry's lowest return rate and why it enjoys many customer relationships that span decades.

Peterson's 450,000-square-foot facility in Grandview, Missouri, houses management, information systems, sales, engineering, research and development, manufacturing and assembly and a warehousing department. Over 650 non-union associates staff this plant and share in the company's success through employee stock ownership and profit-sharing programs.

Peterson Manufacturing Company is the flagship of the Peterson Corporate Group, a family of 11 companies and over 3,000 people working in global transpor-

tation-related industries. In addition to Peterson Manufacturing, these highly specialized companies also contribute to the Peterson corporate success story:
- Anderson Marine—Peterson's marine lighting division.
- Mission Plastics North—plastic injection molding.
- Mission Plastics Arkansas—plastic injection molding.
- Maxi-Seal Harness System—a manufacturer of electrical harness systems for trucks and trailers.
- Vector Tool and Engineering—tooling for plastic injection molding.
- D&D Aviation—air charter services.
- Kansas City Aviation Center—aircraft sales, fuel.
- Renzenberger Inc.—railroad crew transportation services.
- Motorsports Marketing—distributor and retailer of motorsports collectibles.
- Transworld Products, Inc.—an international sourcing company.

Together, these companies have provided Peterson with unique opportunities to excel in a variety of transportation-related industries. Each one seeks to meet tomorrow's needs with cutting-edge innovation and old-fashioned quality—a combination that has taken Peterson from a small manufacturing company to an innovative leader serving customers worldwide.

This combination trailer light performs seven lighting functions and is one of Peterson Manufacturing's best-selling items.

PC & E, INC.

In January 1986, an old door set on shipping boxes served as the first "conference table" for the St. Louis, Missouri, engineering firm of PC & E, Inc. Seventeen years later, the firm functions as a wholly owned subsidiary of Emerson Corporation, an international player that generates, through over 120,000 employees in 60 countries, $15 billion in revenue annually.

Jim Jordan, founder, president and chief executive officer of PC & E, capitalized on the mid-1980s trend toward corporate downsizing to develop a new specialty consulting engineering firm. He was well-qualified to do so, having worked with the engineering giant Monsanto Company over a period of two decades. Jordan signed on with Monsanto after graduation from Washington University in 1964, working at that time as a process control engineer. In 1977 Monsanto appointed him manager of instrument and electrical engineering. During his tenure as manager, Jordan coordinated the efforts of the instrument and electrical design group for a multimillion dollar fiber manufacturing

Jim Jordan speaking at the 15th anniversary of PC & E.

Rick Arnold, Jim Jordan and Ron Lute at the 15th anniversary of PC & E in February 2001.

project. The project came in ahead of schedule and under budget, earning Monsanto an industry award for excellence under Jordan's watch.

In 1981 Jordan moved on to Fisher Controls, an instrument manufacturing and service company. His tenure as manager with Fisher allowed him to develop his idea of "turnkey" engineering and installation for process control projects, a full-service approach that provided clients the development of business plans, preparation of proposals and management for an entire engineering project. Jordan returned to Monsanto in 1984 as manager for their corporate engineering department, where he managed the process control and electrical design group. The firm's layoffs of engineering staff in 1985 prompted him to strike out on his own.

Monsanto engineers Rick Arnold and Ron Lutes joined with Jordan in 1985 to create PC & E, Inc. Both brought impressive credentials to the new St. Louis firm. Arnold, a graduate of the University of Missouri-Rolla, brought to PC & E almost 20 years' experience in corporate engi-

neering, having provided lead instrument and electrical design expertise for Monsanto chemical, petro-chemical and electronic materials projects, including plant design projects in Mexico, Brazil and Australia. Arnold joined the new firm as a process control and electrical engineer. Lutes, also a University of Missouri-Rolla graduate, brought to the new firm over 10 years of experience with Monsanto's corporate engineering department. Both later became vice presidents of PC & E, Inc.

With start-up funds provided by Pioneer Bank, the new operation signed a lease for office space at 1003 Hanley Industrial Court in St. Louis. The new firm officially incorporated on January 1, 1986, and sent out its first invoice, for $36,000, two days later. Salvaged office equipment, an outdated telephone system and a computer constituted the firm's initial technical support. Firm members debated whether a computer hard drive would really be needed. Their vision for the company came into sharper focus during the summer of 1986, when Mon-

santo Electronic Materials Co., now a leading supplier of silicon wafers to the semiconductor industry, hired PC & E for a start-up project in Korea. By December 1986, PC & E had hired eight more Monsanto engineers and designers, again benefiting from that company's reorganizations. By December 1987, total firm revenues were nearing the $2.5 million mark, and by spring of 1989, PC & E had outgrown its original home. The company moved its operations to its current headquarters at 2280 Schuetz Road in St. Louis and opened its first branch office in Decatur, Illinois.

Summer of 1990 saw the establishment of PC & E on-site engineering offices at both MEMC and Shell Oil Refinery. By 1991 company staff had grown to 80, due in part to reorganizations at several other companies. PC & E continued to capitalize on corporate downsizing, drawing experienced talent into its organization as other companies contracted. Revenues in 1991 topped $5.5 million, and in 1992, PC & E spun off its first division, a custom manufacturing firm headed by Joe Farina. They named the new division FABCON.

FABCON, whose name derives from "fabrication concepts," would use Jordan's "turnkey" approach to the provision of engineering services: it was designed to handle all aspects of the manufacturing phase of project development. Client services included project design, construction and installation of instrumentation and equipment. FABCON also offered clients project management, design, fabrication and assembly professionals with decades of experience in electrical and mechanical disciplines. Clients could use their own plans for provision of manufacturing services, using FABCON's personnel to implement them, or they could cede responsibility for complete project management, from design to completion, to PC & E's new fabrication division. Services provided included electrical, with expert electricians qualified to provide power and control wiring for any installation; mechanical, including all piping and tubing systems and automated welding when needed; installation of industrial control systems and analyzer systems; and even shipping, with FABCON providing the correct crat-

PC & E's facilities at 2280 Schuetz Road in St. Louis.

ing and containers to ensure proper delivery around the world.

By 1993 PC & E had topped the 100-employee milestone. Gary Borgens joined the firm that year, and in September, Borgens and Gary Windler launched PC & E's newest division. INCAL, the firm's instrument calibration and field service branch, offered to clients in-house and field instrumentation calibration, along with start-up, tuning, preventive maintenance and repair services. Professionals from the division would check each instrument against design specifications prior to start-up, either on-site or at INCAL's test and calibration lab. After installation, instruments monitor the operation for accurate performance within design specifications. Rapidly changing technologies drives the need for much of INCAL's services: the division has provided plant modernization services to many clients, including Monsanto, MEMC and AmerenUE. INCAL also offers on-site calibration services to help minimize production downtime and costly repairs to clients. Its provi-

PC & E's original Board of Directors in 1986.

sion of routine calibration schedules helps ensure the precision and accuracy of sensitive instruments used in analytical process control operations.

PC & E's new divisions led to a demand for updated technology within their own physical plant. In 1993 the company installed a new computer network system to streamline project management. By the time of its 10th anniversary in 1996, the number of PC & E employees had grown to over 175, with management priding itself on hiring the most qualified applicants available. Company projects had spanned the globe, and included overseas projects in Saudi Arabia, Singapore, South Korea, Australia, Belgium and an especially sensitive project installation that took place in Perm, Russia, 1,000 miles northeast of Moscow, during the breakup of the Soviet Union.

Clients are enthusiastic in their assessment of PC & E's services. A newsletter celebrating the firm's 10th anniversary cites a number of quotes from clients, including that of a manager of control and information systems for Procter and Gamble, who noted that PC & E served "a big need that other contractors can't provide to the industry." An engineering manager from Monsanto charac-

terized PC & E as "a high-quality resource for us," calling the company "an excellent source of supplemental help to our internal resources."

Company president Jordan noted that "by 1996, every bank in town was knocking on the door" to offer financing to the successful firm. Other interests were noticing as well. In 1998 Emerson Electric Company, a global firm with widespread holdings, made a successful bid to acquire the St. Louis start-up. Emerson's acquisition of PC & E would enhance the parent company's capabilities in condition monitoring, diagnostics, electrical testing and custom-engineering solutions. New technological capabilities, new product line and service offerings, and increased market share growth would enhance Emerson's holdings, in addition to providing them with greater presence and scale in rapidly expanding world markets. Although Emerson acquired PC & E in part to provide "turnkey" solution capabilities for Emerson manufactured products, PC & E would maintain brand neutrality with the majority of engineering services associated with non-Emerson manufactured products.

PC & E came under Emerson's jurisdiction as a wholly owned subsidiary, with Jordan, Arnold and Lutes all staying on with the company's new owner. PC & E has been renamed the Emerson Pro-

cess Management, St. Louis Industries Center. Arnold notes that corporate structure brought more organization and policies that helped to "tighten up" the newly owned business. Company philosophy remained intact: clients could still select their desired level of involvement in any given project, from initial conception through start-up, training and maintenance. Its services continued to include pre-funding planning, including process engineering; permitting; compatibility, feasibility studies; cost estimates; site surveys; resource planning; pilot plant prototypes; preliminary layouts and schedules; and process flow diagrams.

PC & E's design services include control logics; control system architecture; equipment and instrument specifications; power studies; detailed schedules of implementation; code reviews; and even studies for material balances and waste minimization. Implementation includes services across the board, from detailed layouts and factory acceptance tests to database development and project management, with PC & E's FABCON division supplying control room construction, control panels and process skids. Start-up commissioning includes site acceptance tests; construction supervision; process safety management; project documentation; training of personnel; regulatory compliance; and instrument calibration provided by PC & E's INCAL division. On-going support and maintenance provided by INCAL includes technical training; inspections and audits; air and water quality monitoring; and both predictive and preventive maintenance of equipment. Under the umbrella of Emerson Process Management, the company also offers financing, addressing operating and capital budget considerations, tax and balance sheet considerations, and clients' unique cash flow requirements.

Benefits of this level of service to clients include an assurance of continuous operations; avoidance of costly down-

Celebrating PC & E, Inc.'s fifth and tenth anniversaries. Top photo left to right: co-founders Ron Lutes, Jim Jordan and Rick Arnold. Bottom photo, left to right: Jim Jordan, Rick Arnold and Ron Lutes.

try brings fresh thinking to projects in other industries. This approach helps greatly in a consulting firm that serves a widely varied client base. PC & E utility projects include power studies and electrical design and start-up services, as well as projects peculiar to the industry, such as coal handling design, burner management, ash management, and motor and draft control. PC & E serves the chemical and petroleum refining industries, concentrating there on process safety system design, and on the updating of control systems, control system software development for DCS/PLCs, electrical area classifications and process and instrument drawings.

The company's range of experience within the food and beverage industry includes bulk materials handling; high speed packaging; soft drink bottling; beer brewing and bottling; dairy processing; and the manufacturing of agricultural and fertilizer products.

PC & E's provision of complete engineering and construction packages proves especially beneficial to engineering clients in a field characterized by constant innovation, where new technology and constantly changing codes and federal regulations mandate continual upgrading of systems. The company's mission statement is: "to provide the highest quality engineering services today, while developing our ability to meet the application challenges of tomorrow." It is well served by the triangle of services provided by FABCON in manufacturing, INCAL in technical support and PC & E in engineering. The firm has expanded its office space as business has grown, and now includes regional branch offices in Decatur, Illinois; Kansas City, Missouri; and Golden, Colorado, in addition to its plant headquarters in St. Louis, Missouri. The company continues to draw skilled staff from the country's finest engineering and trade schools, ensuring a continuance of excellent service to clients as PC & E moves into the new millennium.

time and repairs; and flexibility in terms of labor arrangements. Clients can choose short or long-term staffing, with skilled technicians provided on an as-needed basis. These technicians bring a broad range of experience to their posts, having worked with a wide range of equipment from many different manufacturers. The company has sustained its focus on expanding its international base, as engineers working with a multitude of cultural differences have developed projects from China to Thailand, Venezuela and the United Arab Emirates.

PC & E engineers benefit from a "crossover" approach, where knowledge gained from serving one particular indus-

RICHARDSON PRINTING

Nowhere did the twenties roar louder than in Kansas City, Missouri.

Thomas J. Pendergast had risen quickly through various levels of city government to become the city's powerful political boss, presiding over corrupt local government officials who would dominate the political landscape for 50 years.

Speakeasies and Kansas City jazz attracted revelers throughout the city of 324,410, and happy inhabitants of The Heartland regularly celebrated the nightlife into the wee hours.

Returning from the war, Major Harry Truman was discharged in 1919. He began a men's clothing store with an army friend and married Bess Wallace. By 1920 the business had failed.

Earnest Hemingway had left Kansas City's newspaper, *The Star,* in 1918 to drive ambulances in the war. He did not return afterward, but Walt Disney's career was beginning to flourish creating cartoon ads for a local firm.

As the twenties roared in, it is likely that few other than friends and family took much notice in 1921 when a young businessman established a small, independent in-plant printing operation within Intercollegiate Press, a scholastic yearbook printing firm in Kansas City.

Company delivery truck, "The Mighty Mite" during the early 1950s.

Dick Richardson at his desk in 1958.

Dick Richardson Company, Inc., the printing firm carrying the name of its founder, used the boost it gained from its large parent account to leave the nest, so to speak, and move into quarters in the Graphic Arts Building on Wyandotte Street in Downtown Kansas City just a few years later. Relying primarily on short runs of flyers and broadsides, the company enjoyed continued success and soon moved to its own facility at 2223 Guinotte in an area near the Missouri River just north of downtown, known as the bottoms.

Here Dick Richardson Company added multi-part forms and mailing service to its product mix; with a strong reputation for quality and service in its letterpress operation, it entered the second half of the 20th century on solid footing.

C.C. "Chuck" Richardson grew up in and around his father's business. After returning from service in the U.S. Navy in World War II, he graduated from Carnegie Institute of Technology with a degree in printing management and joined his father in the business.

By the end of the 1950s, Dick Richardson Company had added offset lithography, along with camera and plate-making, to its base letterpress business and even was running four-color process on its one-color, 29-inch press. Machine bookkeeping forms, one-time carbon manifold forms and NCR manifold forms rounded out the product mix.

A fire ended the company's stay in the bottoms, and in the summer of 1961, Dick Richardson found a 25,000-square-foot building at the company's current address, 1600 Truman Road, and moved his company into the former commercial laundry facility.

The most robust of the company's products during the 1960s were the business forms. In 1967 Chuck Richardson headed a group of the company's employees to create a wholly owned subsidiary to be called DeArco Business Forms Company, Inc. The plan was to set up a wholesale operation with local dealers and no direct sales to consumers. A year later, in June 1968, United Business Forms Company or UBF was created as the company's business forms operation.

With Dick retired and Chuck now running the operation, Dick Richardson Company, Inc., and United Business Forms were a firm fixture in the Kansas City graphics arts community when James L. Barker came on the scene as a prospective buyer in 1980.

Barker was no newcomer to the local graphics arts community. After graduating from Kansas City Central High School in 1956, he attended junior college, then the University of Kansas City (later to become the University of Missouri—Kansas City). Military duty took him out of college and into aircrew training with the United States Naval Reserve in Pensacola and Jacksonville, Florida.

He spent the following four years as an electronics warfare officer working out

C.C. "Chuck" Richardson observes reassembly of a press after the move in 1961.

Richardson's current facility at the time of its purchase.

of Subic Bay in the Philippines and in Vietnam. Returning to Kansas City in 1965, he went to work at I.J. Eagle Printing Company where he gained experience in production, estimating and sales.

At Eagle, Barker honed the talents that led to his being hired as sales manager at Spangler Printing in 1975, but his real dream was to run his own company. With no family members interested in the company, Chuck Richardson had put out feelers for potential buyers. He and Barker reached an agreement in 1980, and the new owner's first order of business was to change the name to Richardson Printing Company, Inc. Chuck Richardson stayed on in a sales capacity for a little over five more years.

Nearly 20 years later, while introducing Barker as the Printing Industries of the Heartland's 1997 Executive of the Year, a competitor described the new owner as having "reinvented Richardson Printing."

The equipment on hand in 1980 consisted of one- and two-color letterpresses; a one-color, 29-inch offset press; some camera and plating equipment; three linotype machines and some forms equipment. According to Barker, no new equipment had been added in the preceding 15 years.

During the next two years, Barker purchased the company's first four-color offset press, a 26-inch Komori.

He began weaning the company away from business forms, a product with little promise in a business world turning to computers and electronic business transactions.

In 1982 Barker made a decision that would provide a dramatic impact on the way the company operated and probably ensured its future.

Barker saw the need to cross-train employees in order to accomplish cross-utilization of equipment. After a prolonged period of unsuccessful negotiations during which the union refused even to consider such a move, the union employees began a two-and-one-half-year strike. Barker set about re-hiring an entirely new group of plant employees, and when the pickets went away, no former union workers remained. Wages and benefits for the new employees were on par with union shops, but more flexible work rules allowed Barker to concentrate investment in areas other than an excessively large payroll. It was a key element in the allocation of funds for future growth and, frankly, the survival of the company.

A methodical man, who combined his vision for the future with a practical business acumen, Barker identified the direction the business needed to take,

The Barkers, left to right: Jimmy, David, Jim.

cial management than Barker could handle by himself. Kent White, a CPA with whom Barker had worked previously, was hired to manage the business of the business and eventually became vice president and CFO of the company.

Another new press provided the level of quality and service for which Barker was looking, and it was time to turn attention to the state of electronic prepress.

Barker's elder son, Jimmy, had worked in the plant during summers while in high school and came on board full time after graduation from Northwest Missouri State University in 1985. After paying his dues in the pressroom and bindery, the younger Barker "moved upstairs" to the sales and management offices in 1992. Today he is the executive vice president of Richardson Printing.

Younger brother David tended to be more mechanically inclined with great interest in building and racing stock cars. He joined the company in 1990 and worked his way through the bindery and pressroom and soon became a lead pressman.

One of Jimmy's first major assignments was to research prepress equipment and make a recommendation to his father. In the autumn of 1994, Scitex scanning and processing equipment along with new computers were purchased. During that summer, Barker hired a new vice president for marketing. C. Eugene Jacobs was a long-time friend with nearly 20 years

what he needed to arrive at his goals and how to prioritize the steps once identified.

He wanted a medium-size company capable of producing high-quality, multi-color lithography. He wanted to maintain and even improve the company's long-standing, exceptional reputation for service and customer relations. He wanted equipment that would enable his newly hired and cross-trained craftspeople to perform at the highest level of their abilities.

The first order of business, therefore, was new equipment, an expensive undertaking in a capital-intensive business like commercial printing. Barker determined that manufacturing equipment, i.e., presses and bindery machinery, would continue to become more expensive in the near term. He also determined that the technology in computerized prepress equipment still had room for improvement and would become less expensive through the process.

With the backing of his bankers, Barker fashioned a plan that brought new folders and binders as well as another 26-inch, five-color press to go with the existing 40-inch, two-color press during the next six years.

In 1992 the growing company presented the need for higher level finan-

Architect's elevation drawing of the renovation to take place next door to the current headquarters building.

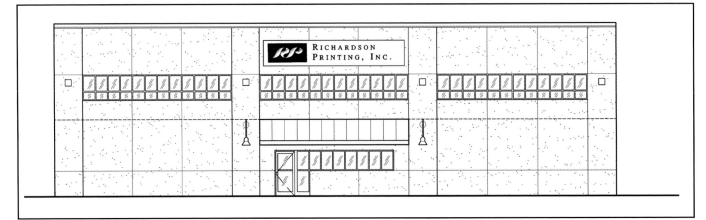

Company officers, from left to right: Jimmy Barker, executive vice president; Jim Barker, owner and president; Kent White, vice president/finance; C. Eugene Jacobs, vice president/marketing.

of experience in graphics arts sales and marketing and, most importantly, experience in companies with in-house prepress.

Jacobs created Richardson Electrical Digital Imaging (REDI) as an independent identification for the company's new capabilities, and "REDI Teddy" became the company's symbol for the new department. As Richardson's new era began, Jimmy Barker was heard to say, "We will ride that bear as far as we can to capture a whole new segment of the market."

Successfully managed growth has been the chief characteristic of Richardson Printing under the direction of Jim Barker. After bringing sales to the $6 million level by the early 1990s, that total doubled in the next several years. Careful management became the key in coping with the combined impact of two important clients relocating and the economy's downturn after the events of September 11, 2001. Barker's sound financial management had the company in a position, not only to cope, but also to take advantage of the new circumstances.

The company backed down from its near capacity schedule that had seen seven-day work weeks too often as the norm. A minor reduction in staff and the new sales level still produced margins well within projection. With a lighter production schedule in effect, Barker aggressively steered the company in another forward move.

Substandard proofing methods had hindered the utilization of computer-to-plate (CTP) technology for companies such as Richardson. The coincidence of new proofing procedures and newly available time for staff training provided Barker with a window of opportunity.

All new Scitex equipment was brought in along with new proofing and plate-making capabilities. The new digital proofing equipment utilized the same file-processing technology as did the plate-making equipment and as such, provided a back-up system for making plates, a critical element in avoiding downtime in the pressroom.

Additional hardware, including PC platforms and state-of-the-art software, was put in place to support sales representatives in addressing the new market place created by desktop publishing and CTP. Sales trends at Richardson Printing once again were on the rise.

In 2002 Barker took note of the only bright aspect of the struggling economy. Interest rates were reaching modern-day, record-low levels. A company with Richardson's sound financial record proved most attractive to the local banking industry, and once again Barker used the situation to facilitate bold, aggressive moves.

By the end of 2003 the company will be completing renovation of a second building next to its current facility. All current presses will be moved to the new facility along with a new 40-inch, six-color unit with all the current technology. A modern, over-night responsive fulfillment center now also is operating successfully a few miles away from the mail plant.

Jim Barker considers this renovation and influx of equipment to be his final brush strokes on the commercial canvas he began in 1980. Throughout nearly a quarter century of planning, managing and building, Barker now leads a company of which he and his sons are immensely proud, and the next generation will assume the controls in the not-too-distant future.

In 2003 Richardson Printing is a bright new company cultivated and shaped from the strong roots of the original. The concept of a high quality product and strong attention to customer service by a staff of trained professionals has, and will continue to be, the philosophy most associated with this highly respected Kansas City corporate citizen.

REDI Teddy, spokesbear for Richardson Electronic Digital Imaging.

SWISHER MOWER AND MACHINE

Swisher Mower and Machine Company includes the phrases "a servant to our customers" and "a shepherd to our employees" in its mission statement and further promises to "work hard and have fun while becoming the premier manufacturer of specialty lawn and garden equipment and accessories."

It begins with the end in mind: Images of perfectly manicured grass, sharp edging, beautiful gardens, neatly bagged leaves—and wood, split and stacked.

Thus, this over-50-year-old family business defines itself, embracing its customers and employees as part of the family.

Swisher began with the ingenuity and resourcefulness of Max Swisher, who grew up on a farm three miles north of Leeton. In 1945 Max, 17, was expected to work on his father's sawmill and threshing machine crews. However, stacking railroad ties and working the harvest weren't for him. Neither was mowing the Swisher's yard. He enjoyed tinkering in the farm's machine shop.

To avoid mowing, Max created, and later patented, a gearbox to convert their Goodall Manufacturing rotary lawn

Swisher lawn vac attachment.

Max Swisher, founder, in 1948 with one of his early self-propelled designs.

mower into a self-propelled unit. He tied one end of a rope to a tree in the middle of the yard and the other end to the mower. As the mower moved, the rope wrapped around the tree and pulled it closer. Max relaxed in a shaded seat on the porch while his invention did the work.

While Max's father, Henry, didn't want him puttering around with lawnmowers, neighbors noticed his modification and asked him to make more. Max did, swapping them for such things as tools to make more and better mowers. His first plant was in his mother's chicken house, where he did everything from welding to casting aluminum parts with battery power; electricity hadn't yet come to rural Missouri. Soon, Max's mowers—under the name "Mohawk"—were being used throughout the area.

In 1951 Max was recruited for the Korean War. This spelled crisis for the business, a one-person operation with a backlog of inventory and a pile of bills. Henry stepped in to keep up his son's credit, delivering orders on weekends in his 1947 Chevy pickup truck. This gave him a sense of the demand for the mowers. Soon Max's brother, Ray, joined in, building investor interest so Swisher could expand.

Max, assigned to the Aberdeen Proving Ground in Maryland, found time to position the company for the future, making good use of the telephone and occasional all-night drives home. Late in 1951, he acquired a 1,600-square-foot building, formerly the Roseland Packing Company.

When it opened at 333 East Gay Street in Warrensberg, Swisher Mower and Machine Company had six employees. Stockholders included Henry; Max, Ray and their third brother, Gene; Max's aunt and uncle, Guy Booth and Ethel Booth, and several local investors. Max was president; Guy, first vice president; Walter Barnes, second vice president; Wallace Cooper, secretary; and Ray, treasurer.

Production equipment for the "Swisherrr" power lawn mower initially occupied part of the building, but quickly spread to exceed the building's capacity. The first of a series of additions—2,500 square feet—came in 1954. In the years that followed, Swisher grew to occupy seven buildings on East Gay. Swisher purchased three buildings on East Market in 1962 from Goodall, and sold them a year later. In 1999 Swisher started building at a new site, 1602 Corporate Drive, adding 80,000 square feet for production, 42,000 for warehousing and 6,000 for offices.

Today's Swisher Zero-Turn mower.

All told, in 2003 Swisher's 330 employees occupied 157,000 square feet.

The standard Swish-errr in 1951 was a self-propelled, pusher-type mower with a suction-type rotary blade, pushed by a single-centered rear wheel and powered by a two-horsepower engine. It came both self-propelled and not, and Swisher offered a saw for cutting brush and a two-and-a-half horsepower motor. The height of the cut was adjustable using a lever instead of changing wheels, as had been done on other mowers. Sales in Swisher Mower's first year totaled $50,000, largely in the area around Warrensburg.

In 1953 Max was discharged from the Army. His inventiveness drove the business, and he was its primary traveling salesman.

In 1954 Max built the original zero-turning riding mower—the Ride King. He and a dealer took a suite of rooms in a Nashville hotel to show it off. Max recalls a man getting off the elevator and walking in. "He saw the rider and wanted to know what it was and, by that time, he was sitting on it. He asked what the price was. I told him $150 to $200, wanting to get him out because obviously he was not a prospective dealer. His reply was, 'That's not bad,' and asked if I would ship one to Memphis. I said sure, as long as he was willing to pay the freight."

It turned out the customer was Elvis Presley, not yet famous but staying in the suite above Swisher's. He'd gotten off at

Swisher log splitter innovations.

the wrong floor and thought the mower was in his room.

The company had planned to test the market with 50 zero-turn riders during the first year. Max took one in his car to the National Hardware show in New York City. The first person to stop and look ordered 50. Swisher made 700 in 1955, all by hand with no tooling or equipment.

Max continued to invent, working in his basement workshop and the machine shop at his expanding facility. His children—sons Jerry and Wayne—now manage Swisher and remember odd noises, power outages and strange happenings from that basement. Those heralded innovations have kept Swisher lawn and garden equipment and All Terrain Vehicle (ATV) accessories strong and dependable. Even products that were produced for only a short time broke new ground. These included solar-powered yard composters and barbecue rotisseries, both produced in 1991 but discontinued because they did not fit with key sales outlets.

Patents earned by Max and his research staff produced and constantly improved on Swisher's self-propelling walk-behind, with quick height adjustment; its zero-turn riding mower; and other products.

Today, Swisher mowers are available in all 50 states, Canada and several other nations, with a line that includes trimmers and mowers, edgers, lawn vacuums, trail cutters and mowers, log splitters—and such ATV accessories as fork lifts, plows, buckets, carts, storage baskets and the quadivator, a multi-purpose garden implement. The company also offers quality fabricating services, partnering with individuals and businesses.

Max remains active on the board, while designing new products. Looking back, he says having a family business can be very rewarding. "Seeing your kids grow up and take charge and continue making a success of it is the greatest."

TRABON-PARIS PRINTING COMPANY

Sometimes it takes years before a person realizes and claims the gifts he's been blessed with. And sometimes it takes years to gain perspective and look back to see that, in spite of obstacles and tragic events, it's been a wonderful life after all. Such is the case of Tim Trabon, owner of Trabon-Paris Printing Company and Trabon Solutions based in Kansas City, Missouri.

A philanthropist at heart, Tim wanted to be a writer when he grew up, so he could create stories that would inspire the masses. It wasn't until later in life that he realized the masses could be reached and inspired through acts of kindness, generosity and a genuine willingness to help.

Tim's father, Michael Trabon, a typographer for the *Kansas City Star*, was a huge inspiration and influence in his son's life. One evening, after a long day at work, he announced to his wife, Mary, that he had purchased a used letterpress and would be starting his own business—while keeping his full-time job at the paper.

"As a child," says Tim, "the melody of the press lulled me to sleep." He also re-

Tim Trabon, owner of Trabon-Paris Printing Company and Trabon Solutions based in Kansas City, Missouri.

members it being educational: "I learned my *ABCs* by distributing individual letters of lead type into the type drawers that my father had marked with a piece of chalk."

Tim's parents managed to build up a good, small business for themselves, and by 1967 they were making about $19,000 per year, in addition to Michael's full-time time job. His new company, which upgraded to a Heidelberg windmill letterpress, specialized in printing items such as business cards, handbills and invoices for other small businesses. Tim helped by keeping the press oiled and hand-collating forms.

Having grown up during the Great Depression, Michael's strong work ethic influenced his son greatly, more than either of them knew at the time. He always encouraged Tim to learn a trade "just in case." Tim was reluctant to follow in his dad's business footsteps, however, and kept his sights on writing.

When Tim was only 15 years old, his father was diagnosed with terminal can-

cer. During his illness, Tim perfected his craft of printing in order to help out. "My dad was my hero," says Tim. "His dying wish was that I might somehow keep our family business going."

At 17 years of age, Tim suddenly found himself as the "chief breadwinner" for his family. Barely getting by, he got working capital from the bank, but soon it was gone. "With the help of my mother and sister, I managed to keep most of the customers my father had acquired. I began to print the newspaper for the private high school I attended in trade for the tuition. I did the same for the college I attended. As the years passed, I had built the business modestly, but never really considered myself successful. I had never worked for anyone and felt my father's early death prevented me from living the life I might have chosen if circumstances had been different. I began to consider what I would have done if my father had lived. I came up with the idea that I would have liked

Michael Trabon in the South Pacific, circa 1943–1944.

Tim Trabon in 1959.

One of four buildings currently occupied in Trabon-Paris's office park.

to have had a life with a little more adventure than working in my basement had provided. I fantacized that if things had gone differently, I might be sailing aboard the *Calypso* with Jacques Cousteau."

Tim's dogged determination to see his dreams come true finally paid off. After familiarizing himself for two years with Captain Cousteau's organization, he studied scuba diving, French—and the art of persuasive letter-writing. It wasn't long before Tim actually found himself onboard. "I convinced the Captain that he needed me as part of his team," says Tim. "I made my dream come true. I found myself sailing *Calypso* across the oceans of the world."

In 1982 Tim was appointed as the financial director of The Amazon Expedition, which would later be the source for *Jacques Cousteau's Amazon Journey*, a six-hour television series. For four months, Tim braved the Brazilian jungle filming goldminers and Indian tribes. For 11 years, Tim traveled with Cousteau's expeditions to the St. Lawrence Seaway, Papua New Guinea, Australia, the British Virgin Islands "and other exotic, remote locations that I never dreamed I might

Inside one of the four production facilities.

see. In between my traveling, I managed to keep my very modest printing business just barely alive."

Ironically, it was when he ruined a printing job that he met his wife, Patti. "She was a client I messed up a job for," he says. "I went over to apologize." At 35, Tim married Patti, and the couple now has three children: Michael, Timothy and Anthony. By this time, extensive traveling had lost its appeal, and Tim was now more focused on running his business and making a good living for his family. "I had learned a great deal about finances while working for the Cousteau Organization," he says. "I had also learned that having a strong desire to accomplish a goal could lead to the successful acquisition of that goal." As he disciplined himself to really learn the business, he found that he was really good at it.

By 1991, Trabon Printing company, as it was then known, surpassed the $3 million mark in sales. That same year, Tim acquired Paris Printing Company, and changed the name officially to Trabon-Paris Printing. He had great respect for the Paris family and wanted to keep their name. He even asked Gene Paris to work for him, and Gene is now in charge of sales management. The company's focus is on "treating everyone very respectfully," says Tim.

Treating people with respect has shown up in all sorts of ways with Tim. Once, when a competitor called and left a rude message, Tim good-naturedly challenged him to a duel—with paintball guns. Word leaked out, and when the two met at the appointed time, so did the media. The following morning, headlines pronounced him the winner.

Trabon Solutions, Tim's second business venture, began when he and his two business partners, Michael Lewer and David Windhausen, saw the potential and need to integrate electronic media with the publishing world. "We focus on providing technology solutions that meet the core business objectives of our clients," Tim says. "We have helped clients increase their productivity; provide a fast, accurate information exchange; along with greater flexibility, lower costs, higher profitability and the ability to stay competitive in a rapidly changing marketplace." Combined, both companies together now draw approximately $25 million per year.

Tim has now been in business for 35 years. He says that a person pursuing a goal should expect many setbacks, but that the secret is to see it as though you're climbing a mountain. "It won't be a steady climb; it's a struggle to get there; you move sideways and backwards once in a while . . . and then you never arrive." Always trying to make it to the designated

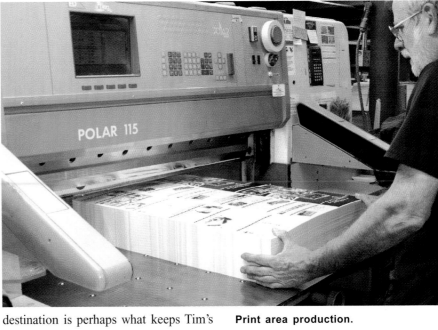

Print area production.

destination is perhaps what keeps Tim's business growing. "It's not about money," he says, and refers to the journey, instead.

Many organizations have been helped by Tim's generous spirit. Among them are The Sunflower House that helps abused children; Seton Center, which assists the poor; the Sisters of Carondelet, a local hospital; and the Children's Place. Tim's company also offers complimentary printing to all charities and gives about $300,000 worth of printing away free every year.

Both he and his wife have a huge soft spot for children. Once, when watching a Barbara Walters special, their hearts were touched as they heard of a brother and sister, separated during the war in Sarajevo. Their parents had been killed by mortar. "I was watching this, thinking about how insignificant my problems were," says Tim. "I wanted to reunite these

children." So, as had always been true to his nature, he acted on those feelings. He called a Croatian photographer, who talked to the director of the television program, who then called the producer of ABC. The producer called Senator Byron Dorgan of North Dakota, and after six weeks, the 17-year-old girl, Delilah, was rescued; her brother had already been sent to the United States. Tim and his family met her at the airport and took her into their home, and she was ultimately reunited with her brother. Although she spoke no English at the time, she eventually earned a degree in international business from DePaul University, got married, and now lives in Kansas City. "She's as much a part of my family as any of my kids," says Tim.

Tim's endearing and colorful anecdotes show that there's still a writer inside him. Exploring that idea just might be his next big adventure—while he continues to use his business and printing skills in the wonderful life he's finally realized. Already in the works is a book of memoirs for his children. He now acknowledges, though, that business is his main creative outlet. "I didn't always see business as being creative," he continues. "We're given the gift of life, and at some time, you've got to do something with that gift." He's using his well—and his father would be proud.

Mary Trabon (center) 1940.

WUNDERLICH FIBRE BOX COMPANY

The St. Louis family firm of Wunderlich Fibre Box Company represents a business bracketed by this country's history. The firm's founder, Charles Wunderlich, established his Monroe Cooper Shop in 1860, before the state of Missouri granted articles of incorporation. Wunderlich sited his cooperage, or barrel-making shop, on the banks of the Mississippi River just blocks from Laclede's Landing in St. Louis, where the city's founder created its first settlement in 1764. The governor of Louisiana, concerned with depressed trade caused by the French and Indian War, had granted trading rights with Indians located along the banks of the Mississippi to two French explorers. Laclede, quick to appreciate the trading possibilities afforded by the powerful river, sited the settlement of St. Louis along its western bank.

Charles Wunderlich built his firm on the thriving Mississippi River traffic and on St. Louis' reputation as the "Gateway to the West." He crafted and supplied barrels to customers ranging from midwestern granaries to homesteaders headed west in Conestoga wagons to riverboats plying their trade on the Mississippi. Historic photographs of the St. Louis levee undoubtedly include barrels made by Wunderlich being rolled into the cargo holds of Mississippi River steamboats. In 1892 Wunderlich incorporated his firm, and the Monroe Cooper Shop became Charles Wunderlich Coo-

Left to right: Rob Wunderlich, Jr.; Robert Wunderlich; and son-in-law Steve Dybus.

perage Company, the first legally incorporated cooper shop in Missouri. At the time of his death, Wunderlich's nine children were variously involved in both the cooperage company and in its twelve barrel stave mills that dotted the Ozark Mountains.

The firm has flourished since that time under five generations of father-to-son leadership and operates now as a leading Midwestern designer and manufacturer of custom corrugated paperboard packaging. Customers in eastern Missouri and in western and southern Illinois benefit from the company's long history of expertise in the design and manufacture of packaging materials.

Wunderlich Fibre Box Company came into being during the 1930s, when the company began producing corrugated shipping containers as an alternative to the heavier wooden barrels. Mass-produced corrugated boxes quickly replaced "hand-raised" barrels, and after 1950 the company's barrel manufacturing operation had been completely phased out. Wunderlich machines were among the first in

the industry to add printed logos to corrugated boxes, reducing customer dependence on hand-painted stencils. Flexographic printing in the firm's manufacturing facilities now offers new possibilities for the use of color, with state-of-the-art equipment allowing for multi-color printing of process screens. Wunderlich's inclusion in the *World Excellence in Corrugated Graphics Yearbook* for three consecutive years, the only St. Louis firm to be so included, attests to the firm's excellence in the design and manufacture of its products.

The Wunderlich family business remains firmly rooted within the shifting influences of commerce and technology. This 19th-century firm is heading into the 21st century under the guidance of Robert A. Wunderlich, Sr.; his son-in-law, Steve Dybus; and Wunderlich's son, Robert, Jr., who points to the loyalty of the firm's 50 employees as a mainstay of its success. Wunderlich, Jr., who recently rejoined the family firm after ten years of service in the Marines, notes that even after their retirement, a number of former employees return to visit the company on a regular basis and even to celebrate birthdays. It appears that to many, this historic midwestern firm really does represent family.

Wunderlich Cooperage front office in 1912.

UNIVERSITY OF MISSOURI - ST. LOUIS

The University of Missouri-St. Louis is a dynamic, metropolitan institution of higher learning. With 15,000 students, 966 faculty members and more than 60,000 graduates, UM-St. Louis has, in just 40 years, taken its place among the great universities of the St. Louis area. With institutional accreditation by the North Central Association Commission on Accreditation and School Improvement and professional accreditation by 15 national academic associations, UM-St. Louis offers a quality education on par with its three sister institutions in the University of Missouri System. That quality is reflected in the success of its alumni, the recognition of its faculty and the growth of its campus.

UM-St. Louis is now the third-largest university in Missouri. The campus, located in northwest St. Louis County, has grown dramatically since its inception in 1963. From one building and 660 students, UM-St. Louis has developed into the vibrant public research university envisioned by its founders. It now encompasses 328 acres and more than 60 buildings. Among its facilities is the Millennium Student Center, a unique, 175,000-square-foot, three-story edifice that houses all student-related services. The newest addition to the campus is the 128,500-square-foot Performing Arts Center. This new performance venue includes a three-level, 1,600-seat performance hall, a 300-seat music and theater hall, a glass-enclosed, two-tiered atrium lobby with promenade and state-of-the-art technical facilities for sound, lighting and set production.

This view shows the interior of the Millennium Student Center on the campus of the University of Missouri-St. Louis.

Bugg Lake, named for James Bugg, the campus's first chancellor, lies just west of the Research Complex at the University of Missouri-St. Louis.

UM-St. Louis provides quality teaching, research and service programs of national and international scope. It currently offers 47 undergraduate, 31 master's, one professional and 11 doctoral programs. These programs, along with their computer components and international elements, are designed to ensure that UM-St. Louis graduates are ready to compete in an increasingly global and technological world. The wide range of programs reflects the diverse needs of Missouri's largest community.

The University is proud of the diverse nature of its student body. More than 50 percent of UM-St. Louis students are non-traditional, meaning they are older than the typical 18- to 22-year-old student, and many hold full- or part-time jobs.

Sixty percent of UM-St. Louis's students are women. Twenty percent are minorities, and UM-St. Louis enrolls and graduates the largest number of African-American students of any university in the state.

The University also boasts an exceptional faculty. The 500 full-time faculty members who teach at UM-St. Louis hold advanced degrees from some of the world's most prestigious universities, and a large number of full-time faculty hold doctoral degrees.

Along with the international components being built into UM-St. Louis's curriculum, the University takes great pride in recognizing individuals who have contributed to the quality of life on a global scale. Its "Global Citizen Award" recognizes people who have effected positive change internationally, and its World Ecology Medal goes to individuals who have made extraordinary contributions to conservation.

UM-St. Louis is proud of its record of community service, and the community has responded to its efforts. Former Chancellor Blanche M. Touhill, who retired in December 2002, was the first woman to be named St. Louis's "Citizen of the Year." UM-St. Louis also is home to the Des Lee Collaborative Vision, a program linking 23 of the University's 32 endowed professorships to local institutions in a

These beautiful flowers along West Drive greet UM-St. Louis students and visitors as they enter campus.

cooperative effort for the betterment of the St. Louis region.

UM-St. Louis is the largest supplier of college-educated workers in St. Louis. The University is constantly striving to improve its partnerships with area school districts, community organizations and business and labor leaders to help St. Louis grow economically and socially.

THE ST. LOUIS MERCANTILE LIBRARY AT THE UNIVERSITY OF MISSOURI - ST. LOUIS

Although St. Louis from its beginnings in the mid-18th century had many cultured, old-world citizens with the means and inclination to buy and read books for their own personal use, public libraries in any sense of the modern meaning were not established until the early 19th century in the growing and bustling trading center. While the city was gaining its reputation as a gateway to the West it also, fatefully, determined to add culture to the frontier, becoming, with the establishment of the St. Louis Mercantile Library, a gateway to the mind and a crossroads to cultural aspirations in the new state of Missouri. The world-famous library thus helped in the state's earliest days to set the "Show Me" tone of its inquisitive citizens and has continued to support learning through its historical research services in St. Louis down to the present day.

Today, the Mercantile Library can look back on its heritage as the oldest library in continuing existence West of the Mississippi River. Founded in 1846 by philanthropic business leaders and wealthy citizens for the public good, the Mercantile became not only the city's first library, its broad collections and interests allowed it to become the first viable art museum, the town's first theater, an early college of sorts, and a home for the city's earliest scientific and other learned societies. It was and is, in other words, the grandparent of all of the cultural institutions of a major Midwestern metropolis, a circumstance in which it takes great pride.

Starting out as a public library, which prosperous merchants planned to occupy the attention of young apprentices from the temptations of the wild goings-on of the St. Louis frontier levee, the Mercantile quickly evolved into a huge collection of books on every subject for the city. Early universities used its law and medical book collections. Soldiers, like the young William T. Sherman, studied the tactics of Alexander and Napoleon in its stacks. Journalists such as Joseph Pulitzer read omnivorously in the library's holdings to learn the craft of writing. Authors

The St. Louis Mercantile Library/Thomas Jefferson Library complex. The glass pyramid overlooks the Mercantile's atrium/reading area.

like Kate Chopin, Sara Teasdale and Eugene Field studied the classics in the Mercantile's stacks. In the process the Mercantile Library's holdings kept enlarging through the common inquiry of a vibrant populace and today, along with the great treasures of rare books that bear witness to this popular St. Louis landmark's own useful past history, the many lesser-known holdings—in art, manuscripts, photos, and prints—make the collections a kind of bibliographic laboratory for the history of reading and learning in America.

The Mercantile was a great forum, an athenaeum, for the city. Its theater boasted many successful performances by Jenny Lind, Lola Montez and the earliest seasons of the world-famous St. Louis Symphony. The library's lecture hall welcomed Oscar Wilde, William Thackeray, Susan Anthony, Ralph Waldo Emerson and Herman Melville, as well as to homegrown talents such as Mark Twain. In serious times the library's halls rang with tumultuous speeches such as Senator Thomas Hart Benton's exhortation on "Westward the Star of Empire"— an impassioned speech on the development of the transcontinental railroad. The Library became a bulwark for the Union in the 1860s, a place where the Emancipation Proclamation was read and ratified by the Missouri Legislature. Clearly, the Mercantile Library has lived its share of great historical events.

Today the Mercantile, from its roots as an early American library, is a national treasure, one that collected the heritage

of the new nation. So much so that this crown jewel of St. Louis' cultural institutions, a favorite of many citizens whose families for generations have visited it as an old, dependable friend, decided that the time had come to make its collections even more accessible by affiliating with St. Louis' only publicly supported, land-grant institution of higher education, the University of Missouri-St. Louis. After observing the passing parade of statesmen, pioneers, Civil War heroes and native Americans, steamboat captains and all the colorful walks of life which made up old St. Louis for nearly 150 years in its location on Locust Street in the heart of downtown, the Mercantile moved to a young, vibrant college campus—one committed, just as the Mercantile in its earliest days, to educating young St. Louis for the future. The newest users of the Mercantile, along with scholars from across the nation and the world, are much like the earliest users of the Library— young men and women bent on new careers tempered by a deep respect for the traditions which the new St. Louis Mercantile Library at the University of Missouri-St. Louis preserves for the past, present and future generations of St. Louis readers and lovers of learning and cultural history—a place where time and history can be imagined by everyone on a vast, engaging scale.

Z-INTERNATIONAL, INC.

Fritz Zschietzschmann's father was a professor of archaeology at the university in Giessen, where Fritz was born in February 1938. The war raging in Germany forced his family to separate locations. His father, who had joined the Nazi party in 1933, fought on the Russian front; George, his 16-year-old brother, fought on the Western front. Fritz and his sister were each placed in separate homes in the countryside. Fritz's mother, who was pregnant with Fritz's younger brother, Hans, was evacuated from Giessen since their home and the entire city was destroyed by American bombers December 6, 1944.

They left Giessen to move to the American occupied section of Berlin, but their shocking discovery that it was going to be under Russian control caused Fritz, his mother, older sister and toddler brother to flee back to the West in the summer of 1946.

In yet another cruel twist of fate, in 1946 doctors discovered tuberculosis in Fritz's left eye and in both lungs, sending him to a lung sanitarium for two years. While a patient at the sanitarium, he received a C.A.R.E. package from America

Friedrich Wilhelm Zschietzschmann, president and founder of Z-International, Inc.

that included a pair of boots. That gift impressed Fritz so much that, at the age of ten, he decided to immigrate to the U.S.A.

After his father returned from a prisoner-of-war camp, he homeschooled Fritz, then 11 years old, who could neither read nor write. Following his father's efforts, Fritz was able to attend public school, but never finished high school or college. In 1962 he met Rex Beach from Olathe, Kansas, the first foreign exchange student from Kansas State

University to attend the Justus Liebig University in Giessen.

Four years later, on May 26 1966, Fritz landed in Norfolk, Virginia, on a coal freighter. Although he came to America as a tourist, he fully intended to stay. By the summer of 1966 he met up with Rex in Kansas City. Twenty dollars a week bought him room and board with the Eugene Funck family. The early years in the U.S.A. were hard for a young German who could speak little English and read practically none. He changed tires for a few months and then worked in a factory for a year. Then he fell in love. "Nancy Kinnamon caught my eye in 1967 in Sunday School at the Country Club Christian Church in Kansas City," Fritz said. "We married in 1968."

That same year Fritz discovered his talent in sales. Bill Clowney gave him a break when he hired him to sell for Dictaphone in Kansas City. In 1968 he became Dictaphone's top salesman in the U.S.A. For the next four years he sold for Dictaphone in New Haven, Connecticut; New York, New York; and back in Kansas City. Fritz learned the label business working for Avery Label from 1972 through 1974 in Kansas City.

At this point Fritz decided there was no reason to be in America unless he was in business for himself. And so, on New Year's Day, 1975, Z-LABEL Systems, Inc., was established in a warehouse at 14th and McGee in Kansas City. It was a trying time for Fritz and Nancy, with two small children and a third on the way.

"We had used my sales bonus from Avery to start Z-LABEL," said Fritz. "By September 1975 we were at the edge; our SBA loan was depleted, and we had placed an order for a new press. We received a $23,000 order from Ron Willett at Hallmark Cards to produce glow-in-the-dark Halloween stickers. With that order we started to grow and seemed to do better. We had two old presses; I worked long hours, selling during the day and detailing orders at night. Nancy typed invoices at night, and we ended the year with $140,000 in sales."

First location in 1975 for Z-International, Inc., 14th and McGee, downtown Kansas City, Missouri.

Custom-printed Z-Label® products.

Sales grew rapidly. They started to produce private brand stock labels for Quill, a mail-order office products company. Sales boomed, many other brands followed, and they saw themselves as the private brand "kings" specializing in stock office and data processing labels. The name was changed from Z-Label Systems, Inc., to Z-International, Inc., to better identify the company's multiple product lines and global markets. Z-International opened a manufacturing plant in Germany in 1989 intending to follow American retailers to Europe, providing them with similar services as in the United States.

In the following years, though, the company lost a lot of business—when Avery changed policy and decided to also manufacture private brands. "We felt

MULTI-PRINT® labels for laser and inkjet printers—pioneered by Z-International, Inc.

powerless against a publicly owned giant company that seemingly had endless cash and resources," said Fritz. To answer the challenge, the company expanded into new product lines such as pre-printed desk top publishing papers, repositionable notes and school/home office accessories. It restructured, but got into financial trouble with product lines that were graphic-design driven and required huge inventories to meet demand from large "super store" retailers. Z-International's entry into the self-stick notes business, competing with 3M's Post-It® notes, placed it in competition with another office product giant.

In spite of the difficulties, Z-International pioneered product lines and innovations such as: laser labels, ink jet labels, Multi-Print™ labels, clear clamshell packaging, color assorted labels, assorted color note pads, neon notes, note cubes, roll notes, desk top publishing papers and products made from recycled materials.

The company's participation in the repositionable notes business and the SOHO accessories business taught it to be importers as well as exporters. Today it is seriously studying the possibilities of opening a manufacturing and packaging facility in China to further reduce its manufacturing costs and to meet major competition coming from Asia. Manufacturing in China will also position it to take advantage of emerging Asia-Pacific consumer market opportunities.

As a small privately owned company with 150 co-workers, Fritz is very optimistic about the future. "There will always be opportunities to compete against giant corporations," said Fritz, "but we are always one step ahead of them." There have been many times at Z-International in the last 28 years that were hard and trying, but never did I give up hope," said Fritz. "I had the confidence that some day it would get better again. I have always tried to run the business on the principles of fairness and honesty. We are grateful for our customers. Every day we want to be the best supplier to our customers, small or large, and our many dedicated associates help to make this happen."

"Even though I am a senior citizen already," Fritz continued, "I never stop dreaming, and I am imagining all that

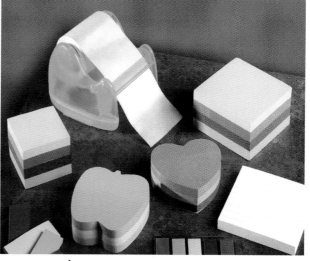

Z-NOTES® products.

could happen yet in my business career and in my life in general. As long as I get to go to work every day, have my children working in the business, get to play soccer every Saturday morning with my friends of 30 years, get to spend some time in our home in Giessen, see my grandson in San Francisco and enjoy my work, I will continue to work every day. God has guided me through all these years—I am a happy person. We have been blessed."

BALDKNOBBERS

In the heart of the Ozarks, Branson, Missouri, is well-known for its growing enclave of entertainment venues, but not everyone knows that the Baldknobbers theatre company started it all.

Performing on street corners and on Saturday nights at the local police station, Bill Mabe and his brothers, Jim, Lyle and Bob, soon began playing at Lake Taneycomo for fishermen and tourists in 1959. They rented out the Branson Community Center for their act and set up 50 folding chairs for audience members. They called their act "The Baldknobbers," and the name stuck. (A "baldknobber" used to refer to a person who was part of a vigilante group that helped take care of thieves and rustlers at a time when no law existed in the Ozarks. They congregated up on a mountain top—a "bald knob"—for their meetings.)

Soon, however, the foursome grew so popular that they needed a bigger space to perform in, so they moved their show to the Sammy Lane Pavilion. That, too, wasn't big enough, so they moved to Branson's 600-seat skating rink. At this point, their wives, dressed in old country dresses, were getting in on the act by carrying signs to advertise the show. During intermission, they sold concessions, and afterwards hawked souvenirs.

Left to right: The four original owners, Jim Mabe, Bill Mabe, Lyle Mabe and Bob Mabe. The other three on the right were band members.

Bill Mabe in 1960.

Wearing overalls and playing on a washtub bass, a Dobro guitar, a mule's jawbone and a washboard, the brothers were a hit. Their love of music started long before their musical act, though. When they were children—and there were 11 brothers and sisters in all—they sang in a church pastored by their parents, Mr. and Mrs. Donald Mabe.

When they weren't performing their own act, the brothers could be found acting in mock-gun fights in Silver Dollar City or performing as the house band in the Shepherd of the Hills Outdoor Drama.

In 1969 the group found that they had a national following and, since they had once again outgrown their performance space, they moved to what is now its present location on 76 Country Boulevard. Smaller than what it is today, the group continued to draw large crowds.

The "Baldknobbers Jamboree," as it's now known, is still a family-owned-and-operated business, which works out of a state-of-the-art, 1,500-seat theatre. It's one of the main attractions for over 7 million visitors annually. Along with the theatre, the complex includes a 75-room motor inn, a swimming pool, a restaurant and two gift shops.

With faith in God and commitment to family, this company insists on entertainment that the whole family can enjoy—patriotic, Gospel and country music, plus good ol' comedy.

"Branson has gone through several transitions, but every performer finds out before long that they have to do a family-oriented show to survive here," Mabe said to Missouri's *New Tribune-Jefferson City.*

Bill and his wife, Joyce, are co-founders and co-owners of Baldknobbers. Their daughter Debbie Bilyeu co-pastors a church with her husband, Hosea, in Nixa, Missouri. Another daughter, Darla Linebaugh, co-manages the Baldknobbers theatre with her husband. Dennis Mabe, Bill and Joyce's son, performs in the show as a lead vocalist and musician—and has for over 17 years.

Jim and his wife, Katie, are also co-founders and co-owners. Their daughter, Marilyn Poitz, and her husband, Lynn, run the Baldknobbers Motor Inn. And, Jim and Katie's son, Tim, plays the part of "Droopy Drawers, Jr.," in the show.

The Mabe family has been honored with several lifetime-achievement accolades and invitations during their years in the entertainment business. In 1988 the group performed for former President Ronald Reagan. And, on April 1, 1989, then-Governor John Ashcroft presented the troupe with the "Official State of Missouri Proclamation" as being the "First Country Music Show in Branson, Mis-

Baldknobbers Country Restaurant and Motor Inn and Theatre Complex.

souri, beginning a major segment of the Ozarks' tourism industry." Former Vice President Dan Quail also gave them a plaque for "Outstanding Achievement and Great Family Values" before a performance.

Television shows that the group has appeared on include ABC's *Good Morning, America*; *Inside Edition*; *The Ralph Emory Show*; CBS's *This Morning* and as well as on TNN. They've also been a part of Nashville's "Fan Fair," and have participated in several national advertising campaigns, including Coca-Cola.

The Mabe family has a heart for helping the community, too, as volunteers. Each year, they assist with Jerry Lewis' Muscular Dystrophy Association's telethons, plus other organizations. Also, for the past few years, the Baldknobbers theatre has hosted the "Tony Orlando Yellow Ribbon Salute to Veterans," which recognizes and honors those who have served and fought for the United States.

The Baldknobbers Jamboree show lasts two hours, starting at 8 p.m. Those who get there early can enjoy a 7:15 p.m. pre-show, called "Ragtime Joe's Warm-up Show," which features a sing-along to old tunes such as "Take Me Out to the Ball Game" and "You Are My Sunshine." The main show is a colorful and high-energy event that showcases top-notch performers—guaranteed to give the audience quality entertainment. When she was younger, even LeAnn Rimes tread the boards singing for the crowds. Performances are held year-round, with time off for the Thanksgiving and Christmas holidays, giving the entertainers a much-deserved break.

Baldknobbers is a popular place for various organizations, such as youth groups and businesses, to enjoy short

Left to right: Tim Mabe, second generation, AKA "Droopy Drawers Jr.," son of Jim Mabe; Joy Bilyea, third generation, granddaughter of Bill Mabe; and Dennis Mabe, second generation, son of Bill Mabe.

meetings or weekend get-aways. Special group rates apply to tour operators, church groups, bank travel, student groups and the military.

With customized packages and pricing to fit all needs, the smallest groups to the largest groups will find what they're looking for. Large groups may use the theatre for their meetings, while smaller ones might make use of breakout meeting rooms to accommodate their groups' sizes. In addition, there is a video department for editing, recording and presentations—plus dining options, with buffet, concessions or menu choices.

The following features are also available for groups: hearing-impaired equipment, separate check-in, promotional gifts, autograph sessions at intermission, driver's lounge and refreshments for driver and escort. Prospective visitors can visit www.baldknobbers.com for more information.

Baldknobbers has grown so much since its small beginnings. Little did the four Mabe brothers know that—when they were humbly playing on the washtub, guitar, jawbone, and washboard—they were setting the stage for something big for Branson, which is now called the "Live Entertainment Capital of the World."

DINO'S TRUCKING, INC.

Many people come to the United States speaking very little English, but few of them build thriving businesses within one generation of their arrival. Dino Vainalis, owner of Dino's Trucking, Inc., in St. Louis, Missouri, came to this country by way of Naousa, an industrial and agricultural town located in the northern Macedonian region of Greece. Roman ruins, cave churches and ancient walled fortresses characterize this region known as the birthplace of Alexander the Great. Vainalis's grandfather set out from the area as a young man to visit this country. His travels influenced his grandson deeply. "It was always my dream to come to the states," said Vainalis. The states have been definitely enhanced by his coming.

Vainalis arrived in the United States in 1975 with the idea of attending St. Louis University. A lack of funds, an increasing debt load, and the challenge of the language barrier had forced Vainalis to seek another path. When the money ran out, he started driving 18-wheelers for other people. His first truck, purchased with a partner, was financed in part by money earned at various odd jobs:

Back row, left to right: Soterios Vainalis and Dave Plumley, seated is Dino Vainalis.

Front of maintenance facility of Dino's Trucking, Inc., in St. Louis, Missouri.

dishwashing, bussing tables, "all of those things that people do." In 1981 Vainalis established Dino's Trucking, operating it initially from his basement in St. Louis. "I fixed it up myself," he said of the company's first office space. His sole customer at the time, a manufacturing concern named So Good Potato Company employed his services to ship potato chips to 20 East Coast and Midwestern states. The business grew and in 1983, now with 10 employees and 10 trucks, Vainalis leased an office on Hoffmeister Street in St. Louis.

The year 1985 saw further expansion, with the So Good Potato Company opening a factory in Atlanta; however, the growing success of So Good would take a critical turn within the next few years. It filed for bankruptcy in 1988, forcing Vainalis to lay off most of his staff and to sell 18 of the 20 trucks he was currently running. In 1989 he started over again, almost from scratch, but this time with two trucks and over 10 years' experience in the freight business.

It was experience that would serve him well. Vainalis went against the advice of his lawyer, who urged him to declare bankruptcy to clear his debts. Notice of So Good's bankruptcy had been in the papers, making lenders hesitant to extend credit to Vainalis. Undeterred, in order to pay his drivers what he owed them, he borrowed money using his house as collateral. He then rebuilt his business, taking on his old jobs of driving, dispatching, working as a mechanic on the rigs,

Aerial photo of Dino's Trucking in St. Louis.

and searching out new clients. His wife, Alexandra, who had helped out with the books in the early days, assumed her former role of bookkeeper. "My wife has helped and supported me from day one," Vainalis says. "I couldn't have done it without her." The business again grew slowly and steadily. One part of the rebuilding process—that of finding drivers—proved easy. When word of the company's rebuilding reached Vainalis's former drivers, they were happy to return where they had been so well treated. Vainalis credits the excellence of his employees with much of his success.

In 1995, driven by a need for more space, the company moved its operations to Continental Industrial Drive in St. Louis, where Vainalis built his first terminal, including office space and service bays for mechanics. Today, Dino's Trucking, Inc., generates $12 million a year in revenue, running 75 trucks and 200 trailers for delivery of general commodities. DTI Freight Brokerage, a subsidiary of

Dino's Trucking established in 1993, generates between $3 million and $4 million dollars annually. Also in 1995 Vainalis and partner Lindell Byron saw the establishment by of the AAA Trailer Services Company, a business that specializes in trailer repair. This company grew as well, moving in 1998 to a site totaling 30,000 square feet. It now employs 45 people. In April 2003 Vainalis and Byron formed AAA Trailer Leasing, a spin-off of AAA Trailer Services.

Each of Vainalis's four children has worked in the business, a number of them while attending college. His daughters Maria and Vicki have since graduated and moved on to Los Angeles. Vainalis's son Sam currently works part-time for his father while pursuing an undergraduate degree in business. His son Nick also works for his father part-time while attending high school. They may or may not choose to follow their father's path, and that seems fine with Vainalis, who is content watching his children pursue their own destinies.

Two employees from the old days of restructuring remain with the company: dispatcher Greg Momroig and Mel

Sanden, Vainalis's 74-year-old bookkeeper. The company is also home to one Russian employee and a number of Bosnian employees, whose children play on the company-sponsored soccer team "Euro-Bosnia." A former softball team for children of company employees disbanded as the children grew older. Sports is also a strong component of the Mathew-Dickey Endowment Fund, an organization sponsored in part by Vainalis that is dedicated to the service of 40,000 children in inner-city St. Louis.

As Vainalis's companies have grown, so has his sense of civic responsibility. The business owner's Greek heritage comes into play very strongly in his sponsoring of various service organizations. In 1996 the Hellenic Spirit Foundation of St. Louis was born. Vainalis served three years as president and still continues to be very active within the organization, which has distributed one-half million dollars to various organizations since its inception. *Hellenic*, meaning "of or relating to Greece, its people or its language," aptly describes this benevolent organization comprised of local Greek Americans. Its beneficiaries include the Multiple Sclerosis Foundation, the Ronald McDonald House and Feed The Children, a nonprofit organization assisting children in need in the U.S. and overseas.

In November 2001, the University of Missouri-St. Louis hosted an art exhibit titled "Expressions of Dual Ethnicity: Greek-American Spirits." The exhibit, sponsored in part by the Hellenic Spirit Foundation, was a celebration of work by Midwestern Greek-American artists. It seemed a fitting project for Vainalis, who, when asked about future projects, said, "If an opportunity comes, I will jump on it."

FLEMING & COMPANY

Thomas Fleming came to the pharmaceutical industry via a circuitous route: that of major league sports. Fleming, a graduate of St. Louis University in St. Louis, Missouri, studied chemistry as an undergraduate and earned a master's in chemistry, but his first love was baseball. In 1951, when professional baseball ousted Happy Chandler as commissioner, it marked the end of Fleming's career as a professional umpire. Fleming's letter of agreement to join the pros in the national league became invalid, but his background in chemistry would now be put to good use. In 1954 he went to work for Storck Pharmaceuticals in St. Louis, enjoying a very successful sales career with the local firm until 1960.

At that point, figuring that "if I could make money for somebody else, I could make it for myself," Fleming decided to start his own company. In July 1960, he opened Fleming & Company's first plant in a medical building in Webster Groves, Missouri. Fleming was the company's sole employee at the time, making the rounds of doctors' offices with his detail bag. A peach-flavored antacid with the trade name Marblen constituted the firm's earliest product. The second product was the first long-acting bronchodilator, Aerolate, which really took off and es-

Pictured in the early '40s, Tom Fleming had yet to start his pharmaceutical career.

In 2000 Mr. Fleming was still reporting for work every day at the age of 82.

tablished the company. The nasal spray Ocean®, a moisturizing saline spray, followed, at which time Fleming and Company had its second major product and became a nationally known company in the pharmaceutical world.

Products in the early years included the prescription drug Extendryl, a root beer-flavored prescription antihistamine, decongestant and anticholinergic. Nephrocaps®, a prescription B-complex multi-vitamin specifically formulated for patients undergoing dialysis treatment, remains a viable product after 20 years. Other company products include RUM-K Liquid, a prescription liquid potassium supplement, and Obegyn® Prenatal Supplement, a prescription multi-vitamin and mineral supplement developed specifically to enhance fetal health.

Fleming & Company developed its Pima syrup, a prescription medication containing potassium iodide, for use as an expectorant. An unexpected use for the medication developed in 1986, when explosions rocked the Chernobyl Power Plant in the former Soviet Union. The explosions released clouds of deadly radioactive material into the atmosphere. Health officials from the region ordered 10,000 pints of Pima from Fleming & Company for use as a prophylactic mea-

sure against the danger of thyroid cancer from exposure to radiation. The current FDA website fda.gov/cder/guidance, reflecting on "the new urgency to be prepared for acts of terrorism," lists Fleming & Company's Pima syrup as one source of potassium iodide for use in reducing "the risk of thyroid cancer following exposure to radioactive iodine through the air or contaminated food."

Fleming's nasal spray Ocean, with its less dramatic applications, remains an extremely popular over-the-counter product. The website for Children's Hospital in St. Louis, Missouri, recommends the product for nasal congestion, encouraging the use of "simple remedies." The Health & Human Services Medical Supply Catalog lists Ocean under decongestants in its Job Corps List of preferred medications. Many medical websites recommend the product by name for post-operative care following nasal surgery.

The physical plant of Fleming & Company has expanded along with its product line, relocating numerous times over the years as demand for space has increased. The firm's current location, on Gilsinn Lane in Fenton, Missouri, houses 80 employees with an additional 50 detail reps around the country. Executive vice-president, Tom Johnson notes that the current site for manufacturing also includes assay, legal, order processing and even printing departments under one roof.

When asked about the impetus behind his product development, Fleming talked about "pearls" (as in "pearls of wisdom"). Discussions with doctors about various ailments and their treatments have led to many of his product development ideas.

Fleming, however, loved being his own boss. "It's nice to see it grow," he said of the company he started. When asked about motivation, he noted that educating his daughters provided motivation enough, even when he "quit a good job" to start his own company over 40 years ago.

Fleming & Company recently commissioned the filming of a videotape of their founder. The footage, much of it filmed at a medical trade show in Denver, shows a lot of give and take between Fleming and various doctors who stop by the booth for information. Some obviously have known the entrepreneur for years. "I use your stuff all the time," said a physician in a sports jacket and tie, who then stopped for the real discussion, the one about baseball. Fleming noted that most of his success in sales to medical professionals was a result of product knowledge. The Denver footage shows a chemist who was passionate about his products.

When thoughts of retirement were spoken of, Mr. Fleming wanted no part of it. He continued to attend medical and dental conventions (about 20 per year) until just months before he died. He was an active leader of his company until his death following hip surgery, at age 85. He is remembered as one of the cornerstones of the pharmaceutical industry.

Above: At the AAAAI allergy convention in Denver, March 2003, Fleming was still promoting his products. Featured with Tom are Sherry DuMont and Mary Bourne, salespeople from Fleming. Also pictured is Sandy Barbercheck, marketing manager.

Below: Umpiring was always Fleming's passion. He continued umpiring until he broke his hip at age 82.

MONNIG INDUSTRIES, INC.

Glasgow, Missouri, is home to the full-range, steel-galvanizing plant, Monnig Industries. This independent, family-owned-and-operated plant has been in business for over 40 years and is still thriving. They galvanize items such as the highway signs and guardrails seen on roads and freeways. They also have the capability of galvanizing large items such as picnic tables and boat docks. With customers throughout the United States, the capacity to galvanize small and large items and their signature, "Monnig Touch," Monnig Industries sets themselves apart from their larger competitors.

Monnig Industries is the only single-source, full-range galvanizing plant in Mid-America. Full-range galvanizing includes two methods for coating steel. The hot dip galvanizing process creates a metalurgical bond between the steel and zinc. Monnig Industries houses one of the largest hot dippers in Mid-America. The other process, mechanical galvanizing, is used mostly on small parts up to 6 inches or one pound. Basically, a barrel turns these parts at such a rate that the energy created beats the zinc into the steel. This galvanizing method was developed by 3M who also monitors every batch for quality. Monnig Industries also can

Hot dip and mechanical galvanizing building.

boast the largest mechanical galvanizing capacity in Mid-America with their two 10-cubic-foot barrels.

Beyond Monnig Industries' ability to be the largest capacity galvanizer in Mid-America, the "Monnig Touch" is another aspect that sets them above their competitors. The "Monnig Touch" is the company's commitment to quality and service. This has been the foundation of its success and growth for the past 42 years. John Monnig, president of Monnig

Industries, knows that the growth of the company is due to the dedication it has to its customers and how it treats them. It's not just about "getting the orders out." They pride themselves with the quality of their galvanizing and timely deliveries.

Dedicated employees at Monnig Industries make the "Monnig Touch" possible. Monnig is committed to his employees and thinks of them as family. They employ 55 people. Pat Westhues, John Monnig's secretary, has been with Monnig Industries for 23 years. She describes the Monnigs as "family-oriented people." Through the years she has always appreciated the company's attitude toward the employees and their families. Westhues said that there were times when her children were young that she needed to attend school functions or attend to family matters, and it was never a problem.

The "Monnig Touch" goes beyond what Monnig Industries promises its customers and how it treats its employees. The community of Glasgow reaps the

Finished structural steel withdrawn from the zinc kettle.

From left to right: Tom Monnig, Tony Monnig, Tim Monnig, John Monnig and Bob Monnig, founder. Not shown: Ron Monnig.

benefits as well. Monnig sponsors a little league baseball team, an adult baseball team and bowling team. It also contributes to area churches and community organizations. Dedication to the community and to family is at the core of Monnig Industries. In fact, it is because of the community that Monnig Industries even exists today.

Glasgow is on the Missouri River halfway between Kansas City and St. Louis and is the place where the first all-steel railroad bridge in the world was completed. Historically its commerce has been predominantly based on agriculture and river industries. By the 1950s, much of the farming was mechanized and farm wages could not compete with factory wages in other larger communities. The town's population and supporting businesses were trickling out of the town, and something had to be done before Glasgow became a ghost town. Thanks to Robert Monnig, the mayor of Glasgow, and several other Glasgow leaders, efforts were made to bring industry to Glasgow and change the inevitable fate of the town. Initially, Robert Monnig acquired a mill and lumber company, employed 13 men and manufactured gunstocks for the

military. Later Monnig was able to expand and manufactured, among other things, wood pallets. In 1961 in partnership with a local steel mill, Monnig began operation of a hot-dip galvanizing plant. The seed of Monnig Industries was planted. Monnig Industries went through several incarnations, including manufacturing farm machinery, before they became the galvanizing plant they are today. Over the years some of the biggest obstacles Monnig Industries has had to face are the ever-fluctuating economy and the changing OSHA requirements. They also take part in a procedure called

"Acid Recover System" which involves turning industry waste into fertilizers.

John Monnig, the president of Monnig industries and the son of its founder Robert Monnig, is quite proud of his father's work and commitment to the Glasgow community. He describes him as a "jack of all trades." Robert Monnig even opened a grocery store in Glasgow when one was needed. John is also proud that the business has been taken to the second generation. As a young man he worked in the plant part-time with his brother and first cousin. Later, when his father's secretary became ill, he helped out in the office and then learned the business side of plant operations. John said that he always knew he would work for Monnig Industries and never considered anything else. Over time, John learned the ropes and was able to take his father's place when he retired.

Very few companies can boast about how important their presence in the community really is. From the start Monnig Industries was established for the community and its preservation. But beyond that, Monnig Industries is a reputable company that takes pride in its work and cares for its employees.

Boat dock frames and boat lift tank.

UNIVERSITY OF MISSOURI-COLUMBIA

The University of Missouri owes its very existence to 900 citizens of Boone County who, in 1839, pledged $117,921 in cash and land to win the bid to locate the new state university in Columbia. Most donors had limited formal schooling, but they willingly and generously invested in an idea, a promise, a hope for a better future for all through public higher education. At the time, there was not a single public university in Missouri—not even in the entire territory stretching west of the Mississippi River to the Pacific Ocean.

Some visionary individuals changed that, adding a university to a small but growing Midwestern town that had eight dry-goods stores, one bookstore and one church. In fact, MU was the first public university in Thomas Jefferson's Louisiana Purchase territory.

Even though there were only two people in the first graduating class of 1843, they were honored with a three-hour commencement ceremony.

Its earliest supporters kept the university going during the lean early years, 27

Memorial Union, with its distinctive gothic clock tower, was built after World War I to honor MU faculty and students who have given their lives for their country in war. The Union also is a favorite place for members of the Mizzou family to gather for meetings, studying and snacks.

Academic Hall was the focus of activity on campus during the 1800s. Built in 1843, with the east and west wings added in 1885, the building housed administrative and department offices, classrooms, a library, chapel and natural history museum. On January 9, 1892, flames consumed the building. For a short time afterward it appeared the University would be forced to leave its home in Columbia. Photo courtesy of the State Historical Society of Missouri, Columbia.

to be exact, before the state legislature began to appropriate money for the university's sustenance. MU persevered and eventually thrived, creating an enduring bond with the local community whose early efforts ultimately produced a university known around the world.

University cultural life began in 1842 with the formation of two literary societies, the Union Literary and the Athenaean Society, which stimulated early intellectual life. The first department of art was directed by George Caleb Bingham, the famous Missouri artist.

In 1849 the first course in civil engineering west of the Mississippi River was taught at MU. Today, the College of Engineering offers courses in everything from biological to nuclear engineering, and its students work on cutting-edge research projects such as designing a better NASA spacesuit, constructing blast-resistant buildings and creating more efficient solar cars.

The "Normal College," now the College of Education, was established in 1867 to prepare teachers for Missouri public schools and enrolled the University's first female students. Women were admitted to all academic classes in 1871. Today the College of Education leads new teachers in efforts to reform the American public school system and develop new classroom technologies.

The real impetus for growth occurred

in 1870 when MU was awarded land-grant status under the terms of the federal Morrill Act and the College of Agriculture and Mechanic Arts, later renamed the College of Agriculture, Food and Natural Resources, opened its doors. The Missouri Agricultural Experiment Station began operation in 1888. Today it encompasses 10 centers and research farms, allowing scientists to test discoveries from University laboratories and share the results of their research with the public.

During those early years, MU also added schools of law and medicine. Undaunted by a disastrous fire in 1892, the University rebuilt around all that remained of its first academic building, six Ionic Columns that now symbolize public higher education in Missouri.

In large part, MU's quality can be traced to Missouri's comprehensive view of education. While other states created separate research and land-grant institutions—such as Michigan and Michigan State, Iowa and Iowa State—Missouri

MU is a land-grant institution emphasizing service to Missourians, and it is the state's largest public research university. Playing a statewide role in professional education, the University is the top provider of practicing physicians for Missouri, two-thirds of the state's veterinarians are MU graduates, one-quarter of all attorneys in Missouri were educated at the University's law school, and MU's academic medical center treats patients from every county in the state.

combines its research and land-grant efforts at one university. MU professors generated new knowledge through research and then shared that knowledge with students in the classroom and with the public through one of the nation's first extension programs.

By the beginning of the 20th century, the university had increased the number of graduates, acquired an affectionate nickname, Mizzou, and blossomed as a major research university. During this time, a number of programs were added, including home economics, later renamed the College of Human Environmental Sciences; nursing, which in 1975 became the Sinclair School of Nursing; the College of Business; and an interdisciplinary graduate school.

In 1908 MU established the world's first journalism school now globally famous for its Missouri Method of teaching students in authentic media outlets, including a daily city newspaper, an NBC-affiliate TV station and one of

National Public Radio's top affiliates.

In addition to academic programs, athletics have always played an important role in the life of the University. Intercollegiate programs date back to 1873 when MU played Westminster College in baseball. Mizzou fielded its first football team in 1890. In 1911 Mizzou invited alumni to "come home" for the MU vs. KU football game, thus beginning the tradition of Homecoming adopted by colleges nationwide. A member of the Big 12 Conference, MU is the only institution in the state that operates all of its sports in NCAA Division I-A, the nation's highest level of intercollegiate athletics.

Following World War II, MU's enrollment escalated, partially due to the GI Bill. It became fully integrated in 1950 when it opened its doors to African-American students. By 1963 the University became a four-campus system with flagship Mizzou as its largest university member.

Today the Mizzou family is a community of more than 26,000 students, some 10,000 faculty and staff members, 200,000 alumni worldwide and countless friends who support the University.

With more than 275 degree programs and 20

colleges and schools, MU is the most comprehensive institution of higher learning in the state of Missouri. It is one of only five universities in the country with medicine, veterinary medicine and law all on one campus. When they are combined with the other academic divisions, Mizzou offers unparalleled opportunities for interdisciplinary collaboration, knowledge creation and educational growth.

MU is one of only 34 public universities, and the only public institution in Missouri, to be selected for membership in the Association of American Universities. AAU members are the most distinguished research universities in the United States and Canada.

Advancing knowledge through teaching, research and service is fundamental to MU's mission as the state's flagship university. Attracting 72 percent of the federal research dollars flowing to Missouri's public universities, MU scientists are doing groundbreaking research in the life sciences to improve human health, food and the environment.

The University community shares its core values with a growing number of students each year: respect, responsibility, discovery and excellence. Today Mizzou is committed to becoming an even greater university, known for the best education from the heart of the nation.

One of the most photographed sites in Missouri, the six 43-foot Ionic Columns that stand in the center of Francis Quadrangle represent the core of MU's pride and tradition. They are all that remain of Academic Hall, completed in 1843 and destroyed by fire in 1892.

A TIMELINE OF MISSOURI'S HISTORY

500 B.C. to 500 A.D. Hopewell culture permeates the Mississippi River Valley.

1000 to 1500 Missouri and Osage tribes dominate the region.

1673 Marquette and Joliet voyage down the Mississippi and discover the Missouri River.

1682 LaSalle takes possession of "Louisiana" for France.

1720 Philippe Renault brings slaves into Missouri.

1750 Ste. Genevieve is founded.

1762 France cedes Louisiana to Spain, but the Spanish government doesn't take control until 1770.

1764 Pierre Laclede and Auguste Chouteau establish a post and name it for Saint Louis.

1769 Louis Blanchette founds St. Charles; it will become Missouri's first capital.

1780 British and Indian forces attack St. Louis.

1793 Cape Girardeau is founded.

1797 Moses Austin founds Herculaneum in the lead belt.

1798 Daniel and Rebecca Boone move to Defiance, Missouri.

1800 Louisiana is returned to France.

1803 President Thomas Jefferson

Many of the 18th century French homes in Ste. Genevieve have been lovingly restored and maintained. Courtesy, Missouri Division of Tourism

authorizes the purchase of Louisiana from France.

1804 Lewis and Clark begin their exploration of Louisiana Territory by way of the Missouri River.

1808 Ste. Genevieve Academy, the first organized school in Missouri is formally established. William Clark designs and builds Fort Osage on the Missouri River, north of present-day Kansas City.

1809 The Missouri Fur Company is formed, one of a dozen fur companies that will bring wealth to St. Louis.

1811 An earthquake centered near New Madrid changes the course of the Mississippi River.

1817 The *Zebulon Pike* docks at

St. Louis, the first steamboat to reach the city.

1818 Mother Philippine Duchesne brings Sacred Heart to Missouri; in 1988 she will be canonized.

1821 The Missouri Compromise is hammered out in Congress, and Missouri is brought into the union. Trader William Becknell heads for Mexico and opens the Santa Fe Trail.

1826 Jefferson Barracks is established as an army outpost. Stephen Watts Kearny, Philip Sheridan, Zachary Taylor, William T. Sherman, Jefferson Davis, Robert E. Lee, U. S. Grant, and Dwight Eisenhower will all serve here. Jefferson City is established as Missouri's permanent capital.

1827 Mary Sibley founds Lindenwood College for young ladies in St. Charles.

1831 Mormons settle in Jackson County; they will be driven out of their homes two years later by intolerant neighbors.

1832 The Catholic college that will become Saint Louis University is chartered.

1836 The first Jewish congregation in the state meets in St. Louis.

1838 Cherokees march from

Fort Osage, now a National Historic Landmark in Jackson County, was established in 1808 by Gen. William Clark to facilitate trade with the Osage Indians. Courtesy, Gregory M. Franzwa

Georgia through southern Missouri on the Trail of Tears. The state militia is called to drive Mormons out of Missouri.

1839 The City of Kansas is established.

1841 The University of Missouri is chartered.

1846 The Oregon Trail, with jumping-off points in Independence and St. Joseph, opens. It will take hundreds of thousands of emigrants West.

1847 The Lutheran Synod of Missouri is organized, and the great wave of German immigration begins.

1849 The Missouri-Pacific Railroad is chartered. A cholera epidemic decimates St. Louis, followed by a devastating fire along the riverfront

1853 The state's first public high school opens in St. Louis; Eliot Seminary (later Washington University) is chartered.

1855 A railroad bridge over the Gasconade River collapses. A hun-

In 1899 engineers began an effort to control the Missouri River. Here they are building gabions in an effort to straighten out the river's flow. Courtesy, U.S. Army Corps of Engineers.

dred passengers are injured and 34 killed.

1857 The Dred Scott Decision confirms that slaves are property and have no rights as persons.

1858 The Border War with Kansas begins. Many Missourians will lose their homes to the marauding Jayhawkers.

1861–1865 Civil War battles rage in Missouri at St. Louis, Boonville, Lexington, Cole Camp, Carthage, Springfield, and Westport.

1865 Slavery is abolished in Missouri as a new state constitution is adopted.

1870 The Rolla School of the Mines opens.

1874 The Eads Bridge across the Mississippi opens, and railroads finally connect Missouri to the East.

1878 St. Louis City separates itself from St. Louis County. The First American Royal Livestock show is held in Kansas City. The stockyards there have become the terminus of cattle drives beginning in Texas, Oklahoma, and Kansas.

1880 The *Kansas City Star* begins publication.

1882 Outlaw Jesse James is killed.

1888 The Baldknobbers gang is suppressed in southwest Missouri.

1896 A devastating cyclone levels much of St. Louis; 118 are dead.

1902 Political boss Ed Butler is indicted.

1904 The World's Fair opens in St. Louis to universal applause.

1907 Missouri adopts the primary election law.

1911 Champ Clark is elected Speaker of the U.S. House.

1912 Lake Tanneycomo is completed, the first of several projects in the Ozarks.

1916 At the National Democratic Convention held in St. Louis, 7,000 women dressed in white stand in silence along the route to the

In June 1927 at Sportsmen's Park in St. Louis, baseball legend Rogers Hornsby (far left) and aviation legend Charles Lindbergh present a Cardinal player with the championship ring for winning the 1926 World Series as a smiling Mayor Victor Miller looks on. Courtesy, Mercantile Library at the University of Missouri-St. Louis

convention hall, hoping to influence delegates to make a commitment to women's suffrage.

1917 Missourian General John J. Pershing is named commander of the American Expeditionary Forces in the Great War.

1919 Prohibition is enacted. It will be all but ignored in the urban areas. Anheuser-Busch stays in business by producing several nonalcoholic drinks and marketing yeast.

1920 A $60 million "Good Roads" bill is enacted to "get Missouri out of the mud."

1921 WEW of St. Louis is the state's first radio station.

1927 Lindbergh lands in Paris in the *Spirit of St. Louis*, funded by St. Louis businessmen.

1933 The Union Station Massacre shocked Kansas Citians.

1934 Harry S. Truman is elected as U.S. senator.

1939 Sharecroppers organize a protest in the bootheel, bringing national

The seven *Mercury* astronauts visit the home of their capsule—McDonnell Aircraft Company in St. Louis. Courtesy, The Boeing Company

attention to the poverty there.

1942 Mallinkrodt Chemical Co. begins to produce uranium oxide blocks for a secret government project, the *A-bomb!*

1944 The MGM film *Meet Me in St. Louis*, based on the book by Sally Benson, premiers in the title city.

1945 "The Man from Independence," Harry S. Truman, becomes president on the death of Franklin Roosevelt. Japan surrenders aboard the U.S.S. *Missouri* ending World War II.

A jubilant Harry Truman holds the *Chicago Tribune* erroneously announcing his defeat. Courtesy, Mercantile Library at the University of Missouri-St. Louis

1954 The U.S. Supreme Court rules that "separate" does not mean "equal," and public school desegregation begins throughout the state.

1959 The McDonnell plant in St. Louis builds the first human-controlled spacecraft, called project Mercury. Both Alan Shepard and John Glenn will take the *Mercury* into space.

1965 The Jefferson National Expansion Memorial, known popularly as The Arch, is topped out on the St. Louis Riverfront, revitalizing the city.

1972 Democratic presidential candidate George McGovern names Senator Tom Eagleton as his running mate. When the media discloses that Eagleton has been treated for depression, he resigns from the ticket.

1985 The first "I-70 World Series" is played between the St. Louis Cardinals and the Kansas City Royals. Kansas City wins.

1993 The Great Flood inundates much of the state.

2000 Governor Mel Carnahan is killed in an airplane crash.

BIBLIOGRAPHY

Barnes, Harper. *Standing on a Volcano: The Life and Times of David Rowland Francis*. St. Louis: Missouri Historical Society Press, 2001.

Brown, A. Theodore, and Lyle W. Dorsett. K. C.: *A History of Kansas City, Missouri*. Boulder, Colo.: Pruett Publishing Company, 1978.

Brownlee, Richard S. *Grey Ghosts of the Confederacy*. Baton Rouge: Louisiana State University Press, 1958.

Burbank, David T. The Reign of the Rabble: the *St. Louis General Strike of 1877*. New York: Augustus M. Kelley Publishers, 1966.

Burnett, Betty. *St. Louis at War: the Story of a City 191-46*. St. Louis: Patrice Press, 1983.

Burnett, Betty, ed. *The Flood of 1993: Stories from a Midwestern Disaster*. Tucson, Ariz: Patrice Press, 1994.

Chagnon, Stanley A., ed. *The Great Flood of 1993: Causes, Impacts, and Re sponses*. Westview Press, 1996.

Chambers, William N. *Old Bullion Benton: Senator from the New West*. Boston: Little, Brown and Co., 1956.

Dorsett, Lyle W. The Pendergast Machine. New York: Oxford University Press, 1968.

Foley, William F. A *History of Missouri: Volume 1, 1673 to 1820*. Columbia: The University of Missouri Press, 1971.

Franzwa, Gregory. *The Story of Old St. Genevieve*. St. Louis: Patrice Press, 1990. Schneider, Sue. *Old St. Charles*. St. Louis: Patrice Press, 1990.

Garwood, Darell. *Crossroads of America, the Story of Kansas City*. New York: W.W. Norton, 1948.

Gerlach, Russel L. *Immigrants in the Ozarks*. Columbia: The University of Missouri Press, 1976.

Greene, Lorenzo J., Gary R. Fremer, and Anthony F. Holland. *Missouri's Black Heritage*. St. Louis: Forum Press, 1980.

Hagan, William T. *The Sac and the Fox Indians*. Norman: The University of Oklahoma Press, 1958.

Hall, Leonard. *Stars Upstream: Life along the Ozark River*. Columbia: The University of Missouri Press, 1969.

Houck, Louis. *A History of Missouri*. 4 vols. Chicago: R.R. Donnelley & Sons Co., 1908.

Kirkendall, Richard S. A *History of Missouri: Volume V, 1919 to 1953*.

Columbia: The University of Missouri Press, 1986.

Kirschten, Ernest. *Catfish and Crystal*. Garden City: Doubleday, 1960.

Lasch, Christopher. *The New Radicalism in America, 1889-1963: The Intellectual as Social Type*. New York: W.W. Norton & Co., 1965.

March, David D. The History of Missouri. 4 vols. New York and West Palm Beach: Lewis Historical Publishing Co., 1967.

Matthews, John Joseph. *The Osages*. Norman: The University of Oklahoma Press, 1961.

McCandless, Perry. *A History of Missouri: Volume II, 1820 to 1860*. Columbia: The University of Missouri, 1972.

Meyer, Duane G. *The Heritage of Missouri*. St. Louis: River City Publishers, Ltd., 1982.

Mitchell, Franklin D. *Embattled Democracy: Missouri Democratic Politics, 1919-1932*. Columbia: The University of Missouri Press, 1968.

Montgomery, David. *The Fall of the House of Labor*. Cambridge: Cambridge University Press, 1987.

Moore, Glover. *The Missouri Compromise*. Lexington: The University of Kentucky Press, 1953.

Nagel, Paul C. *Missouri: A Bicentennial History*. New York and Nashville: AASLH Press and W.W. Norton & Company, Inc., 1977.

Oglesby, Richard E. *Manual Lisa and the Opening of the Missouri Fur Trade*. Norman: The University of Oklahoma Press, 1963.

Parrish, William E. *A History of Missouri*: Volume III, 1860 to 1875. Columbia: The University of Missouri Press, 1973.

Parrish, William E., Charles T. Jones, Jr., and Lawrence O. Christensen. *Missouri: The Heart of the Nation*. St. Louis: Forum Press, 1980.

Penick, James, Jr. *The New Madrid Earthquakes of 1811-1812*. Columbia: The University of Missouri Press, 1976.

Primm, James Neal. *Economic Policy in the Development of a Western State, Missouri, 1820-1860*. Cambridge: Harvard University Press, 1954.

——. *Lion of the Valley*. Boulder, Colo.:

Preutt Publishing Company, 1981.

Schirmer, Sherry Lamb, and Richard D. McKinzie. *At the River's Bend: An Illustrated History of Kansas City*. Northridge, Calif.: Windsor Publications, Inc., 1982.

Schneider, Sue. *Old St. Charles*. St. Louis: Patrice Press, 1990.

Shoemaker, Floyd C. *Missouri and Missourians: Land of Contrasts and People of Achievement*. Chicago: Lewis Publishing Co., 1943.

——. *Missouri's Struggle for Statehood*. Jefferson City: Stephens Printing Co., 1916.

Sprague, Marshall. *So Vast a Land: Louisiana and the Purchase*. Boston: Little, Brown and Co., 1974.

Troen, Selwyn K., and Glen Holt, eds. *St. Louis: A Documentary Anthology*. New York: New Viewpoints, 1977.

Truman, Harry S. *Memoirs*. 2 vols. Garden City, N.Y.: Doubleday, 1955-1956.

van Ravensway, Charles. *The WPA Guide to 1930s Missouri*. Lawrence: University Press of Kansas, 1986.

Violette, E.M., and F.E. Wolverton. A *History of Missouri*. St. Louis: State Publishing Company, 1955.

Williams, Walter, and Floyd Calvin Shoemaker. *Missouri, Mother of the West*. 5 vols. Chicago and New York: American Historical Society, 1930.

INDEX